D1509151

The
Client–Consultant
Handbook

The Client-Consultant Handbook

*Twenty-one experts tell managers
how to choose, negotiate with,
and get the most from
a consultant.*

Edited by Chip R. Bell
and Leonard Nadler

**Gulf Publishing Company
Book Division
Houston, London, Paris, Tokyo**

The Client—Consultant Handbook

Library of Congress
Catalog Card Number 78-67437
ISBN 0-87201-113-5

Building Blocks of Human Potential Series
Leonard Nadler, Series Editor

The Adult Learner: A Neglected Species, by Malcolm Knowles

The Adult Educator—A Handbook for Staff Development, by Harry G. Miller and John R. Verduin

Managing Cultural Differences, by Philip R. Harris and Robert T. Moran

The Conference Book, by Leonard Nadler and Zeace Nadler

The Client—Consultant Handbook, by Chip R. Bell and Leonard Nadler

Human Resource Development: The European Approach, by H. Eric Frank

Leadership Development for Public Service, by Barry A. Passett

People, Evaluation, and Achievement, by George Nixon

The NOW Employee, by David Nadler

Handbook of Creative Learning Exercises, by Herbert Engel

Contents

v

Preface

In our own experience as clients as well as consultants, we found that the real key to effectiveness in those encounters was the quality of the rapport between the parties involved—the nature of the human relationship between client and consultant.

And so it was alarming when a search of the social-science literature revealed that no book dealt adequately with how to manage the relationship between client and consultant. Despite widespread writing on the consulting process, the relational aspects of consulting seem to have been neglected. We believe the client-consultant relationship is the most crucial and the most vulnerable aspect of the consulting process. Thus, the key to maximizing the potential of a positive client-consultant relationship is attaining mutual understanding as well as self-understanding.

We have assembled articles we find useful to clients *and* consultants. We have discovered it is not unusual for consultants to train their clients to use a consultant. This puts the client in a potentially dependent position which can ultimately doom the consultation to mediocrity. This book was compiled to prevent that dependence and to enhance the effectiveness of consultation.

The book was written for people who use or plan to use the services of a consultant. It provides insight and understanding to professionals who devote a part of their working lives to helping clients. There are many suggestions and techniques throughout the book that are useful in achieving and maintaining a positive and productive client-consultant relationship.

Graduate students in behavioral science, management, human resource development, adult education, and organizational psychology will find this to be a practical tool to understanding the subtle issues involved in managing such a complex interpersonal relationship.

We wish to express our appreciation to the authors and publishers who so kindly gave us permission to reprint their works. We are also grateful to Bruce Fritch for his creative editing and to Nancy Chapman for typing and proofing the manuscript. Finally, we express our warm appreciation for the love and patience of Nancy Bell and Zeace Nadler.

Chip R. Bell
Leonard Nadler
March 1979

Introduction to the Client-Consultant Relationship

Consultation is fundamentally the act of helping. As such, it holds the dramatic vibrance and reality which characterizes life itself. Consultation is not simply the mechanical tossing of expertise toward a painful client; it is an experience in shared resources. There is an appropriate place for technique, tactic, and form. However, it is the substance and spirit in the helping process which gives consultation its unique humanness.

The core of the act of helping is the interaction of two or more people relating in order to improve some person, situation, or thing. The quality of those dynamics determines if the encounter results in more help than harm, more joy than sorrow, and more growth than death.

Many years ago there were tribes who ceremonially ate the raw meat of a mountain lion before embarking on a hunt. They believed that in the process of integrating with the lion they would assume some of the lion's strength and cunning. The analogy characterizes the client–consultant relationship in its most ideal form — the consultant and client becoming so integrated (Martin Buber called it an I–Thou relationship) that the client discovers personal power through the strength of the consultant.

The ingredients in an ideal client–consultant relationship are many. Each is not easy to come by. Even if attained, they remain slippery; all parties involved must work constantly to keep them at hand. This book is anchored to the belief that as one increases sensitivity to the dynamics of helping, the chances for effectiveness likewise climb.

The book has been assembled with the primary purpose of assisting insight and facilitating discovery by the players currently in the consultative drama and those desiring to learn it's character. It is our opinion that growth occurs in serving, as well as in being served. This book is therefore as much about growing as it is about helping.

An Overview of Consulting

Consultation has come to be a broad label for a variety of relationships. Principally, it is a two-way process of seeking, giving, and receiving help. We use

1

the word consulting in a very specific sense. It is the provision of information or help by a professional helper (consultant) to a help-needing person or system (client) in the context of a voluntary, temporary relationship which is mutually advantageous.

The plea for professional help is precipitated by the client's recognition that he or she lacks certain kinds of resources. It may be that the specialized expertise required to solve some current or potential problem is not readily available within the client system and must thus be secured outside. It may be that the client needs a type or level of objectivity which only an outsider could provide. It could be that the client simply lacks the time to do what he or she could normally do and hires an outsider with available time.

The words "client," "client system," "consultant," and "outsider" are used in very specific ways and thus require additional clarification. Client refers to the person responsible for the outcome of the consultation. This may be a different person from the individual who served as the initial contact, go-between, or sponsor in securing a particular consultant. Client system refers to the organizational unit most directly affected by the consultation and is generally lead by the client.

The consultant is the person who, because of competence, experience, status, reputation, or a combination of these, is deemed by the client to be capable of providing needed information or help. The consultant is always external to the client system, but may be internal to the organization in which the client is an employee. The consultant is therefore sometimes a physical outsider and always a psychological outsider.

The many varied types of consultation add to the confusion of words. Throughout the following readings, authors may refer to organization development consulting (OD), management consulting, human resource development consulting (HRD), and a few others. We prefer to combine these and use the broader label of behavioral science consulting. If someone is contracted to run a training program for an organization, we would not call such an activity consulting. If, on the other hand, a person was hired to help solve a problem and if a diagnosis revealed that a training program was a solution, we would be more likely to label the activity consulting.

There are numerous ways of perceiving the consulting process. Writers differ on their words for process steps and on the models or conceptual framework they utilize. Most agree there is entry, some type of diagnosis, some response or action, and, at a point, termination of the consultation. Most agree there is a defined beginning and a defined end.

The model we have elected to use (Figure I-1) is a straightforward, simple five-step process. While the model reflects distinct phases, we would underscore that in reality these distinctions are less precise.

The following is a brief review of the meaning of each phase and the tasks which are typically associated with each of these phases.

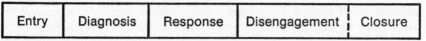

| Entry | Diagnosis | Response | Disengagement | Closure |

Figure I-1. The five phases of the consulting process.

Entry

Because of some pain or disequilibrium experienced or expected to be experienced by the client and/or client system, a consultant is called onto the scene. The entry phase begins with some contact of one by the other. Problems are jointly explored, perceived needs and symptoms are discussed, relationships are clarified, goals and roles are defined, resource parameters are identified, methodology is clarified, and ultimately a contract (written or psychological) is negotiated.

The time which elapses during entry may range from a brief telephone call to numerous meetings. Throughout the entry phase, both parties are scouting to ascertain the degree to which the consultation will be a potentially advantageous relationship.

Diagnosis

Diagnosis is essentially the process of determining by examination the cause and nature of a problem. It generally begins with the understanding of the problem as perceived by the client. It includes an appreciation of the client's goals, resources, and the client system's culture, values, norms, and beliefs.

The consultant is charged with identifying the subsystem(s) in which the problem is perceived to be located and the interrelationships between that subsystem and the other parts of the system. Another important issue in the diagnosis phase is the extent and degree to which the client system is willing to commit its resources to a resolution of the problem.

Questionnaires, interviews, observation, and analysis of previous performance data are the most common methods used in obtaining an assessment of the situation.

Response

The literature in social and behavioral science is unclear regarding when diagnosis stops and response begins. Many models of consulting place a planning phase between the two to separate them more distinctly. Should the feedback of the diagnosis be in the diagnosis phase or response phase? Technically, data feedback is, in fact, a response and may be all that was contracted. We chose to place data feedback and presentation of alternative responses in the diagnosis phase.

The response or action phase includes the selection of a course of action, redefinition of the consultative goals, and identification of appropriate objectives, strategies, and roles. Likewise, the response phase includes the planning and engagement of structured activities or interventions employed to correct the problem or improve the situation which was spelled out in the contract.

Disengagement

This book combines disengagement and closure since most writers treat them as one phase. Despite this, we feel the actions undertaken in the disengagement phase and closure phase are sufficiently different to warrant separating them into two distinct phases. The model (Figure I-1) shows a dotted line separating the two phases. This reflects the confusion regarding whether they are indeed separate. We believe writers at some point in the future will view disengagement and closure as related, but different, phases in consultation.

The disengagement phase includes the evaluation of results conducted to determine not only if the response has been successful and is progressing as planned, but also whether there is a need for response revision or additional resources. Based on that evaluation, planning for continuous process maintenance is conducted to insure permanent integration and lasting change.

An effort is made to decrease the client's dependency on the the consultant and develop within the client system the ability to use self-generated data by involving the client system in monitoring progress and evaluating results. Change can only be sustained if the client and client system attain sufficient growth during the consultation.

Closure

Presuming the consultant has taken steps during disengagement to insure continuity and internal support, he or she should be ready for a mutually satisfying termination of the working relationship. Termination may mean leaving the client system or may mean ceasing one effort and starting another. The challenge of the helpers is to bring the party being helped to a point at which a helper is no longer necessary.

Organization of the Book

The major foundation of this book is the presentation of relevant theory and practice pertinent to the client–consultant relationship. The book begins and ends with an issues look at the relational consultant and chapters on the relationship dimensions of each phase of consulting.

In our search for material, we tried to find articles which most clearly presented a particular phase. Few articles did in total what we wanted an article to do. Two articles (one by Chalofsky and one by Furr) were written specifically for this book and have not been previously published. Where gaps appeared, we have attempted to fill them in with the introductions to each part.

An effort was also made to present articles from diverse journals, including some not likely to be read by the practitioner (client or consultant). Most articles were published in the last ten years. The few exceptions are considered classics in their particular areas. Despite the proliferation of material on consultation (reflected in the Bibliography), surprisingly few articles dealt with the relationship aspects.

The part introductions provide a major service beyond filling voids caused by the scarcity of subject-related works. They are designed to serve as mental-setting devices to enhance the growth derived from the articles. The articles provide a wide diversity of thought within each chapter. We have not attempted to resolve the conflict in positions. Hopefully, the part introductions will quell some of the abruptness inherent in diversity.

Uses of the Book

This book was written for clients who currently use or plan to use the services of a consultant. The behavioral sciences have been inundated with theory and practice texts for the consultant; those for the client are few and far between. We hope this book provides insight and understanding useful to clients in managing a very complex relationship.

This book is also for the growing number of professionals who devote a portion of their working lives to providing help to clients. We feel this particular group will gain from this book a deeper appreciation for the world of the client. We have made sure there are many suggestions and techniques throughout the text that will prove useful in more effectively achieving and maintaining a positive and productive client–consultant relationship.

Finally, we view this as a comprehensive textbook dealing with the client–consultant relationship, particularly for graduate students in the fields of human resource development, behavioral science, business management, adult education, and organizational psychology. We believe the text will enhance their perceptiveness of the subtle issues surrounding the relationship of client and consultant.

For all readers, the book was designed as a ready reference. Reading the book through will provide a comprehensive view of the subject. We trust that some chapters will prove sufficiently helpful to elicit a second and third reading. The Bibliography includes most of the major works (and many of the minor works) related to consultation. All were reviewed for possible inclusion in this work.

The Bias of the Authors

Our deepest bias related to the client–consultant relationship is reflected in the old story of the grasshopper and owl. A grasshopper, having suffered during two cold winters, went to an expert owl for assistance. The owl listened carefully to the grasshopper's problem and then prescribed a solution. "All you have to do is turn yourself into a cricket and hibernate throughout the winter," the owl said. The grasshopper happily departed only to return later to the owl disappointedly. "Look," said the owl curtly when the grasshopper asked how one performs metamorphosis, "I gave you the principle, it's up to you to work out the details."

Our conviction is that the extent to which knowledge can be effectively used by clients depends in a large measure on the nature of the relationship between the client and consultant. We suspect that too frequently clients, in their frantic search for a solution, and consultants, in their drive to demonstrate their expertise, pass each other in the night without realizing that at the root of giving and receiving help is the richness of human encounter.

We believe with Carl Rogers that the only learning which significantly influences behavior is self-discovered learning — truth that has been personally assimilated in experience. This puts the helper in the role of the facilitator of discovery rather than the dispenser of information.

Lastly, we think consultants have a responsibility to be impeccably ethical in their dealings with clients. By ethical, we mean the consultant should be up front regarding his or her motives with the client. Central to his or her motives is taking to heart the best interests of the client.

Introduction to the Readings

The introductory readings are either etched in consultative issues or provide thoughts useful as a frame of reference. We felt it would be helpful to begin with a macroview of the client–consultant relationship before consultation was diced up in later chapters for a close look at smaller pieces.

At the bottom of the first page of each reading, we have provided its source. A brief statement about the author(s) has been placed at the end of each article. We have been as accurate as possible in stating the correct title and organization for each author. However, given the mobility of the practitioners in this field, some biographical data is likely to be dated.

Chapter 1
"Developing a Successful Client–Consultant Relationship"
Charles H. Ford

Clarity is a primary theme in the writing of Ford. He elbows through the quagmire of philosophical navel gazing and succinctly uncovers key causes for client–consultant disharmony.

The lack of consultant competence is the source of poor relationships on the consultant side of the equation. Failure to identify the real problem, promising too much too soon, failure to specify role, recommending actions not feasible — each are samples of consultant inadequacies Ford discusses.

The lack of effective communication lies at the heart of most of client-caused causes of poor relationships. Failure to clarify what his or her money will buy, failure to clarify how the consultant will operate, failure to inform his or her client system of the consultant's role and goals and failure to explain resource limitations are some of the problems outlined.

The article provides a useful opening piece in its pragmatic treatment of common pitfalls which doom client—consultant relationships to failure. Both clients and consultants can find helpful hints for optimizing consultation.

Chapter 2
"The Characteristics of a Helping Relationship"
Carl Rogers

Carl Rogers defines a helping relationship as one in which at least one party has the intent of promoting the growth, development, maturity and improved functioning of the other. The definition is very compatible with the definition of a consulting relationship. This reading is among the most notable of Rogers' works and is taken from his classic *On Becoming a Person*.

It is widely known that Rogers is occupationally a psychotherapist. His writings were primarily focused on helping practitioners in one-to-one counseling develop greater genuineness, openness, and warmth in their counseling. The article is included here because we feel it has a cogent message for clients and consultants applicable to their developing a mature, positive and creative relationship.

Chapter 3
"Feedback: The Art of Giving and Receiving Help"
Cyril R. Mill

Like the Carl Rogers article, this classic provides an important philosophical base for looking at the helping relationship. The key to most consultative efforts is the communication of feedback by the helper to the helpee. The suggestions, if used, may not reduce the receiver's pain which sometimes accompanies feedback, but clearly increases the chance that the information will be heard in a way useful to the receiver. The reading is taken from the *NTL Readings in Laboratory Training*.

Developing a Successful Client-Consultant Relationship

Charles H. Ford

The next time you are with a group of say, ten businessmen and the conversation begins to lag, try slipping in the word "consultant" and watch the conversation pick up as passions heat. No doubt, the words "crooks" and "incompetents" and "conmen" will be the more printable ones used. One of the participants is bound to throw in the old cliche, "A consultant is nothing more than an unemployed executive with a briefcase." Almost everyone will have had either an unfortunate experience with a consultant or, more likely, will have *heard* of someone who has.

In short, as more businesses operating in today's complicated, ultra-competitive, shortage-ridden business climate can profitably use a consultant's services, the profession's reputation is sliding down hill.

Let's try to add some perspective to the situation: Business has become and is becoming even more compartmentalized in terms of specialized functions. Ten years ago, for example, few businesses were concerned with the ecological impact of their operations. Equality of employment opportunity was on the basis of race; today sex must be considered as well. OSHA is a new force to contend with. New computer applications appear almost daily. Shortages have introduced both new production problems and marketing problems.

Couple all this with the on-going situation of new marketing and new product opportunities and new manufacturing techniques, both procedural and equipmental; throw into the equation the pervasive problem of in-bred management whose perspective is sometimes obscured by being too close to a problem and whose frames of reference are based on "What we've always done," and a pretty good case can be made for the outsider who has a high level of expertise in one or more fields, whose experience is based on the experience of a multiplicity of companies, and whose frames of reference are not bound by in-bred company habits and attitudes.

Reprinted from *Human Resource Management,* Vol. 13, No. 2, Summer, 1974, pp. 2-11, Graduate School of Business Administration, University of Michigan, Ann Arbor, MI 48109.

Why, then, the rancor? The answer is two-fold. First, an increasing number of client–consultant relationships have simply not worked out. And as the cost of most everything else has gone up, so has the cost of this failure. In very simple terms, in those cases which did not work out, either the consultant did not do what he should have done or the client did not do what he should have done. More likely, the answer lies in a combination of mutual culpability.

Secondly, one does not hear with the same expression of heat and passion of successful client–consultant relationships for the same reason that newspapers do not bother to print good news. Thus, the failures take on added significance and tend to tarnish the whole aspect of consulting.

We here, of course, are concerned with why these relationships are not successful and what a client should do to insure that they will be.

We cannot help, unfortunately, the fact that most of the reasons for failure once stated appear painfully obvious. Even though the reader might conclude that "This couldn't happen to me," one must remember that client–consultant relationships are often new experiences for the client, and thus he lacks the perspective of previous experience. The obviousness of failure becomes first a product of 20–20 hindsight and second, is often lost in the welter of recrimination that follows an unsuccessful relationship.

The examples we will use are typical of what has and is happening. They will not tax the reader's imagination — nor are they meant to. Rather they seek to serve by illustration the pitfalls that client companies fall into and how they can be avoided. Let the reader be assured that if the causes of failure were profound, we would illustrate our points by profundities, but to do so in the light of reality would only serve to obscure the real simplicities of the problem. Now let us examine the causes of failure based on what the consultant should have done or did not do.

The Consultant Fails to Identify the Real Problem. A large ladies lingerie manufacturer found its sales slipping. Its salesmen complained that its high prices were making the line noncompetitive.

"Not so," humphed the president. "These guys have had it too soft too long. Now that things have gotten rough competitively, they've forgotten how to sell. We'll get them back to fundamentals."

Enter the Sales Engineering Consultant. After analyzing the situation he agreed with the president's conclusion. He went to work holding sales meetings, setting up incentive programs and quotas, holding classes in salesmanship. "We don't need him to teach us how to sell," the salesmen complained. "Some of us were selling before he was out of diapers." For emphasis, four of the company's twelve salesmen promptly quit. Sales continued to slide. Exit the sales engineer.

"Perhaps," thought the president, "I'd better look into my costing procedures." Enter the Cost Consultant. He was appalled at the simplicity and looseness of the present costing system and agreed that the problem must be there.

He proceeded to set up an elaborate costing and cost control system that would have required two extra people to administer. No one could fault his in-depth approach but when his unit costs came out approximately the same as what the company was already using, he too got his walking papers.

"That's it for consultants," said the president. "All I've got to show for them is four less salesmen and a bigger hole in my bank account." "Try one more," suggested his worried banker. "Let's try a manufacturing specialist." Enter the manufacturing specialist. "Your plants are ten years behind the times," he suggested. He laid out a program for modernizing equipment, methods, and cost controls. The company and the bank went along with the program. Result: Costs came down, prices followed; sales went up.

Two consultants (and the company president) had attacked the symptoms of the problem rather than the root cause. Regardless of their competence within their fields, their failure was pre-ordained simply because they failed to look sufficiently beyond their specialties to determine whether they (their specialties) were really the problem areas that needed solving in order to achieve the client's objective, namely to increase sales.

The Consultant Promises Too Much Too Soon. No one calls in a consultant unless he has a problem. This in itself generally creates a susceptibility to the consultant's expansive expression of confidence in his ability to solve the problem.

Many problem solutions look easy when discussed across a desk. The problem is often stated in such a way as to make the solution seem textbook. At this point, in the absence of specifics and problem nuances, it is often discussed in abstract terms. As a result, the consultant sometimes tends to tie his promise of success to the obvious simplicity of the solution. The client, often desperate, is eager to accept it. Thus, we have the elements of a potential explosion.

In actually addressing himself to the solution, however, the consultant often finds nuances that he hadn't expected — and the possibility of which he hadn't advised the client — perhaps elements of the problem that were not discussed at the interview because of the client's prejudicial point of view or because of his failure to attach significance to them. Perhaps the consultant finds other problems that flow into the main problem which gives it a different complexion from what he expected. As a result, he finds that the easy solution upon which he based his promises has changed along with his ability to deliver.

For example, a consultant was called to help reorganize a metal works company. The average age of the top 12 executives was 59. The president, 64, felt that the company's decline was due to the rigid thinking of his deeply patterned executives. He asked the consultant to run an executive evaluation of each department head and to recommend executive replacement where necessary. "I just can't get these people to move. The industry is passing us by and we just sit and look at each other. These people have been with me a long time. Too long perhaps."

Not an unusual situation, thought the consultant. Finding the weak sisters ought not to be too difficult, he assured the president. He'd soon have things turned around. The president was blissfully reassured. The consultant accepted the president's premise that the latter's dynamism was being sabotaged by the conservativeness of his key people. "It's like punching a balloon," complained the president. "My inputs just don't come out the other side when they're filtered through my key people."

The deeper the consultant probed, however, the more apparent it became that the problem lay principally with the president himself and the executive vice president — a presidential brother-in-law, a relationship which had not been explained at the interview. Both were in reality quite antagonistic to change ("I built this company, dammit, and I know what built it") and in a position to shift the responsibility of the company's resultant decline to the department heads.

Virtually every executive the consultant interviewed could pull program and ideas out of his desk that had been submitted and rejected. To the consultant, most of these made sense.

Final result? The consultant suggested that it might be a good idea if the president turned the reins over to someone else and went fishing. And while he was doing it, he might take his brother-in-law with him. The reaction, predictably, was explosive. Consulting had incurred another vocal enemy simply because the consultant promised expansively what he couldn't deliver. Even though he had the answer, it was not the one he had promised.

The Consultant Fails to Specify His Role. Often a consultant will accept an assignment and not indicate clearly to the client what form his help will take.

A consultant was hired by a large stereo equipment manufacturer to re-organize the company. The company felt it needed to regear itself to meet new changes in consumer buying habits and increased foreign-made competition. "Our organization functioned well during the growth years because we developed a good product line and the market was waiting for us. Now we're being hurt by a contracting market and not only is our domestic competition importing components from abroad but foreign competition itself is exporting to this country. We need to shift gears both organizationally to cut our costs and functionally to meet the shift in consumer buying habits."

The consultant agreed with the need. In came his associates with pencils and clipboards. Surveys were made, executives were evaluated, new production methods and techniques were developed. Two months later, the consultant submitted his report — all 104 pages of it single-spaced. He followed this up with his final bill.

The client hit the ceiling. "The report is fine," he said, "if I had the time to read it, digest it and could understand it. I thought the consultant would hold us by the hand during the reorganization and follow-up on it to make sure it worked — and to make adjustments where it didn't. By the time I got through reading this report, I could have done the job myself."

The report now reposes in the president's desk drawer. The company is out nearly $44,000 and the company's executives have very unkind things to say about consultants and consulting.

The Consultant Fails to Adapt to the Individuality of the Client's Problems. Consultants, as anyone else, often develop patterns of approaches based on their experiences. Often they view situations as they should be rather than as they are.

An "expert" on organization was called in by a growing conglomerate to help the company work in the newly acquired management teams it was absorbing. Coincidentally, he (the consultant) had just performed the same job for another conglomerate. The previous company had a strong operations-oriented management team. Its philosophy was to buy ailing companies at bargain prices and turn them around. With this company, the consultant had strengthened the bonds of corporate management and weakened the authority of the absorbed managements. It worked. The strong-willed competent corporate management made itself felt with success on the less competent absorbed managements.

The consultant was delighted. In his enthusiasm, he wrote an article on the subject based on his successful experience. Conglomerates, he concluded, should have strong central managements. With his previous success as a blueprint, he promptly proceeded to reorganize the latest client the same way. The result was chaos.

Theoretically, it should have worked and he would die, if necessary, defending his approach. After all, it had worked before. He had the experience to prove it. The client must be doing something wrong, he contended.

Unfortunately, although the circumstances appeared to be the same, obviously they were not. The top management of the latter client was financially oriented — not operationally oriented. Its philosophy was to buy moderately successful companies and infuse additional capital necessary to help them grow further. The absorbed managements were far more competent to operate their companies, to assess the risks, etc., than corporate management.

The company saved itself by reversing the consultant's blueprint and delegating more authority to the absorbed managements — the same managements that had built the successful subsidiaries in the first place and needed only the motivation of increased authority to make them continue to grow. The company's president made a vow never again to hire a consultant even if, at a later date, the firm faced disaster.

The consultant often fails to tailor his approach to the unique and different circumstances of his client. And every company is unique and different, with different people, different attitudes, operating under different pressures. The gap in communication so frequently complained about between the client's people and the consultant is most often due to the consultant's failure to adapt his approach to the specifics of the client-company.

The Consultant's Recommendations Are Not Feasible. There is a marked difference, obviously, between a good theoretical recommendation and a feasible practical one. And one consequential difference is a satisfied client and an unsatisfied one.

A medium-sized toy manufacturer had grown rapidly in the past few years. Its staff was located in three buildings in two different cities, 40 miles apart. Two of these buildings also housed its two factories. The third building housed only part of its staff. All three buildings were older types and low rental. Like Topsy, the company had just grown. It had concentrated its capital efforts in new equipment and product development to the point where it was skating on a thin edge of working capital.

It discovered that, as it grew, staff coordination became a problem. It called in an organization specialist to help solve the problem. He analyzed the communications break-down and concluded that the obvious and best solution was to house the staff in one building. This noble bit of intelligence cost the client $3100.

"I didn't need to spend $3100 for that answer," said the company president, not without heat. "If we had the money to build or lease a new headquarters we'd have already done it. We're not that stupid." Discarding the consultant report, the company, although disenchanted with consultants, was prevailed upon to hire a communications specialist. He promptly proceeded to set up a time-controlled system of interoffice, interplant communications.

Although it was not the optimum solution, everyone agreed, at least it "will help us grease the wheels to keep things moving until we can retrench our capitalization to the point where we can consolidate our staff into one building."

Optimum solutions, defensible on paper, are often not the "best" solutions for a particular time. When the consultant fails to distinguish this difference, the client–consultant relationship is doomed to failure.

The Consultant Lacks Competence. And here, reluctantly, we must include the "con man." Many consultants simply lack the expertise or temperament with which to solve a company's problem. The "con man" is the one who, despite this, attempts to sell his services — and, unfortunately, often does. He relies on glibness, rash promises, name-dropping, and often a working knowledge of the language used in his field of "expertise."

For example, the principle of a consulting firm visited a glove plant. He had never before been in one. Before going in he asked one of his senior consultants who had made the contact and who had toured the plant to name an operation. "Thumb setting." "How many do they do an hour?" "About 120."

When he too was given the tour, he stopped at the thumb-setting operation, turned to the company's vice president of manufacturing and noted, "Hmm, thumb setting. What do you run an hour, about 120?" This established him as an "expert" on manufacturing gloves.

Incompetence, of course, goes beyond the realm of deceit. A consultant may have worked for one or two companies, specializing in one area of operations. His successful experience, he feels, qualifies him to give counsel and advice. It may — and it may not. The problems he faced previously may not be the same problems, even within the same field of specialty, that the client-company faces. Or he may not be accountable in the same way as he was when he worked for an employer, and his solutions to problems may be more conservative or more radical than those he would have made when he was accountable.

Or his previous method of problem-solving may have been through trial and error — a luxury a client can ill afford if he's paying for outside expertise. Or his employment experience may have been such that he had had competent guidance — a factor that may be missing when he goes out on his own.

The reasons for incompetence are many and diverse and we need not dwell on them any further except to note in summary that consultants, as any other group of people, range from good to bad.

Some General Observations

Before getting into the client's contributions to the failure of a client–consultant relationship, we should make some observations. The reader will note that some of these contributions are so basic as to belong in an elementary primer on management. In substance, for example, we will point out that the client should exercise care in selecting a consultant and should know how the consultant will operate before he starts. Most readers, sophisticated and hard-headed, will smite their foreheads in anguish over the basic advice. "Come on, now," is apt to be the plea. "We didn't come this far only to be told this."

Unfortunately, between the smite and practice, something frequently happens. While admittedly many prospective clients are likely to establish the client–consultant relationship on some pretty firm ground, we are concerned here with the failure of these relationships, not the successes — and how these failures can be reduced.

With this in mind, let's look at why an experienced manager may commit a fundamental error which seems quite obvious when viewed in retrospect or when committed to paper.

Most consultants "sell" very well. They have to. They are selling an expensive intangible service to a very sophisticated market — top managements — and the cultivation of a good selling approach is a must. Virtually every consultant makes a good appearance. He generates an enthusiasm and climate of confidence that is often infectious — especially to a man who has lived with and brooded over a problem and who perhaps has reached the point where he's given up on it and recognizes the need for outside help. The consultant is almost always well-spoken with a glibness in the language of the trade. He is generally well-read and can cite the latest concepts in management technique that may or may not be applicable to the prospective client's problem — but which are impressive nonetheless.

He is often familiar with the problems of other companies (either through his experience, his reading, or his conversations with others) and how they did or did not solve their problems. This increases the client's receptivity to the consultant's "selling" because he is made to feel that the consultant knows a whole lot more about his problem than he (the prospective client) because the consultant either explicitly or implicitly indicates a familiarity with this type of problem.

Thus, what may appear to the prospective client a crisis problem oftens feeds back as just another easily soluble run-of-the-mill job for the consultant. The relief in being able to turn this over to the latter, to be able to turn his attention to other problems and opportunities with the feeling that the present problem is in capable, knowledgeable hands, can often make the prospective client a little careless in laying the proper groundwork for the resultant relationship.

The prospective client is often isolated from the specific problems of other companies and their company peculiarities. He recognizes the insularity produced by his company's in-bred attitudes and limited frames of reference. There is the feeling (and generally true) that the consultant because of his third-party perspective can bridge the gap between these attitudes and the rest of the industry "out there." Most companies' top executives harbor the subconscious feeling that someone else may be doing something better and they won't find out about it until it's too late.

The consultant's experience may criss-cross the industry and can provide this information — especially when the consultant drops the right tactical hints. This too tends to make some prospective clients, if caught at the right time, less prone to do their homework.

Many prospective clients don't delve as much as they should into how the consultant will operate. The reason is simple. They assume the consultant knows his business and they (prospective clients) are often results-oriented. Most top managements adhere pretty strongly to the principle of delegation, e.g. delegate responsibilities and evaluate results (even though in practice this principle is all too often ignored) and carry it over to the operation of a client–consultant relationship. This type of delegation is fine and desirable if the delegatee is an executive of the company building a career and risking this career constantly by his success or failure to achieve results. However, the consultant does not risk this. Obviously, he wants to succeed. But his relationship with the prospective client is not a career one. It may, and most likely will be, a one-time shot. Therefore, his mode of operation should become an important evaluative consideration to the client in determining whether to consummate the client–consultant relationship. All too often, unhappily, it is not.

With this background in mind, let's now look at the client's contributions to the failure of a client–consultant relationship and, more specifically, what he can do to reduce the incidence of failure.

Now, about the Client

As we stated previously, this coin has two sides. From the consultant's side of responsibility, we've covered some of the reasons why the client–consultant relationship doesn't work. We cannot leave the client out of this negative equation because he too may share the culpability. At the same time that we analyze his contribution to it, we will also note what steps he can take to insure that his experience with a consultant is both profitable and nonexplosive.

The Client Fails to Properly Screen a Prospective Consultant. Consultants come in all shapes and forms — from the one-man generalist to the one-man specialist, from the large firm with many consultants and many specialties to the moonlighting academician. Their specialties may vary from organization to data processing, from decision-making courses to fair employment practices, from labor relations to definition of management goals. The list is endless and if one probed deeply enough, one would even find consultants to consultants.

The prospective client, therefore, has a wide field to choose from. In selecting one, the client should exercise the same caution he uses in selecting a top executive. What is the consultant's experience? Whom did he work for and what did he accomplish? Does the consultant's field of expertise tie in with the client's needs? Is the consultant's personality such as to permit him to work with the company's people or will he generate negative-productive antagonism?

The client should check references and previous clients to verify the consultant's claims to success. Any consultant's refusal to cooperate in this background check should in itself raise a red flag of caution. Many consultants come to a client through one referral. Yet the new client's problems may not have the same mixture as the referral client's. Therefore, the former should, where possible, check beyond the one reference.

It has been a constant source of amazement to us how many hard-bitten, tough-minded, normally cynical executives accept at face value the man with whom they are ready to make a generally very expensive commitment — both in terms of fees and potential internal disruption.

The Client Does Not Seek Clarification of How the Consultant Will Operate. At the interview stage, a prospective client should have a clear-cut understanding of the approach the consultant intends to use and basically his method of operation.

These are the types of questions that should be asked: Will the consultant simply observe? Will he use a stopwatch? Will he be interviewing executives and/or employees? If so, which ones? How long will the job take? Will the consultant's services be intermittent or continuous until completion? What help will he need from the company? What records will have to be made available to him? Will he provide interim reports? Will he conduct expensive surveys that perhaps the company has already made? How many people will be assigned to the job? What are the potentials for disruption of the company's day-by-day operations? In short, the client should clearly understand what this comparative stranger will be doing around the company during his tenure.

The Client Fails to Seek Clarification of What His Money Will Buy. Here again, a clear-cut understanding should be reached at the interview stage. What exactly will the consultant do in terms of solving problems? Will he simply submit a report? Will he survey and do nothing more than re-define the problems from his perspective? Will he follow up on his recommendations? Will he provide interim reports, written or oral? Will he hold the client's hand and implement his recommendations? Will the client be doing business with the consultant or the consultant's staff? Does the consultant plan return visits to check on the implementation of his recommendations and adjust them where necessary?

If, for example, he finds a piece of equipment antiquated, will he simply note that fact or will he be specific in terms of suggesting a replacement by brand, cost, and anticipated results? How much will this service cost? If the consultant operates on a per diem basis, how many days should it take? And if the fee includes "expenses", just what do these expenses include?

Obvious? Seemingly so. Yet, surprisingly, many clients engage consultants without ever really knowing what final product they are buying until the very end of the consultant's tenure. By then, it's too late.

The Client Fails to Accurately Identify the Problem. We have already covered this facet from the point of view of the consultant. Let's look at it now from the client's. A small tool manufacturer found his costs were excessively high — as evidenced by the fact that while his prices were competitive, his competition was making money. High costs, he concluded, could only mean low productivity from equipment and/or personnel. His profit structure had been keeping pace with the rest of the industry up until a year ago. He called in a consulting firm heavily experienced in manufacturing.

After seven weeks of effort, the consulting firm, by re-vamping assembly lines, reduced manufacturing costs by 3¾%. Within his field of specialty, the consultant apparently did a competent job. The economics of the situation, however, were such that his bill, $11,000, absorbed the first 16 months of savings. The client was not ecstatic over the results, especially since the resultant savings did not really solve his problem.

Four months later, quite by accident, the client discovered that he had been buying a raw material alloy that was 12% higher in cost than what his competition was buying for a slightly different but equally functional material. Somewhere along the line the industry had changed alloys and he hadn't gotten the word. His purchasing department had been exposed to the new material but somehow between purchasing, engineering, and manufacturing, this exposure came to a dead end. As his company had a 58% material factor, a switch to the new material added almost 7% to his profits.

Identifying this type of problem is, of course, difficult. If it does elude identification or if there is any possibility that the problem itself lies elsewhere, then the client should enlist the aid of the consultant.

When interviewing the latter, the client should explain his definition of the problem and, if necessary, have the consultant spend a few days verifying it before committing both the client and consultant to a long-term expensive committment. In the above case, the client should have explained that his profits were about 2% of sales as opposed to about 9% for the rest of the industry. He should then have had the manufacturing consultant determine whether, after an analysis, he (the consultant) saw the possibility of saving enough by altering manufacturing procedure to increase the profitability of the company up to the industry average. And if so, how?

The Client Fails to Explain Its Resource Limitations. At the initial interview or shortly after the consultant has assessed the problem, the client should explain what resources the company has available for solving the problem plus any other limitations not at once apparent. The obvious purpose is to permit the consultant to either tailor his solutions to what is available or to very quickly assess whether he can indeed develop a useful product with these limitations.

For example, a consultant was called in by a medium-sized luggage manufacturer to reorganize its manufacturing plant. The plant was housed in an old building and its equipment reflected the age of the building. The consultant drew up a list of recommendations for the purchase of new equipment. With it, he recommended a new production flow line. "This will result," he reported proudly 3 weeks later, "in approximately $200,000 in labor savings per year. In addition, using the same space now being used, production output will increase 15–20%."

"How much will it cost?" asked a suspicious company president.

"The major pieces of equipment will run about $850,000 and ancillary equipment perhaps another $75,000."

"Beautiful!" said the president. "If we were General Motors, which we are not. We're up to our neck at the banks as it is. We thought if we went something less than first class, we could make a good start for something like $250,000 and then with the savings from that investment continue a program of modernization."

The consultant submitted his bill for $8500 and went off into the sunset mumbling something about "Why didn't someone tell me?" The president mumbled also. "That's the trouble with consultants. It's not their money. What do they care how they spend it?"

The Client Fails to Adequately Inform His Organization of the Consultant's Role and Goals. An electric appliance manufacturer projecting a substantial increase in his sales volume decided that his middle and lower levels of management needed to reorganize for this expansion. New responsibilities would have to be assigned; decision making at these levels would now have a greater impact as volume increased.

He called in an organizational specialist. "I've got good people. But I'm not sure we've delegated enough responsibility to make them maximally effective. I can visualize hiring more people as our sales increase but before I do, I want to make sure I'm using the people I've got to the fullest."

The client then passed the word along in memo form: "On Sept. 6th, Mr. _____ will, as an outside consultant, work with us in reorganizing our management structure. Your fullest cooperation is requested." Panic hit the ranks. There is a natural inclination to equate "reorganization" with "reductions in force." And an outside consultnat is often considered a euphemism for "hatchet man."

Instead of getting cooperation, the consultant got inflated definitions of the responsibilities from the people he interviewed. Knives were sharpened as most of the executives attempted to defend their own jobs. It was every man for himself. The only unity was in mutual distrust of the consultant. The resistance fed on itself and reached the point where the consultant reported that his efforts were coming to nought. "They're pulling in one direction. I'm pulling in another. I can't get a straight story from anyone." The client blamed the consultant. "I can't hold your hand on this. Maybe it's the way you're going about it." The consultant's departure was imminent.

Fortunately, when the dust of recrimination cleared, the president issued a clarifying memo stressing that the reorganization would not result in reductions of force but rather would involve more individual responsibilities with greater personal opportunities through more visible efforts.

Failure to establish a cooperative climate for the consultant by top management is one of the chief reasons for the failure of the client—consultant relationship. It is often not recognized because the latter's natural tendency is to lay the blame for an antagonistic nonproductive climate on the consultant's techniques and personality.

The Client Fails to Adequately Try to Solve Its Own Problems. A medium-sized food processing company found its sales slipping. It called in a marketing specialist firm.

The consulting firm spent the first six weeks doing market surveys. It developed a very comprehensive picture of the company's marketing position, market potential, product acceptance, etc. Once it felt it had the tools with which to work, it went to work to try to solve the problem. During the course of its efforts, the senior consultant on the job lunched with the assistant manager. He posed the question, "What do you think is wrong?"

"I don't think. I know. Our salesmen were put on salary. They should be on commission. Our sales manager, my boss, is a driver. His idea of sales managing is to climb on his salesmen's backs. Their morale is shot and with little possibility of seeing their efforts more tangibly rewarded, their retaliation is to lay down on the job."

"Why haven't you told anyone?"

"I have. My boss. He told me that this is the way he did it with his previous company, not incidentally a food processing company, and this is the way we're going to do it here. I can't go over his head."

The consultant recommended that the salesmen be put on commission and that the sales manager be replaced. His fee for 7½ weeks of work including the surveys came to $38,000 — equivalent to slightly less than three years salary for the assistant sales manager. The company had the answer all the time. It just never looked for it, never probed deeply enough within its own organization for the answer. The company, therefore, had, in reality, no need for an outside consultant. When the story came out, it felt bilked. It hadn't been bilked. The consultant simply did what the company could have and should have done itself. This logic, however, had not abated its new-found antipathy toward consultants.

How Contacts Are Made

We should perhaps say a word about how contacts are made between client and consultant.

The Client Looks for a Consultant. This occurs when the prospective client recognizes the need for a consultant either to evaluate a course of action before it is taken, to solve a particular problem, or to evaluate a potential opportunity. Sources available to a prospective client to help him zero in on a consultant include friends, relatives, business acquaintances, trade associations, mailings from consultants, chance reading of a consultant's writings that touch a nerve, deans of graduate business schools (for moonlighting faculty members with generally very good in-depth skills), consultant's associations, etc. The list is endless. One might even find a consultant by cruising cocktail parties where someone is bound to be a "consultant." Finding a consultant is easy. One need, in fact, go no further than the yellow pages. Finding the right consultant is not so easy. Of the list above, trade associations, business acquaintances, and graduate business school deans probably represent the most reliable sources.

The Consultant Looks for a Client. Here again, we touch on mailings which generally include brochures and the inevitable copies of testimonials, etc. Mailings, however, are not generally productive to the prospective client unless the consultant is a specialist and his specialty hits a bull's-eye on a current or incipient problem with which a prospective client might be wrestling.

A second way is for the consultant to make a referral part of his deal with another client. "Mr. Smith, we do expect and hope that after we do a good job for you, you will perhaps call one or two business acquaintances and suggest that it might be useful if they see us." Sometimes they add, "It is this quid pro quo that reduces our selling costs and the savings, of course, are reflected in our fee schedule." This method can be useful if there is some relationship between the problem the referral had and the problem the prospective client has.

The third method is the cold call. This may be to sell a specific service (setting up a computerized bookkeeping system, for example) or a general service ("For a moderate fee, we'll send our people in to survey your business and make appropriate recommendations.") The latter consultant generally has a list of people that may be called for referrals. Unfortunately, the list of less-satisfied clients is generally larger, and of course, is tactfully omitted. This type of consultant, incidentally, is the most prone to make recommendations that are not feasible or which do not take into account the peculiarities of a particular business. At best, the prospective client would be taking pot luck.

Summary

Although most of the examples we've used relate to medium-sized companies, the principles apply also to small and large corporations. We believe the reader will share our conclusion that developing a higher rate of successful client-consultant relationships depends primarily on what safeguards the client takes initially. Despite the fact that the principle of caveat emptor applies in full force to this relationship, the company that feels the need for outside help ought not be deterred from seeking it.

A one-time expenditure to organize an on-going operation or a facet of management can be an extremely profitable investment. Nothing in this article should be inferred to discourage such investments. The inference, rather, is an exhortation to make them judiciously with a minimum of risk and a maximum of return. This judicious process starts with a recognition of the potential pitfalls.

Charles H. Ford is an author, lecturer, and consultant on organizational problems and co-owner of Duval Corporation in Canton, Massachusetts.

The Characteristics of a Helping Relationship

Carl R. Rogers

I have long had the strong conviction — some might say it was an obsession — that the therapeutic relationship is only a special instance of interpersonal relationships in general, and that the same lawfulness governs all such relationships. This was the theme I chose to work out for myself when I was asked to give an address to the convention of the American Personnel and Guidance Association at St. Louis, in 1958.

Evident in this article is the dichotomy between the objective and the subjective which has been such an important part of my experience during recent years. I find it very difficult to present an article which is either wholly objective or wholly subjective. I like to bring the two worlds into close juxtaposition, even if I cannot fully reconcile them.

My interest in psychotherapy has brought about in me an interest in every kind of helping relationship. By this term I mean a relationship in which at least one of the parties has the intent of promoting the growth, development, maturity, improved functioning, improved coping with life of the other. The other, in this sense, may be one individual or a group. To put it another way, a helping relationship might be defined as one in which one of the participants intends that there should come about, in one or both parties, more appreciation of, more expression of, more functional use of the latent inner resources of the individual.

Now it is obvious that such a definition covers a wide range of relationships which usually are intended to facilitate growth. It would certainly include the relationship between mother and child, father and child. It would include the relationship between the physician and his patient. The relationship between teacher and pupil would often come under this definition, though some teachers would not have the promotion of growth as their intent. It includes almost all counselor–client relationships, whether we are speaking of educational counseling, vocational counseling, or personal counseling. In this last-mentioned area it would include the wide range of relationships between the psychotherapist and the hospitalized psychotic, the therapist and the troubled or neurotic individual, and the relationship between the therapist and the increasing number of so-called "normal" individuals who enter therapy to improve their own functioning or accelerate their personal growth.

These are largely one-to-one relationships. But we should also think of the large number of individual–group interactions which are intended as helping relationships. Some administrators intend that their relationship to their staff groups shall be of the sort which promotes growth, though other administrators would not have this purpose. The interaction between the group therapy leader and his group belongs here. So does the relationship of the community consultant to a community group. Increasingly the interaction between the industrial consultant and a management group is intended as a helping relationship. Perhaps this listing will point up the fact that a great many of the relationships in which we and others are involved fall within this category of interactions in which there is the purpose of promoting development and more mature and adequate functioning.

The Question

But what are the characteristics of those relationships which *do* help, which do facilitate growth? And at the other end of the scale is it possible to discern those characteristics which make a relationship unhelpful, even though it was the sincere intent to promote growth and development? It is to these questions, particularly the first, that I would like to take you with me over some of the paths I have explored, and to tell you where I am, as of now, in my thinking on these issues.

The Answers Given by Research

It is natural to ask first of all whether there is any empirical research which would give us an objective answer to these questions. There has not been a large amount of research in this area as yet, but what there is is stimulating and suggestive. I cannot report all of it, but I would like to make a somewhat extensive sampling of the studies which have been done and state very briefly some of the findings. In so doing, oversimplification is necessary, and I am quite aware that I am not doing full justice to the researches I am mentioning, but it may give you the feeling that factual advances are being made and pique your curiosity enough to examine the studies themselves, if you have not already done so.

Studies of Attitudes

Most of the studies throw light on the attitudes on the part of the helping person which make a relationship growth-promoting or growth-inhibiting. Let us look at some of these.

A careful study of parent–child relationships made some years ago by Baldwin and others[1] at the Fels Institute contains interesting evidence. Of the various clusters of parental attitudes toward children, the "acceptant-democratic" seemed most growth-facilitating. Children of these parents with their warm and equalitarian attitudes showed an accelerated intellectual development (an increasing I.Q.), more originality, more emotional security and control, and less excitability than children from other types of homes. Though somewhat slow initially in social development, they were, by the time they reached school age, popular, friendly, nonaggressive leaders.

Where parents' attitudes are classed as "actively rejectant," the children show a slightly decelerated intellectual development, relatively poor use of the abilities they do possess, and some lack of originality. They are emotionally unstable, rebellious, aggressive, and quarrelsome. The children of parents with other attitude syndromes tend in various respects to fall in-between these extremes.

I am sure that these findings do not surprise us as related to child development. I would like to suggest that they probably apply to other relationships as well and that the counselor or physician or administrator who is warmly emotional and expressive, respectful of the individuality of himself and of the other, and who exhibits a nonpossessive caring probably facilitates self-realization much as does a parent with these attitudes.

Let me turn to another careful study in a very different area. Whitehorn and Betz[2, 18] investigated the degree of success achieved by young resident physicians in working with schizophrenic patients on a psychiatric ward. They chose for special study the seven who had been outstandingly helpful, and seven whose patients had shown the least degree of improvement. Each group had treated about fifty patients. The investigators examined all the available evidence to discover in what ways the A group (the successful group) differed from the B group. Several significant differences were found. The physicians in the A group tended to see the schizophrenic in terms of the personal meaning which various behaviors had to the patient, rather than seeing him as a case history or a descriptive diagnosis. They also tended to work toward goals which were oriented to the personality of the patient, rather than such goals as reducing the symptoms or curing the disease. It was found that the helpful physicians, in their day-by-day interaction, primarily made use of active personal participation — a person-to-person relationship. They made less use of procedures which could be classed as "passive permissive." They were even less likely to use such procedures as interpretation, instruction or advice, or emphasis upon the practical care of the patient. Finally, they were much more likely than the B group to develop a relationship in which the patient felt trust and confidence in the physician.

Although the authors cautiously emphasize that these findings relate only to the treatment of schizophrenics, I am inclined to disagree. I suspect that similar facts would be found in a research study of almost any class of helping relationship.

Another interesting study focuses upon the way in which the person being helped perceives the relationship. Heine[11] studied individuals who had gone for psychotherapeutic help to psychoanalytic, client-centered, and Adlerian therapists. Regardless of the type of therapy, these clients report similar changes in themselves. But it is their perception of the relationship which is of particular interest to us here. When asked what accounted for the changes which had occurred, they expressed some differing explanations, depending on the orientation of the therapist. But their agreement on the major elements they had found helpful was even more significant. They indicated that these attitudinal elements in the relationship accounted for the changes which had taken place in themselves (the trust they had felt in the therapist; being understood by the therapist; the feeling of independence they had had in making choices and decisions). The therapist procedure which they had found most helpful was that the therapist clarified and openly stated feelings which the client had been approaching hazily and hesitantly.

There was also a high degree of agreement among these clients, regardless of the orientation of their therapists, as to what elements had been unhelpful in the relationship. Such therapist attitudes as lack of interest, remoteness or distance, and an over-degree of sympathy were perceived as unhelpful. As to procedures, they had found it unhelpful when therapists had given direct specific advice regarding decisions or had emphasized past history rather than present problems. Guiding suggestions mildly given were preceived in an intermediate range — neither clearly helpful nor unhelpful.

Fiedler, in a much quoted study,[7] found that expert therapists of differing orientations formed similar relationships with their clients. Less well known are the elements which characterized these relationships, differentiating them from the relationships formed by less expert therapists. These elements are: an ability to understand the client's meanings and feelings; a sensitivity to the client's attitudes; a warm interest without any emotional over-involvement.

A study by Quinn[14] throws light on what is involved in understanding the client's meanings and feelings. His study is surprising in that it shows that "understanding" of the client's meanings is essentially an attitude of *desiring* to understand. Quinn presented his judges only with recorded therapist statements taken from interviews. The raters had no knowledge of what the therapist was responding to or how the client reacted to his response. Yet it was found that the degree of understanding could be judged about as well from this material as from listening to the response in context. This seems rather conclusive evidence that it is an attitude of wanting to understand which is communicated.

As to the emotional quality of the relationship, Seeman[16] found that success in psychotherapy is closely associated with a strong and growing mutual liking and respect between client and therapist.

An interesting study by Dittes[4] indicates how delicate this relationship is. Using a physiological measure, the psychogalvanic reflex, to measure the anxious or threatened or alerted reactions of the client, Dittes correlated the deviations on this measure with judges' ratings of the degree of warm acceptance and permissiveness on the part of the therapist. It was found that whenever the therapist's attitudes changed even slightly in the direction of a lesser degree of acceptance, the number of abrupt GSR deviations significantly increased. Evidently when the relationship is experienced as less acceptant, the organism organizes against threat, even at the physiological level.

Without trying fully to integrate the findings from these various studies, it can at least be noted that a few things stand out. One is the fact that it is the attitudes and feelings of the therapist, rather than his theoretical orientation, which is important. His procedures and techniques are less important than his attitudes. It is also worth noting that it is the way in which his attitudes and procedures are *perceived* which makes a difference to the client, and that it is this perception which is crucial.

"Manufactured" Relationships

Let me turn to research of a very different sort, some of which you may find rather abhorrent, but which nevertheless has a bearing upon the nature of a facilitating relationship. These studies have to do with what we might think of as manufactured relationships.

Verplanck,[17] Greenspoon,[8] and others have shown that operant conditioning of verbal behavior is possible in a relationship. Very briefly, if the experimenter says "Mhm," or "Good," or nods his head after certain types of words or statements, those classes of words tend to increase because of being reinforced. It has been shown that using such procedures one can bring about increases in such diverse verbal categories as plural nouns, hostile words, and statements of opinion. The person is completely unaware that he is being influenced in any way by these reinforcers. The implication is that by such selective reinforcement we could bring it about that the other person in the relationship would be using whatever kinds of words and making whatever kinds of statements we had decided to reinforce.

Following still further the principles of operant conditioning as developed by Skinner and his group, Lindsley[12] has shown that a chronic schizophrenic can be placed in a "helping relationship" with a machine. The machine, somewhat like a vending machine, can be set to reward a variety of types of behaviors. Initially it simply rewards — with candy, a cigarette, or the display of a picture — the lever-pressing behavior of the patient. But it is possible to set it so that many pulls on the lever may supply a hungry kitten — visible in a separate enclosure — with a drop of milk. In this case the satisfaction is an altruistic one. Plans are being developed to reward similar social or altruistic behavior directed toward another patient, placed in the next room. The only limit to the kinds of behavior which might be rewarded lies in the degree of mechanical ingenuity of the experimenter.

Lindsley reports that in some patients there has been marked clinical improvement. Personally I cannot help but be impressed by the description of one patient who had gone from a deteriorated chronic state to being given free grounds privileges, this change being quite clearly associated with his interaction with the machine. Then the experimenter decided to study experimental extinction, which, put in more personal terms, means that no matter how many thousands of times the lever was pressed, no reward of any kind was forthcoming. The patient gradually regressed, grew untidy, uncommunicative, and his grounds privilege had to be revoked. This (to me) pathetic incident would seem to indicate that even in a relationship to a machine, trustworthiness is important if the relationship is to be helpful.

Still another interesting study of a manufactured relationship is being carried on by Harlow and his associates,[10] this time with monkeys. Infant monkeys, removed from their mothers almost immediately after birth, are, in one phase of the experiment, presented with two objects. One might be termed the "hard mother," a sloping cylinder of wire netting with a nipple from which the baby may feed. The other is a "soft mother," a similar cylinder made of foam rubber and terry cloth. Even when an infant gets all his food from the "hard mother" he clearly and increasingly prefers the "soft mother." Motion pictures show that he definitely "relates" to this object, playing with it, enjoying it, finding security in clinging to it when strange objects are near, and using that security as a home base for venturing into the frightening world. Of the many interesting and challenging implications of this study, one seems reasonably clear. It is that no amount of direct food reward can take the place of certain perceived qualities which the infant appears to need and desire.

Two Recent Studies

Let me close this wide-ranging — and perhaps perplexing — sampling of research studies with an account of two very recent investigations. The first is an experiment conducted by Ends and Page.[5] Working with hardened chronic hospitalized alcoholics who had been committed to a state hospital for sixty days, they tried three different methods of group psychotherapy. The method which they believed would be most effective was therapy based on a two-factor theory of learning; a client-centered approach was expected to be second; a psychoanalytically oriented approach was expected to be least efficient. Their results showed that the therapy based upon a learning theory was not only not helpful, but was somewhat deleterious. The outcomes were worse than those in the control group which had no therapy. The analytically oriented therapy produced some positive gain, and the client-centered group therapy was associated with the greatest amount of positive change. Follow-up data, extending over one and one-half years, confirmed the in-hospital findings, with the lasting improvement being greatest in the client-centered approach, next in the analytic, next the control group, and least in those handled by a learning theory approach.

As I have puzzled over this study, unusual in that the approach to which the authors were committed proved *least* effective, I find a clue, I believe, in the description of the therapy based on learning theory.[13] Essentially it consisted (a) of pointing out and labeling the behaviors which had proved unsatisfying, (b) of exploring objectively with the client the reasons behind these behaviors, and (c) of establishing through re-education more effective problem-solving habits. But in all of this interaction the aim, as they formulated it, was to be impersonal. The therapist "permits as little of his own personality to intrude as is humanly possible." The "therapist stresses personal anonymity in his activities, i.e., he must studiously avoid impressing the patient with his own (therapist's) individual personality characteristics." To me this seems the most likely clue to the failure of this approach, as I try to interpret the facts in the light of the other research studies. To withhold one's self as a person and to deal with the other person as an object does not have a high probability of being helpful.

The final study I wish to report is one just being completed by Halkides.[9] She started from a theoretical formulation of mine regarding the necessary and sufficient conditions for therapeutic change.[15] She hypothesized that there would be a significant relationship between the extent of constructive personality change in the client and four counselor variables: (a) the degree of emphatic understanding of the client manifested by the counselor; (b) the degree of positive affective attitude (unconditional positive regard) manifested by the counselor toward the client; (c) the extent to which the counselor is genuine, his words matching his own internal feeling; and (d) the extent to which the counselor's response matches the client's expression in the intensity of affective expression.

To investigate these hypotheses she first selected, by multiple objective criteria, a group of ten cases which could be classed as "most successful" and a group of ten "least successful" cases. She then took an early and late recorded interview from each of these cases. On a random basis she picked nine client–counselor interaction units — a client statement and a counselor response — from each of these interviews. She thus had nine early interactions and nine later interactions from each case. This gave her several hundred units which were now placed in random order. The units from an early interview of an unsuccessful case might be followed by the units from a late interview of a successful case, etc.

Three judges who did not know the cases or their degree of success, or the source of any given unit, now listened to this material four different times. They rated each unit on a seven-point scale, first as to the degree of empathy, second as to the counselor's positive attitude toward the client, third as to the counselor's congruence or genuineness, and fourth as to the degree to which the counselor's response matched the emotional intensity of the client's expression.

I think all of us who knew of the study regarded it as a very bold venture. Could judges listening to single units of interaction possibly make any reliable rating of such subtle qualities as I have mentioned? And even if suitable reliability could be obtained, could eighteen counselor–client interchanges from each case — a minute sampling of the hundreds or thousands of such interchanges which occurred in each case — possibly bear any relationship to the therapeutic outcome? The chance seemed slim.

The findings are surprising. It proved possible to achieve high reliability between the judges, most of the interjudge correlations being in the 0.80s or 0.90s, except on the last variable. It was found that a high degree of empathic understanding was significantly associated, at a .001 level, with the more successful cases. A high degree of unconditional positive regard was likewise associated with the more successful cases, at the .001 level. Even the rating of the counselor's genuineness or congruence — the extent to which his words matched his feelings — was associated with the successful outcome of the case, and again at the .001 level of significance. Only in the investigation of the matching intensity of affective expression were the results equivocal.

It is of interest too that high ratings of these variables were not associated more significantly with units from later interviews than with units from early interviews. This means that the counselor's attitudes were quite constant throughout the interviews. If he was highly empathic, he tended to be so from first to last. If he was lacking in genuineness, this tended to be true of both early and late interviews.

As with any study, this investigation has its limitations. It is concerned with a certain type of helping relationship, psychotherapy. It investigated only four variables thought to be significant. Perhaps there are many others. Nevertheless it represents a significant advance in the study of helping relationships. Let me try to state the findings in the simplest possible fashion. It seems to indicate that the quality of the counselor's interaction with a client can be satisfactorily judged on the basis of a very small sampling of his behavior. It also means that if the counselor is congruent or transparent, so that his words are in line with his feelings rather than the two being discrepant, if the counselor likes the client unconditionally, and if the counselor understands the essential feelings of the client as they seem to the client, then there is a strong probability that this will be an effective helping relationship.

Some Comments

These then are some of the studies which throw at least a measure of light on the nature of the helping relationship. They have investigated different facets of the problem. They have approached it from very different theoretical contexts. They have used different methods. They are not directly comparable. Yet they seem to me to point to several statements which may be made with some assurance. It seems clear that relationships which are helpful have different characteristics from relationships which are unhelpful. These differential characteristics have to do primarily with the attitudes of the helping person on the one hand and with the perception of the relationship by the "helpee" on the other. It is equally clear that the studies thus far made do not give us any final answers as to what is a helping relationship, nor how it is to be formed.

How Can I Create a Helping Relationship?

I believe each of us working in the field of human relationships has a similar problem in knowing how to use research knowledge. We cannot slavishly follow findings in a mechanical way or we destroy the personal qualities which these very studies show to be valuable. It seems to me that we have to use these studies, testing them against our own experience and forming new and further personal hypotheses to use and test in our own further personal relationships.

So, rather than try to tell you how you should the findings, I should like to tell you the kind of questions which these studies and my own clinical experience raise for me, and some of the tentative and changing hypotheses which guide my behavior as I enter into what I hope may be helping relationships, whether with students, staff, family, or clients. Let me list a number of these questions and considerations.

1. Can I *be* in some way which will be perceived by the other person as trustworthy, as dependable or consistent in some deep sense? Both research and experience indicate that this is very important, and over the years I have found what I believe are deeper and better ways of answering this question. I used to feel that if I fulfilled all the outer conditions of trustworthiness — keeping appointments, respecting the confidential nature of the interviews, etc. — and if I acted consistently the same during the interviews, then this condition would be fulfilled. But experience drove home the fact that to act consistently acceptant (for example, if in fact I was feeling annoyed or skeptical or some other nonacceptant feeling) was certain in the long run to be perceived as inconsistent or untrustworthy. I have come to recognize that being trustworthy does not demand that I be rigidly consistent but that I can be dependably real. The term "congruent" is one I have used to describe the way I would like to be. By this I mean that whatever feeling or attitude I am experiencing would be matched by my awareness of that attitude. When this is true, then I am a unified or integrated person in that moment, and hence I can *be* whatever I deeply *am*. This is a reality which I find others experience as dependable.

2. A very closely related question is this: Can I be expressive enough as a person that what I am will be communicated unambiguously? I believe that most of my failures to achieve a helping relationship can be traced to unsatisfactory answers to these two questions. When I am experiencing an attitude of annoyance toward another person but am unaware of it, then my communication contains contradictory messages. My words are giving one message, but I am also in subtle ways communicating the annoyance I feel and this confuses the other person and makes him distrustful, though he too may be unaware of what is causing the difficulty. When as a parent or a therapist or a teacher or an administrator I fail to listen to what is going on in me, fail because of my own defensiveness to sense my own feelings, then this kind of failure seems to result. It has made it seem to me that the most basic learning for anyone who hopes to establish any kind of helping relationship is that it is safe to be transparently real. If in a given relationship I am reasonably congruent, if no feelings relevant to the relationship are hidden either to me or the other person, then I can be almost sure that the relationship will be a helpful one.

One way of putting this which may seem strange to you is that if I can form a helping relationship to myself — if I can be sensitively aware of and acceptant toward my own feelings — then the likelihood is great that I can form a helping relationship toward another.

Now, acceptantly to be what I am, in this sense, and to permit this to show through to the other person, is the most difficult task I know and one I never fully achieve. But to realize that this *is* my task has been most rewarding because it has helped me to find what has gone wrong with interpersonal relationships which have become snarled and to put them on a constructive track again. It has meant that if I am to facilitate the personal growth of others in relation to me, then I must grow, and while this is often painful it is also enriching.

3. A third question is: Can I let myself experience positive attitudes toward this other person — attitudes of warmth, caring, liking, interest, respect? It is not easy. I find in myself, and feel that I often see in others, a certain amount of fear of these feelings. We are afraid that if we let ourselves freely experience these positive feelings toward another, we may be trapped by them. They may lead to demands on us or we may be disappointed in our trust, and these outcomes we fear. So, as a reaction, we tend to build up distance between ourselves and others — aloofness, a "professional" attitude, an impersonal relationship.

I feel quite strongly that one of the important reasons for the professionalization of every field is that it helps to keep this distance. In the clinical areas, we develop elaborate diagnostic formulations, seeing the person as an object. In teaching and in administration we develop all kinds of evaluative procedures, so that again the person is perceived as an object. In these ways, I believe, we can keep ourselves from experiencing the caring which would exist if we recognized the relationship as one between two persons. It is a real achievement when we can learn, even in certain relationships or at certain times in those relationships, that it is safe to care, that it is safe to relate to the other as a person for whom we have positive feelings.

4. Another question the importance of which I have learned in my own experience is: Can I be strong enough as a person to be separate from the other? Can I be a sturdy respecter of my own feelings, my own needs, as well as his? Can I own and, if need be, express my own feelings as something belonging to me and separate from his feelings? Am I strong enough in my own separateness that I will not be downcast by his depression, frightened by his fear, nor engulfed by his dependency? Is my inner self hardy enough to realize that I am not destroyed by his anger, taken over by his need for dependence, nor enslaved by his love, but that I exist separate from him with feelings and rights of my own? When I can freely feel this strength of being a separate person, then I find that I can let myself go much more deeply in understanding and accepting him because I am not fearful of losing myself.

5. The next question is closely related. Am I sure enough within myself to permit him his separateness? Can I permit him to be what he is — honest or deceitful, infantile or adult, despairing or over-confident? Can I give him the freedom to be? Or do I feel that he should follow my advice, or remain somewhat dependent on me, or mold himself after me? In this connection I think of the interesting small study by Farson[6] which found that the less well-adjusted and

less-competent counselor tends to induce conformity to himself, to have clients who model themselves after him. On the other hand, the better-adjusted and more-competent counselor can interact with a client through many interviews without interfering with the freedom of the client to develop a personality quite separate from that of his therapist. I should prefer to be in this latter class whether as parent or supervisor or counselor.

6. Another question I ask myself is: Can I let myself enter fully into the world of his feelings and personal meanings and see these as he does? Can I step into his private world so completely that I lose all desire to evaluate or judge it? Can I enter it so sensitively that I can move about in it freely, without trampling on meanings which are precious to him? Can I sense it so accurately that I can catch not only the meanings of his experience which are obvious to him, but those meanings which are only implicit, which he sees only dimly or as confusion? Can I extend this understanding without limit? I think of the client who said, "Whenever I find someone who understands a *part* of me at the time, then it never fails that a point is reached where I know they're *not* understanding me again... What I've looked for so hard is for someone to understand."

For myself I find it easier to feel this kind of understanding and to communicate it to individual clients than to students in a class or staff members in a group in which I am involved. There is a strong temptation to set students "straight," or to point out to a staff member the errors in his thinking. Yet when I can permit myself to understand in these situations, it is mutually rewarding. And with clients in therapy, I am often impressed with the fact that even a minimal amount of empathic understanding — a bumbling and faulty attempt to catch the confused complexity of the client's meaning — is helpful, though there is no doubt that it is most helpful when I can see and formulate clearly the meanings in his experiencing which for him have been unclear and tangled.

7. Still another issue is whether I can be acceptant of each facet of this other person which he presents to me. Can I receive him as he is? Can I communicate this attitude? Or can I only receive him conditionally, acceptant of some aspects of his feelings and silently or openly disapproving of other aspects? It has been my experience that when my attitude is conditional, then he cannot change or grow in those respects in which I cannot fully receive him. And when — afterward and sometimes too late — I try to discover why I have been unable to accept him in every respect, I usually discover that it is because I have been frightened or threatened in myself by some aspect of his feelings. If I am to be more helpful, then I must myself grow and accept myself in these respects.

8. A very practical issue is raised by the question: Can I act with sufficient sensitivity in the relationship that my behavior will not be perceived as a threat? The work we are beginning to do in studying the physiological concomitants of psychotherapy confirms the research by Dittes in indicating how easily individuals are threatened at a physiological level. The psychogalvanic reflex — the measure of skin conductance — takes a sharp dip when the therapist responds with some word which is just a little stronger than the client's feelings. And to a phrase such

as, "My you *do* look upset," the needle swings almost off the paper. My desire to avoid even such minor threats is not due to a hypersensitivity about my client. It is simply due to the conviction based on experience that if I can free him as completely as possible from external threat, then he can begin to experience and to deal with the internal feelings and conflicts which he finds threatening within himself.

9. A specific aspect of the preceding question, but an important one, is: Can I free him from the threat of external evaluation? In almost every phase of our lives — at home, at school, at work — we find ourselves under the rewards and punishments of external judgements. "That's good"; "that's naughty." "That's worth an A"; "that's a failure." "That's good counseling"; "that's poor counseling." Such judgments are a part of our lives from infancy to old age. I believe they have a certain social usefulness to institutions and organizations such as schools and professions. Like everyone else I find myself all too often making such evaluations. But in my experience, they do not make for personal growth and hence I do not believe that they are a part of a helping relationship. Curiously enough, a positive evaluation is as threatening in the long run as a negative one, since to inform someone that he is good implies that you also have the right to tell him he is bad. So I have come to feel that the more I can keep a relationship free of judgment and evaluation, the more this will permit the other person to reach the point where he recognizes that the locus of evaluation, the center of responsibility, lies within himself. The meaning and value of his experience is in the last analysis something which is up to him, and no amount of external judgment can alter this. So I should like to work toward a relationship in which I am not, even in my own feelings, evaluating him. This I believe can set him free to be a self-responsible person.

10. One last question: Can I meet this other individual as a person who is in process of *becoming*, or will I be bound by his past and by my past? If, in my encounter with him, I am dealing with him as an immature child, an ignorant student, a neurotic personality, or a psychopath, each of these concepts of mine limits what he can be in the relationship. Martin Buber, the existentialist philosopher of the University of Jerusalem, has a phrase, "confirming the other," which has had meaning for me. He says, "Confirming means...accepting the whole potentiality of the other...I can recognize in him, the person he has been...*created* to become...I confirm him in myself, and then in him, in relation to this potentiality that...can now be developed, can evolve."[3] If I accept the other person as something fixed, already diagnosed and classified, already shaped by his past, then I am doing my part to confirm this limited hypothesis. If I accept him as a process of becoming, then I am doing what I can to confirm or make real his potentialities.

It is at this point that I see Verplanck, Lindsley, and Skinner, working in operant conditioning, coming together with Buber, the philosopher or mystic. At least they come together in principle, in an odd way. If I see a relationship as only an opportunity to reinforce certain types of words or opinions in the other, then I tend to confirm him as an object — a basically mechanical, manipulable object. And if I see this as his potentiality, he tends to act in ways which support this hypothesis. If, on the other hand, I see a relationship as an opportunity to "reinforce" *all* that he is, the person that he is with all his existent potentialities, then he tends to act in ways which support *this* hypothesis. I have then — to use Buber's term — confirmed him as a living person, capable of creative inner development. Personally I prefer this second type of hypothesis.

Conclusion

In the early portion of this article I reviewed some of the contributions which research is making to our knowledge *about* relationships. Endeavoring to keep that knowledge in mind, I then took up the kind of questions which arise from an inner and subjective point of view as I enter, as a person, into relationships. If I could, in myself, answer all the questions I have raised in the affirmative, then I believe that any relationships in which I was involved would be helping relationships, would involve growth. But I cannot give a positive answer to most of these questions. I can only work in the direction of the positive answer.

This has raised in my mind the strong suspicion that the optimal helping relationship is the kind of relationship created by a person who is psychologically mature. Or to put it in another way, the degree to which I can create relationships which facilitate the growth of others as separate persons is a measure of the growth I have achieved in myself. In some respects this is a disturbing thought, but it is also a promising or challenging one. It would indicate that if I am interested in creating helping relationships, I have a fascinating lifetime job ahead of me, stretching and developing my potentialities in the direction of growth.

I am left with the uncomfortable thought that what I have been working out for myself in this paper may have little relationship to your interests and your work. If so, I regret it. But I am at least partially comforted by the fact that all of us who are working in the field of human relationships and trying to understand the basic orderliness of that field are engaged in the most crucial enterprise in today's world. If we are thoughtfully trying to understand our tasks as administrators, teachers, educational counselors, vocational counselors, therapists, then we are working on the problem which will determine the future of this planet. For it is not upon the physical sciences that the future will depend. It is upon us who are trying to understand and deal with the interactions between human beings — who are trying to create helping relationships. So I hope that the questions I ask of myself will be of some use to you in gaining understanding and perspective as you endeavor, in your way, to facilitate growth in your relationships.

References

1. Baldwin, A. L., J. Kalhorn, and F. H. Breese, "Patterns of parent behavior," *Psychol. Monogr.* Vol. 58, No. 268 (1945), pp. - 75.

2. Betz, B. J., and J. C. Whitehorn, "The relationship of the therapist to the outcome of therapy in schizophrenia," *Psychiat. Research Reports #5. Research techniques in schizophrenia*, Washington, D.C., American Psychiatric Association, 1956, pp. 89 – 117.
3. Buber, M., and C. Rogers, Transcription of dialogue held April 18, 1957, Ann Arbor, Mich. Unpublished manuscript.
4. Dittes, J. E., "Galvanic skin response as a measure of patient's reaction to therapist's permissiveness," *J. Abnorm. & Soc. Psychol.* Vol. 55 (1957), pp. 295 – 303.
5. Ends, E. J., and C. W. Page, "A study of three types of group psychotherapy with hospitalized male inebriates," *Quar. J. Stud. Alcohol.* Vol. 18 (1957), pp. 263 – 277.
6. Farson, R. E., Introjection in the psychotherapeutic relationship. Unpublished doctoral dissertation, University of Chicago, 1955.
7. Fiedler, F. E., "Quantitative studies on the role of therapists feelings toward their patients," In Mowrer, O. H. (Ed.), *Psychotherapy: Theory and Research*, New York: Ronald Press, 1953, Chap. 12.
8. Greenspoon, J., "The Reinforcing Effect of Two Spoken Sounds on the Frequency of Two Responses," *Amer. J. Psychol.*, Vol. 68 (1955), pp. 409 – 416.
9. Halkides, G., An Experimental Study of Four Conditions Necessary for Therapeutic Change. Unpublished doctoral dissertation, University of Chicago, 1958.
10. Harlow, H. F., "The Nature of Love," *Amer. Psychol.*, Vol. 13 (1958), pp. 673 – 685.
11. Heine, R. W., A Comparison of Patients' Reports on Psychotherapeutic experience with Psychoanalytic, Nondirective, and Adlerian Therapists. Unpublished doctoral dissertation, University of Chicago, 1950.
12. Lindsley, O. R., "Operant Conditioning Methods Applied to Research in Chronic Schizophrenia," *Psychiat. Research Reports #5. Research techniques in schizophrenia*. Washington, D.C.: American Psychiatric Association, 1956, pp. 118 – 153.
13. Page, C. W., and E. J. Ends, A Review and Synthesis of the Literature Suggesting a Psychotherapeutic Technique Based on Two-factor Learning Theory. Unpublished manuscript, loaned to the writer.
14. Quinn, R. D., Psychotherapists' Expressions As an Index to the Quality of Early Therapeutic Relationships. Unpublished doctoral dissertation, University of Chicago, 1950.
15. Rogers, C. R., "The Necessary and Sufficient Conditions of Psychotherapeutic Personality Change," *J. Consult. Psychol.*, Vol. 21 (1957), pp. 95-103.
16. Seeman, J., "Counselor Judgments of Therapeutic Process and Outcome," In C. R. Rogers, and R. F. Dymond (Eds.), *Psychotherapy and Personality Change*, University of Chicago Press, 1954 Chap. 7.
17. Verplanck, W. S., "The Control of the Content of Conversation: Reinforcement of Statements of Opinion," *J. Abnorm. & Soc. Psychol.* Vol. 51 (1955), pp. 668 – 676.
18. Whitehorn, J. C., and B. J. Betz, "A Study of Psychotherapeutic Relationships Between Physicians and Schizophrenic Patients," *Amer. J. Psychiat.*, Vol. 111 (1954), pp. 321 – 331.

Carl R. Rogers is a resident Fellow at the Center for Studies of the Person in La Jolla, California.

Feedback: The Art of Giving and Receiving Help

Cyril R. Mill

Feedback is a way of helping another person to consider changing his behavior. It is communication to a person which gives him information about some aspect of his behavior and its effect on you. As in a guided missile system, feedback helps an individual know whether his behavior is having the effect that he wants; it tells him whether he is "on target" as he strives to achieve his goals.

Criteria for Useful Feedback

The giving and receiving of feedback is a skill that can be acquired. When feedback is attempted at the wrong time or given in the wrong way, the results will be, at best, useless and may be disastrous. Therefore, developing feedback skills can be important. Here are some criteria for useful feedback:

It is descriptive rather than evaluative. It is helpful to focus on what the individual *did* rather than to translate his behavior into a statement about what he *is*. "You have interrupted three people in the last half hour" is probably not something that a person really wants to hear, but is is likely to be more helpful than, "You are a bad-mannered oaf."

It focuses on the feelings generated in the person who has experienced the behavior and who is offering the feedback. "When you interrupt me I feel frustrated," gives the individual clear information about the *effect* of his behavior, while at the same time leaving him free to decide what he wants to do about that effect.

It is specific rather than general. For example, it is probably more useful to learn that you "talk too much" than to have someone describe you as "dominating."

It is directed toward behavior which the receiver can do something about. Frustration is increased when a person is reminded of some shortcoming over which he has no control.

Reproduced by special permission from *Reading Book*, pp. 18-19. Copyright by NTL Institute, 1976.

It is solicited rather than imposed. Feedback is most useful when the receiver feels that he needs and wants it, when he himself has formulated the kind of question which those observing him can answer.

It is well-timed. In general, feedback is most useful at the earliest opportunity after the given behavior, depending, of course, on the receiver's readiness to hear it, support available from others, and so on.

It is checked to ensure clear communication. One way of doing this is to have the receiver try to rephrase the feedback in question to see whether the receiver's version corresponds with what the sender meant.

When feedback is given in a training group, both giver and receiver have opportunity to check its accuracy with others in the group. Thus the receiver will know whether this is one person's impression or an impression shared by others.

Feedback should not be given primarily to "dump" or "unload" on another. If you feel you *have* to say this to the other person, then ask yourself who it is you are trying to "help."

Feedback does not ask "Why?" It stays within the bounds of behavior and one's reactions to that behavior. To theorize about or ask why a person does a certain thing is to plumb the depths of motivation and, perhaps, of the unconscious. Avoiding the "whys" will help one to avoid the error of amateur psychologizing.

Why Do We Resist It?

Given the premise that properly given feedback can be a fine way to learn about oneself, what are some reasons that we resist it? For one thing, it is hard to admit our difficulties to ourselves. It is even harder to admit them to someone else. We are not sure that the other person can be trusted or that his observations are valid. We may be afraid of learning what others think of us; we often expect to hear only negative opinions about ourselves, tending to overlook our positive qualities.

We may have struggled so hard to make ourselves independent that the thought of depending on another individual seems to violate something within us. Or we may during all our lives have looked for someone on whom to depend, and we try to repeat this pattern in our relationship with the helping person.

We may be looking for sympathy and support rather than for help in seeing our difficulty more clearly. When the helper tries to point out some of the ways *we* are contributing to the problem, which might suggest that we as well as others will have to change, we may stop listening. Solving a problem may mean uncovering some of the sides of ourselves which we have avoided or wished to avoid thinking about.

We may feel our problem is so unique no one could ever understand it and certainly not an outsider.

On the other side of the interchange, it is not always easy to give feedback to others. Most of us like to give advice. Doing so suggests that we are competent and important. We get caught up in a "telling" role easily enough without testing whether our advice is appropriate to the total issue or to the abilities, the fears, or the powers of the person we are trying to help.

If the person whom we are trying to help becomes defensive, we may try to argue or pressure him. Defensiveness or denial on the part of the receiver is a clear indication that we are going about trying to be helpful in the wrong way. Our timing is off or we may be simply mistaken about his behavior, but in any case, it is best to desist until we can reevaluate the situation. If we respond to the receiver's resistance with more pressure, resistance will only increase.

To be fruitful the helping situation needs these characteristics:

1. Mutual trust
2. Perceiving the helping situation as a joint exploration
3. Careful listening, with the helper's listening more than the individual receiving help
4. Behavior from the helper which will make it easier for the receiver of help to talk

Feedback takes into account the needs of both the receiver and the giver. Positive feedback is welcomed by the receiver when it is genuine. If feedback is given in a training laboratory under the conditions described here, it can become one of the primary means of learning about self.

Cyril R. Mill is president of Behavioral Science Associates, Inc., in Vienna, Virginia.

Client-Consultant Roles

Despite its apparent obviousness, the roles of the client and the consultant are often overlooked or glossed over in treatments of helping endeavors. Here "role" is used to mean those behaviors which are appropriate for individuals in a relationship. The roles characterize the relationship, with the client operating with certain expectations of the consultant, and vice versa.

Within the literature, there is a severe lack of material concerning the role of the client. A few articles can be found, but these typically are batterings on the "beware of the consultant" drum. Such tom-tom articles sound warnings to the prospective client, spelling out what to look for to avoid being taken by the consultant. Rarely do the writings emphasize the mutuality of the roles of consultant and client.

Further, there is lack of agreement regarding the roles of the consultant, as will be seen in the following article. There are, however, certain trends. One trend is a growing emergence of similarity in terminology. Not only is this a boon to communication, it leads to clarity in uncovering the obvious overlaps and redundancies. Another trend is the growing interest in consultative competencies, that is, identifying required skills and knowledge needed to effectively function in a specific consultant role.

An understanding of the roles in the client–consultant relationship is important in order to (1) aid both parties in the search, (2) specify mutual expectations and minimize confusion, and (3) help the consultant identify the skills and competencies associated with different roles.

Aid in the Search

Consultants are constantly seeking clients, for without clients there are no consultants! The client is enticed with repeated brochures, mailings, office visits, public seminars, and the offer of article reprints. The assessment of appropriate roles can aid the consultant in more effectively targeting his or her marketing to the most likely client-prospect, and can aid the client in selection of the appropriate helper.

Few consultants can function in all the roles that will be discussed in the following article. To maximize marketing efficiency and consultative effectiveness, a consultant should begin by identifying those roles in which he or she has had the most success. This success can be parlayed into positioning statements aimed at likely client markets. Consultant self-assessment requires objective self-awareness and the ability to articulate the findings in a client-oriented manner. For example, if the consultant has particular strength as a facilitator, he or she might be advised to project to prospects who need help in problem solving rather than those requiring an expert opinion.

For the client, the process must start with identifying the need or intention. When the client has some feel for the dimensions of the problem or need, it is easier to identify the kind of consulting roles which could be helpful. This facilitates the client's search for the appropriate helper.

Specify Mutual Expectations

The roles, when agreed upon by both parties, allow for a clarification of mutual expectations. A consultant can use role clarification as a way of communicating more effectively with the client. By surfacing the behaviors the client expects of the consultant, the problem and need can be more easily clarified and the end result can be more readily anticipated.

Both parties might begin role clarification by looking at expected behaviors and then labeling these behavioral roles. Clearly defined roles facilitate clear communication. If correctly employed, they enable the parties to resolve differences and negotiate agreements with mutuality and understanding.

Consultant Skills and Competencies

We can expect competent professionals to be constantly engaged in personal growth and development. The assumption that one has acquired all the useful skills and competencies is a reckless departure from the humility which leads to the maintenance of competence.

The need for a particular competency often surfaces when one is involved in a consulting relationship. The consultant may encounter an area of weakness (or even blindness) which requires work. Role clarification and perpetual reassessment enable the consultant to better forecast personal growth needs and plan required means of meeting those needs.

Roles are a way of helping the consultant identify needs before becoming involved in a client–consultant relationship. If a consultant recognizes the variety of roles which can be performed, he or she is better able to build the competencies which will facilitate successful performance in that role. Beyond identification, however, the consultant must take time for academic learning and personal growth experiences in order to remain current and prepared to deal with the future.

The past 20 years have brought massive changes in what has been required of consultants. With the changes, the use of consultants and the number of consultants have significantly increased. Some of the people new to the field have a much stronger theoretical and conceptual base than those who have been practicing successfully for many years. Obsolesence can catch up with even the most successful consultant who has not identified new material and trends in the field.

At this stage in the emergence of the field, there is continuing struggle with the appropriate roles and competencies. It has not yet been possible to provide the type of "laundry list" frequently sought by those wishing to grow. Some organizations have produced such lists for their members. On closer examination, these lists have turned out to be lists of cognitive areas rather than competencies.

The client competencies have not yet been identified to a point where they could be helpful. At best, we can only suggest some cautions. As we gain greater confidence in our understanding of consultation, it will become easier to spell out client competencies.

Consultants need to be clearer about their own roles and those they wish to perform. If the consultant intends to respond to the newer trends, it becomes more important to identify the competencies needed which the consultant does not have. It is not sufficient to do the "old wines in new goatskins" routine— taking existing competencies and giving them new names.

Internal vs. External Consultant Roles

One of the periodic disputes in the field takes place over the question of whether one can be a consultant to one's own organization. Usually none of the parties has bothered to define "internal" and "external." One way of looking at this is to recognize that the consultant may be either internal or external to the organization, but always is external to the problem or need. The consultant may be an employee of the organization, but not directly related to the unit, group, or individual seeking help.

Internal and external consultants in their ideal form are more alike than different. Both have no direct power or control over implementing the change needed but instead must depend on others. Both desire to be effective helpers.

There are differences. The external consultant typically has more freedom than his or her internal counterpart. The internal consultant is more likely to be politically astute regarding the culture of the client. The external consultant often has the power inherent in being an independent, "objective" influence, while the internal consultant may be a part of the problem.

Donald Swartz suggests the internal consultant can enhance the effectiveness of consultation by carefully clarifying consultant and client roles. Doing some external consulting can broaden the internal consultant's perspective and increase his or her personal confidence and organizational credibility.

For the external consultant, Swartz recommends never taking an assignment if the gut says "no." Collaboration with internal helpers is a suggestion the result of which not only improves the probability of success, but leaves the internal consultant with increased power.

Chapter 4
"Emerging Roles of the Training Director"
Gordon Lippitt and Leonard Nadler

This article was selected not only because of its status as a classic in the field, but also because it represents one of the earliest attempts to categorize the roles of the consultant. Only the portion of the article related to the training director as consultant has been included.

Chaper 5
"The Consultant's Role in Organizational Change"
Neil G. Davey

The significance of this article is in its emphasis on the client–consultant relationship. Although Davey concentrates on organizational change, it is obvious that consultants do perform other tasks and other roles. It is suggested that if the characteristics of the client–consultant relationship could be clearly identified, they could provide clues to how the relationship could be made successful and rewarding for both parties.

Chapter 6
"The Trainer's Role as an Internal Consultant"
Gordon L. Lippitt

It is obvious to most consultant users that external consultants are on the increase. New directories and increased listings of external consultants are published each year. What about the internal consultant? Are organizations trapped in the mode of thinking that the only person who can help must be someone from the "outside"? Do organizations have internal resources they are neglecting?

Gordon Lippitt sees an increasing role for the internal consultant. Here too, he relies on the roles approach to help the internal consultant and management identify their mutual expectations. The relationship of these roles to those appearing earlier in the book are obvious. There is a direct relationship but not an absolute similarity. This article reflects some later thinking than that represented in Chapter 4. This is done, in part, to help the reader understand some of the prevalent thinking as we explore the role models and their evolution.

Chapter 7
"The Evolving Role of the Federal Training Consultant"
Neal E. Chalofsky

The evolution of the federal training consultant provides a sense of history that aids in preparing to move the field further. The Chalofsky article was written for this book to give the reader this historical perspective as well as acquaintance with the skills and competence related to consultant roles. That acquaintance should foster better understanding on the part of client and consultant regarding how the consultant might function.

Emerging Roles of the Training Director

Gordon L. Lippitt
Leonard Nadler

We feel that the most important function in the training portfolio is serving as a problem-solving consultant to the management of an organization.

We have always recognized the need for management to *support* the training effort. The relationship of management to training has been explained in the following way:

"The reporting relationship of the person responsible for the formulation of training plans and programs is particularly important, for if the job is to be done with optimum efficiency, he must be able to present his ideas and plans to people in the management who recognize the value of such plans and who are able to act on them with a minimum of discussion and other time-consuming maneuvers."[1]

It is not, however, the support of training by management that is the major need. The major need is for training to be recognized and used as a valuable tool for management problem solving.

Effective training is helping people "learn how to learn" from every aspect of our life. Most problems faced by organizations can be solved by effective application of problem solving, which is itself a *learning process*.

The training office should serve as an example and a resource to management in the *solution of problems:*

"Earlier theorists of organization were content to talk of measuring effectiveness in terms of adequate profits, efficient service, good productivity, or effective employee morale. These are not adequate in and of themselves. Managers of an organizational system need to define its effectiveness in terms of its capacity to survive, maintain itself, adapt, and to develop toward its own goals and in the performance of multiple functions that also affect society."[2]

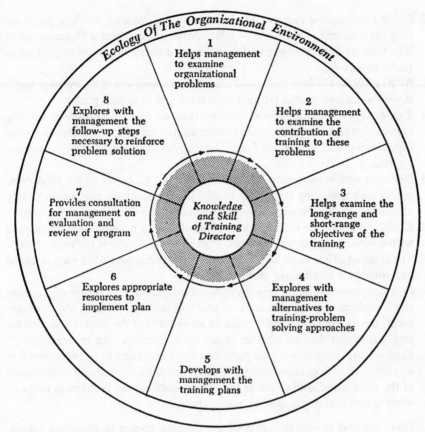

Figure 4-1. Problem-solving function of the training director.

An Increasing Role

The new challenge, then, for a training director and department is to develop their skills and role in the organization as *internal organizational consultants* on problem solving, change, and organizational development.

In Figure 4-1 we have illustrated the way in which the training office can serve as a consultant to management.

Let us examine these steps further:

1. *Helps management examine organizational problems* (e.g., organizes a management retreat for problem-identification in relation to the relations between home and field-office personnel).

2. *Helps management examine the contribution of training to these problems* (e.g., in relation to home/field — office problems, explores with management how training in interpersonal relationships and communications might lead to problem solving).

3. *Helps examine the long-range and short-range objectives of the training* (e.g., involves management in refining objectives and in setting goals).

4. *Explores with management alternatives to training-problem solving approaches* (e.g., encourages the examination of the effect of different forms of organization and managerial leadership, as contrasted with solely a training approach).

5. *Develops with management the training plans* (e.g., based on the objectives, works with a steering committee to develop the program, rather than simply submitting an independently developed plan to management for sanction).

6. *Explores appropriate resources to implement plan* (e.g., provides management with a variety of training resources, both inside and outside the organization. The training office must help management to understand what each resource can contribute to effective problem solution).

7. *Provides consultation for management on evaluation and review of program* (e.g., evaluation must be in terms of problem solving. Working with management, the training office must make an assessment of the current status of the problem, rather than on whether or not the trainees like the program).

8. *Explores with management the follow-up steps necessary to reinforce problem solution* (e.g., encourages management to look at the nontraining implications of the steps taken, and to assess the current status of the problem in terms of other action that might now be necessary).

This "internal consultant" role of the training person is important for the changing organizations of today's society. This role will require increased professionalization and skills in the training field.

"In a sense everyone is a consultant. Everyone has impulses to give advice, information, or help. Teachers, parents, and friends are consultants. Specialists in management, human relations, or finance are consultants. Also, everyone at times feels the need for help. In order that the consultantship between the helper and the recipient optimally meets the needs of both parties, appropriate relationships must be built. It is necessary that both parties have certain kinds of skills, knowledge, and awareness in order to establish these relationships."[3]

ASTD and Other Resources

It is the feeling of these authors that more attention needs to be given by the American Society for Training and Development, Universities, and other professional organizations to providing the skills necessary for an effective consultant.

As Beckhard put it,

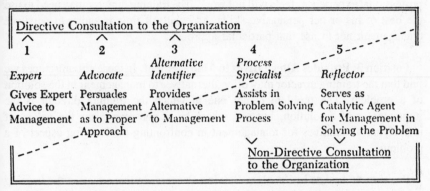

Figure 4-2. Multiple consulting approaches of the training director.

"The consultant (or person in a helping role) always enters such a relationship as a person with authority — achieved either through position or role in the organization or through the possession of specialized knowledge. To achieve an effective consultative relationship, it is essential that he understand the nature of this power and develop skills to use it in a way which will be viewed as helpful by the person receiving the help. A person entering a consulting or helping relationship must have the ability to diagnose the problem and goals of the person being helped, and be able to assess realistically his own motivations for giving the help. He must also recognize the limits of his own resources to help in the particular situation."[4]

In carrying out a "helping" relationship to management, a training director will find himself operating along a continuum of consulting roles (Figure 4-2). In the diagram we have illustrated some of these major helping relationships from directive to primarily nondirective consultations.

Role Choices

Let us examine these different choices in response to management need.

Position 1: Gives Expert Advice to Management. There will be numerous occasions when management will expect the training director to give an answer when asked about a technical question, for example, about the value of a certain kind of training and its utilization in the organization.

Position 2: Persuades Management as to a Proper Approach. In certain circumstances the management of the organization may be attempting to solve a problem by using a medium or a method which the training person from his or her professional experience, feels will not work. The training director may need to use the best of his or her persuasive skills, especially if time is short, to persuade management not to use that particular approach.

Position 3: Provides Alternatives to Management. In these circumstances we find that the training director may offer alternatives to management in the solution of a problem. The problem is not one in which the training director is the implementer of a solution, but one where he or she recognizes the values of identifying alternatives for management in confronting the learning aspect of a problem.

Position 4: Assists in Problem-Solving Process. In this situation the training person serves as a process observer and consultant to management. He or she does not get involved in the "content" of the problem, which may be outside his or her area of competence. Rather, he or she helps management maintain the quality of its problem solving, through his or her skill as a specialist in this field.

Position 5: Serves as Catalyst for Management Problem Solving. In this last category, the training person may only ask questions for management to take into account as it considers a certain direction or action.

Choice Factors

The choice of which position to take at any given time as a consultant to management is conditioned by these factors:

A. Factors in the trainer as a person:
   — Skills as a consultant
   — Ability to work with others
   — Experience in the area of the problem
   — Self-image
   — Level of knowledge and skill as a learning specialist
B. Factors in the relationship between management and the training director:
   — Status in the organization
   — Previous role in management problem solving
   — Familiarity with organization history and objectives
   — Ability to influence management
   — Previous successes and failures in working with other elements of the organization
C. Factors in the problem situation:
   — Knowledge of the content of the problem
   — Time available for solution
   — Ability to see alternatives.

The Challenge to Training

We have tried in this article to present an inclusive view of the emerging role of the training director. With the greater demands for training, increased specialization of training, and the increased needs of organizations, we feel these functions are needed. In many cases, management is not aware of the potential help from its training officer:

"Even so, many otherwise imaginative administrators find it difficult to think of training in other than the most conventional terms. It has taken so much effort to persuade myopic legislators, councilmen, and organizational seniors to establish a training division or add a qualified professional trainer that they are unable to perceive its immense functional possibilities."[5]

It should be said, however, that sometimes the training director and office has not been creative, innovative, or professional enough to see all three roles and functions and to prepare and develop the skills necessary for their fulfillment. .

This is the challenge to all of us who seek to meet the increasing demands placed on the training function in modern society.

References

1. Frank A. DePhillips, William M. Berliner and James J. Cribbin. "Management of Training Programs," Richard D. Irwin, Inc., pp. 235-236.
2. Gordon L. Lippitt, "Implications of the Behavioral Sciences for Management," *Public Personnel Review,* July 1966.
3. Jack R. Gibb "The Role of the Consultant," *The Journal of Social Issues,* Vol. XV, No. 2, 1959.
4. Richard Beckhard, "The Leader Looks at the Consultative Process," Leadership Resources, Inc., 1961.
5. David S. Brown, "An Old Tool Holds New Promise for Management," *Public Management,* Nov. 1965. Reprint Series, Leadership Resources, Inc.

Gordon L. Lippitt is professor of behavioral science in the School of Business Administration, George Washington University.

Leonard Nadler is professor of human resource development and adult education in the School of Education, George Washington University.

The Consultant's Role in Organizational Change

Neil G. Davey

In meeting the challenges and demands of change, organizations frequently seek assistance from *external* agents to play some role in the process of need identification (diagnosis), program evaluation and planning, and the introduction or implementation of change programs. Substantial sums are spent annually by American organizations on the services of external consultants. Although on the whole they appear to be getting their money's worth, there is some evidence that the business clients are less than completely satisfied with the effectiveness of the help they receive in at least some instances.[1] Of even greater import, there is little or no evidence to explain the different levels of consultant effectiveness or organizational satisfaction with these relationships. Clearly, there is need for an empirical study of the relationship which develops between an organization and any consultant it retains.

The fundamental hypothesis underlying this study is that the effectiveness of consultant-assisted change efforts is a function of the relationship between an organization and the consultant it has retained. The question posed is whether an organization–consultant relationship which possesses some particular characteristics is typically associated with successful consultant-assisted change efforts, and whether a relationship with discernibly different characteristics is typically associated with unsuccessful or ineffective change efforts.

While it appears to have been little researched, the idea that the organization–consultant relationship is a vital factor in the effectiveness of consultant-assisted change efforts has appealed — either intuitively, logically, or experientially — to other authors. W. G. Bennis suggests that

"Acceptance (of change) also depends on the relationship between the change agent and client system: the more profound and anxiety-producing the change, the more a collaborative and closer relationship is required. In

From *MSU Business Topics*, Spring, 1971, pp. 76–79. Reprinted by permission of the publisher, Division of Research, Graduate School of Business Administration, Michigan State University.

addition, we can predict that an anticipated change will be resisted to the degree that the client system possesses little or incorrect knowledge about the change, has relatively little trust in the source of change, and has relatively low influence in controlling the nature and direction of the change"[2]

R. Lippitt, J. Watson, and B. Westley, in their book *The Dynamics of Planned Change*, considered that the success of the change effort rests heavily on the quality and workability of the relationship between the change agent (consultant) and client system (organization) — and that many vital aspects of this relationship are established very early in the association. For example, a crucial feature is how the client system begins to think about the change agent.[3] A similar notion was employed by S. Tilles in suggesting that the determinants of the ultimate outcome of a client–consultant relationship are probably manifested much before the final stages of the relationship.[4]

Considerations Prior to Decision

The considerations of organization members which lead to the securing of consultant assistance will inevitably have an effect on the ensuing organization–consultant relationship. These prior considerations may have taken a variety of forms.

The board of directors or personnel of a parent company may decide on the engagement of a consultant and "impose" him on the organization. The organization's chief operating executive may make a decision to engage a consultant and proceed to do so, maintaining himself as the sole point of contact with the consultant, or "imposing" the consultant on other subordinate organization members. Then again, the decision may be made at a lower management level or could perhaps originate as a recommendation from a lower management level. A similar variety of possibilities exists with respect to the selection of a particular consultant and the process through which this is accomplished.

Whether only one consultant is asked to assist the organization, perhaps on the basis of a previously established personal relationship with an organization member, or for any reason, or whether a number of consultants are invited for preliminary discussions or to make preliminary diagnostic investigations could have an influence on the nature of the organization–consultant relationship which ultimately develops. Also, there will be variation in the timing at which consultant help is sought. An urgent appeal to assist with a dramatically serious situation, resulting from the ineffectiveness or inappropriateness of internally sponsored attempts, will likely produce a different type of relationship from one developed in a situation where the request for help is timely and made on more of a preventive basis.

Nature of Consulting Assignment

In addition to those preliminary considerations of seeking consultant help and the decisions actually relating to the consultant engagement, there are the questions which relate to the scope and nature of the intended consulting assignment. Relevant features here include:

— Whether the selected consultant is required by the organization to conduct preliminary diagnostic investigations and submit a proposed program for the organization's consideration and acceptance, or whether he is commissioned to proceed immediately with tasks designated by the organization;
— The scope of the consulting assignments as regards the phases of investigation, program development, recommendations, and implementation, and the manner in which this scope is determined;
— The extent to which the organization's expectations with respect to the required outcomes from the consulting assignment were identified, made explicit, and formalized in an agreement between the organization and consultant;
— The extent to which organization members were formally advised of the proposed introduction of the consultant and of the objectives of his assignment;
— the constraints or restrictions imposed on the consultant by the organization, with respect to areas in which the consultant should not work or to people or information to which he should not have access;
— The definition or shared understanding of the respective duties to be assumed by the consultant and organization members and their division of responsibilities; and
— The definition or shared understanding of the point at which the consultant's work would be regarded as complete.

Working Arrangements

There are many factors relating to the nature of the consultant's intervention or entry into the organization which will also influence the organization–consultant relationship. Proceeding beyond the consultant's period of entry, there are other features of the modus operandi which would appear to further influence the nature of this developing relationship. These concern the selection of an organization member as a point of contact and liaison with the consultant, the working methods and approach the consultant will be required to adopt, and the informing of organization members as to the intended introduction of the consultant into the organization. Whether such considerations are made prior to the establishment of contact with the consultant, or whether the consultant is made a party to such considerations (and in either case) the nature of the arrangements which do eventuate will all have an influence on the nature of the relationship.

More specifically, the relevant factors for this phase of development are:

1. The nature of the arrangements for collaboration, contact, and liaison between the organization and consultant during the working phases of the consultant's assignment;
2. The nature of the arrangements made for the consultant to report on his activities and progress during the consulting assignment and also at its completion;
3. The manner in which the consultant attempted to involve organization members in the assignment and secure their commitment to the programs he wanted recommended;
4. The consultant's relative emphasis on diagnosis and identification of the organization's problems;
5. The nature of any changes made in the scope, extent, objectives, or timing of the consulting assignment which were made during its progress on the recommendation of either the consultant or organization members; and
6. The extent to which the consultant participated in the implementation of any of the programs he recommended.

A Study of the Relationship

While there is an abundance of sources which emphasize the importance of the organization–consultant relationship, such references are almost exclusively homiletic and unsupported by significant empirical evidence which alone can confirm their veracity.

In this study the fundamental research hypothesis concerning the effectiveness of consultant-assisted change efforts and the organization–consultant relationship required: the identification of organizations which have used the services of external consultants; the means for distinguishing between different types or natures of organization–consultant relationships; and measures, or descriptions, of resulting effectiveness of the consultant-assisted change efforts.

Responses were received from the chief operating executives of 133 organizations, although only 91 of these described a consulting experience that took place during the preceding three-year survey period.[5] The research questionnaire sought information about the organizational arrangements before and during a consulting engagement, and also about its ultimate effectiveness as measured by subjective evaluations by key organization members on a scale ranging from *completely effective* to *no worthwhile results achieved*. In all of the analyses of the data, consultant assignments were judged as completely effective in less than 40 percent of all cases, and the recommendations made by consultants were completely accepted by the different levels of management in the responding organizations in less than 30 percent of all cases reported.

Prescriptions for Effectiveness

A review of the tentatively or "directionally" confirmed hypotheses indicates the following arrangements should be observed in order for consultant assistance to be most often judged as completely effective.

1. In considering consultant help, an organization should allow that some changes may be necessary and should reflect this by its identification and explication of specific objectives as bases for the engagement of a consultant.
2. An organization should regard a consultant as an expert resource, and a collaborating equal, and ensure his participation in the consideration of any changes which should be made in the assignment during its progress.
3. An organization should use a consultant-initiated suggestion that his services be retained as a basis for internal considerations which may lead to the identification of needs and explication of goals.
4. Rather than impose a possibly unwanted consultant on subordinate managers, a chief executive should encourage the initiation of pro-consultant discussions at this lower level and/or seek to secure consensus among subordinate managers before making a decision to engage a consultant.
5. Several management members of an organization should participate in pre-engagement discussions concerning consultant help, as well as in the decision that a consultant be retained.
6. Besides participating in the pro-consultant decisions, subordinate managers should participate with the chief executive in identifying and agreeing on the particular consultant to be appointed.
7. Before commencing a consulting assignment, an organization should identify and make explicit to the selected consultant its specific objectives and expectations with respect to the required outcomes from the assignment.
8. An organization should not closely direct a consultant's work, nor unreasonably constrain him by restricting personal contacts or access to organizational information.
9. Before commencing a consulting assignment, an organization should ensure that the respective duties to be undertaken by the consultant and by organization members are identified and understood. Such understanding should preferably be reached by mutual agreement between the parties, or otherwise through its clear explication by the chief executive.
10. A consultant should work closely and directly with members of the client organization and provide for their participation in the consulting assignment either by assignment to specific working roles, discussion of findings, or an opportunity to initiate proposals.
11. An organization should establish a specific point of contact and liaison for a consultant — either the assignment sponsor or other organization member — who can initiate other organization contacts and through whom the consultant can report.

12. An organization should select a consultant from among two or three who have been invited by the organization for preliminary discussions prior to a final appointment being made.

These prescriptions appear as a useful framework for the development of an organization–consultant relationship which will result in a high level of effectiveness of the ensuing collaborative effort.

References

1. Wilson Seney reported that 8% of his survey respondents indicated "unfavorable experiences" with consultants (Wilson, Seney, *Effective Use of Business Consultants* [New York: Financial Executives Research Foundation, Inc., 1963]). Fifty-three percent of C. L. Quittmeyer's sample were less than completely satisfied with their consultant experiences (C. L. Quittmeyer, "Management Looks at Consultants, " *Management Review* 50 [March 1961]). A study by R. F. Amon revealed that 30% of the business responding to that survey regarded the recommendations they had received from the external consultant as unsatisfactory or inadequate. (R. F. Amon et al., *Management Consulting* [Cambridge, Mass.: Harvard University Graduate School of Business, 1958]).
2. W. G. Bennis, *Changing Organizations* (New York: McGraw-Hill, 1966), p. 175.
3. R. Lippit, J. Watson, and B. Westley, *The Dynamics of Planned Change* (New York: Harcourt, Brace and World, Inc., 1958).
4. S. Tilles, "An Exploratory Study of the Relationship Between the Executives of Small Manufacturing Companies and Consultants," Ph.D. diss., Harvard University, 1960.
5. A random sample (from Dun and Bradstreet's *1968 Million Dollar Directory*) of 1,575 business organizations each having a reported net worth of $1 million or more and employing 100 or more people was collected, to which was added 120 federal government departments and agencies. The 133 responses were distributed among the principal categories as follows: industrial manufacturing, 44%; financial institutions, including banks and insurance, 19%; federal government agencies, 17%; merchandising and distribution, 9%. The small response reflects the lack of any, or any recent, consultant experience as well as disinterest in the inquiry.

Neil G. Davey was associated with P.A. Management Consultants Pty. Ltd., in Melbourne, Australia when this article was written.

The Trainer's Role as an Internal Consultant

Gordon L. Lippitt

In an earlier article[1] I discussed four major roles performed by training and development departments or offices in modern organizations:

Role No. 1: As a *learning specialist* and instructor.
Role No. 2: As *administrator* of training and development staff and programs.
Role No. 3: As an *information co-ordinator*.
Role No. 4: As an *internal consultant* to the management of the organization.

It is my feeling that each of these four roles or functions requires different skills and abilities. In a small organization, the training director may perform all four functions, whereas in a larger organization the "head of a department" might well be the consultant to management for problem solving while those on his staff administer, design and conduct training and educational programs. In recent years it has been demonstrated that many management problems require for their solution a broader approach than that furnished by the usual training programs or methods.

An Increasing Role

The new challenge, then, for a training director and department is to develop their skills and role in the organization as *internal organizational consultants* on management problems, economic and social change, and organizational development. This "internal consultant" role of the training person is important for helping the changing organization and will require increased professionalization and skills of those in the training field.

The Training Director, in carrying out this internal consultant role, will not work from a power base, as is typical of a line manager, but as a staff specialist will use *influence power* that comes from four sources:

— influence by *competence*
— influence by *ideas*

Reprinted with permission, *Journal of European Training*, Vol. 4, No. 5, copyright © 1975, M.C.B. Publications, Ltd., Bradford, England.

Figure 6-1. Multiple directive and nondirective roles and approaches of consultants.

— influence by *acceptance*
— influence by *one's role* (legitimization)

These influence methods will have to be "earned" by the training professional. Influence power will not emerge without demonstrated skills and professionalism. As Beckhard put it,

> "The consultant (or person in a helping role) always enters such a relationship as a person with authority — achieved either through position or role in the organization or through the possession of specialized knowledge. To achieve an effective consultative relationship, it is essential that they understand the nature of this power and develop skills to use it in a way which will be viewed as helpful by the person receiving the help. A person entering a consulting or helping relationship must have the ability to diagnose the problem and goals of the person being helped, and be able to assess realistically their own motivations for giving the help. A consultant must also recognize the limits of their own resources to help in the particular situation."[2]

In carrying out a "helping" relationship to management, a training director will find himself operating along a continuum of consulting roles. In Figure 6-1 is illustrated some of these major helping relationships from directive to primarily nondirective consultations. By directive I refer to those behaviors where the consultant assumes a leadership position or initiates activity. In the nondirective role the consultant provides data for the client to use or not to use.

Situational Role Choices[3]

Situational roles are not mutually exclusive; they may manifest themselves in many ways in a particular client relationship. We see these roles as "spheres of expertise" rather than as a static continuum of isolated behavior.

Let us examine these different role choices in response to management need.

Advocate Role

In an advocate role, the consultant endeavors to influence the client. There are two quite different types of advocacy:

1. Positional or "content" advocacy is a role posture of trying to influence the client to choose particular goals or to accept particular values.
2. Methodological advocacy is a role posture of trying to influence the client to become active as a problem solver — and to use certain methods of problem solving — but being careful not to become an advocate, for any particular solution (which would be positional advocacy). In this role, the behavior of the consultant is derived from a "believer" or "valuer" stance about a content or methodological matter.

Technical Specialist

One of the roles of an internal consultant is that of technical specialist. The more traditional role of a consultant is that of a specialist who, through his special knowledge, skill, and professional experience is engaged, either through internal employment or under contract, to provide a unique service to an organization. Within this realm of augmenting client expertise, the client is mainly responsible for defining the problem and the objectives of the consultation. Thereafter, the consultant assumes a directive role until the client is comfortable with the particular approach selected. Later in the relationship, the consultant may act as a catalyst in implementing the recommendations he had made.

Either the internal or the external consultant may be a content specialist on the client's problem or a process specialist on *how* to cope with a problem. This particular role brings out the consultant's substantive knowledge.

Trainer/Educator

Innovative consultation frequently may require the use of periodic or continuous training and education within the client system. In this aspect of the helping relationship, the consultant can play a role in bringing to bear the learning process which best can be employed critically and creatively — depending upon the situation and the need. The consultant may be a designer of learning experiences or a direct teacher. In a sense, this role requires the consultant to have the skill of a learning methodologist and manager. A familiar role to most training specialists.

Collaborator in Problem-Solving

The helping role assumed by the consultant in the problem-solving mode utilizes a synergistic approach to complement and collaborate with the client in the perceptual, cognitive, and action-taking process needed to solve the problem. The consultant helps to maintain objectivity while stimulating conceptualization during the formalizing of the problem. Additionally, the consultant must help to isolate and define the "real" dependent and independent variables which influenced the problem's cause, and ultimately its solution. He also assists in weighing alternatives, aids in sorting out salient causal relationships which may affect alternatives, and synthesizes and develops a course of action for an effective resolution. The consultant in this role is involved in the decision making as a peer member.

Alternative Identifier

There are direct costs associated with decision making. While the value of a decision is dependent upon the attainment of a given set of objectives, in selecting an appropriate solution to a problem there normally can be proposed several identifiable alternatives, along with their attendant risks. The alternatives, either because of economics or other identifiable implications, should be discovered jointly with the client and the consultant. In this helping relationship the consultant must establish relevant criteria for assessing alternatives and develop cause–effect relationships for each alternative along with an appropriate set of strategies. In this particular situational role, however, the consultant is *not* a participant in the decision making itself, but a retriever of appropriate alternatives facing the problem-solver.

Fact Finder

Fact-finding is an integral part of the consulting process, whether it be for developing a data base or for resolving intricate client problems. It is perhaps the most critical area, and often the one that receives the least attention in actual problem solving and decision making. It first requires the development of criteria and guidelines to be used in the performance of the actual fact-finding process and related analysis. It ends when all available facts have been analyzed and synthesized. The result of this process is the obtaining or giving of information for problem solving by the client. Fact-finding can be as simple as listening or as complex as a formal survey utilizing a number of techniques. In this role, the consultant is functioning basically as a researcher.

Process Specialist

Here the consultant attempts to help the client to be more effective and responsive. The consultant must be specifically concerned with the work process itself as a way of achieving client adaptability.

As a process specialist, the consultant must sharpen all of his multiple role skills to help the client. The consultant works on developing joint client–consultant diagnostic skills for addressing specific and relevant problems in order to focus on *how* things are done rather than what tasks are performed. He helps the client to integrate interpersonal and group skills and events with task-oriented activities, and to observe the best match of relationships. In this role, the consultant functions as a "feedbacker."

Reflector

When operating in the mode of a reflector, the consultant stimulates the client to make decisions by asking reflective questions which may help to clarify, modify, or change a given situation. In utilizing this attribute, the consultant may be an arbitrator, an integrator, or an empathetic respondent who experiences along with his client those blocks which provided the structure and provoked the situation initially. In this role the consultant finds himself being an "overviewer" as well as a philosopher.

Skills and the Consulting Function

What kind of person is able to perform these multiple roles appropriately? For the staff person who carries the training and development portfolio, it will require the proper knowledges, skills and attitudes.

The effective development of the human resources of an organization is essential to its continued growth and viability. In most organizations someone with a training and development responsibility is expected to assist the organization in this respect.

What qualifications does this kind of person need to have? Must he be a behavioral scientist? Does he need to be an expert on communication systems? Does he have to be so courageous or personally active in initiating change, at a risk to his own job, that unusual psychological maturity is required?

Whoever is responsible for initiating human resource development will need to manifest *professional* behavior and leadership. Any list of the professional capabilities of a consultant is extensive. It looks like a combination of the Scout Laws, requirements for admission to heaven, the essential elements for securing tenure at a distinguished university.

It seems to me that the qualities a consultant needs fall into two broad categories. On the one hand such a person needs a number of distinctly intellectual abilities, and on the other he needs a number of distinctly personal attributes[4].

Dilemma Analysis Ability

Intellectually, the consultant needs what I call the ability to make a dilemma analysis, because an organization which uses a consultant is probably faced with a situation that appears insoluble. If the difficulty could be solved easily by the operating manager, a consultant would not be needed. The consultant must recognize that a dilemma, whether real or not, does exist in the minds of those within the organization. The consultant's role is to discover the nature of the dilemma and to determine the real causes of it, rather than what are thought to be the causes.

To accomplish this, the consultant must have a special type of diagnostic skill. He or she should approach a study of the organization's dilemma by means of an existential pragmatism[5] that takes into account the total organization setting and all situational variables. It is only through skillful examining of the organization's fabric that one can see the structural relationships between the various subsystems that comprise the total organization and the interdependent nature of its individuals, groups, substructures, and its environmental setting.

In order to make this kind of dilemma analysis, insight or perception and intuition are necessary. Insight or perception is vital because the problem and solution pertinent to almost any dilemma requiring outside assistance are going to be part of a very complex situation. The ability to penetrate the complexity and isolate the key situational variables is the toughest task. Unless the important factors can be sifted from the maze of detail and causes separated from symptoms, accurate diagnosis is impossible.

Sense of "Organizational Climate"

Intuition or "sensing" must be coupled with perception in order to assess the nature of power and politics in the organization. From my experience in bureaucratic structures, both public and private, these organizations are not just functional. Underlying and intermingled with the functional operations the organization performs are the crucial dynamics of internal power and politics. Invariably, people are vying with other people for organizational influence or for some internal political reason. Very often the consultant has been asked to help not just to provide needed assistance, but also as an instrument of a strategy designed to secure an influence objective.

Unless the consultant has the intuition to sense the organizational climate, he runs the risk of being nothing but a pawn in a game of organizational politics. If he has the ability to recognize and understand the dynamics of the internal power and political relationships, the consultant can masterfully utilize them in pursuit of whatever change objectives the client and consultant conclude are appropriate.

Apart from the diagnostic abilities, the consultant needs implementation skills. Obviously, he must have some basic knowledge of the behavioral sciences and the theories and methods of his own discipline. But more than these, the individual needs imagination and experimental flexibility. Dilemma-dissolving is essentially a creative enterprise. No real life situation is going to fit perfectly the mold suggested by typical techniques or textbook methods. Diversity and unique circumstances will almost always exist. The consultant must have imagination enough to innovate adaptations and tailor his concepts to meet real demands.

The consultant must be able to visualize the impact or ultimate outcome of the actions proposed or implemented[6]. But, like most things, this is as much a process of experimental trial and error as it is one of *a prior* solutions. The courage to experiment and the flexibility to try to discard as many approaches as needed to solve the problem are important ingredients in the practitioner's make-up.

Integrity Is Essential

The other major aspects involved are what I call the consultant's *personal attributes*. Above all, he must be a professional in attitude and behavior. To be successful, I think one must be as sincerely interested in helping the organization as any good doctor is interested in helping his patient. The consultant must not conceive of himself as, or portray the image of, being a huckster of patent medicines. The consulting role is no different from that of any other profession. If the training director's first concern as a consultant is to make an impression or build an "empire," and only secondarily to help the organization, the organization leaders will soon recognize the individual as a phoney and deal with him accordingly. People in top management generally are astute individuals. They can identify objectivity, honesty, and above all integrity.

When entering a client system, a strong tolerance for ambiguity is important. From my experience, the first acquaintance with an organizational problem is marked by a certain amount of bewilderment. It takes time to figure out the situation and during this time one is going to experience a certain amount of confusion. One must expect this to occur and not let it worry one.

Coupled to this type of tolerance must be patience and a high frustration level. Curing a client's ills is likely to be a long and trying experience. Quick results, full co-operation, and complete success are unlikely in the short run. Inevitably, attempts to change people's relationships and behavior patterns are going to be met with resistance, resentment, and obstructionism on the part of those who are, or who think they may be, adversely affected. It is important for the training professional as a consultant to have the kind of maturity and realism which recognizes that many of his actions and hopes for change are going to be frustrated. Such maturity is necessary to avoid the reaction of defeatism and withdrawal that commonly accompanies the frustration of a person's sincere efforts to help others.

Sense of Timing

Finally, the consulting practitioner should have a good sense of timing, a stable personality, and good interpersonal skills. Timing can be crucial. The best conceived and articulated plans for change can be destroyed if introduced at the wrong time. Timing is linked to a knowledge of power and political realities existing in the change situation and to the kind of patience that overrides the enthusiasm surrounding a newly conceived idea or training intervention that one can't wait to try out.

Obviously, consulting involves people dealing with people, more than people dealing with machines or mathematical solutions. The consultant must have good interpersonal skills. He must be able to communicate and deal with people in an atmosphere of tact, trust, politeness, friendliness and stability. This is important because the impact of the practitioner's personality must be minimized to keep it from becoming another variable in the existential setting and making a contribution to the existing complexity. Beyond this, his success will depend on the persuasiveness and tact he has in confronting the interpersonal contact on which the helping situation is based.

Professional Development of Consulting Skills

It is a prerequisite for effective consulting that those practicing such a role manifest professional behavior.

This cannot be merely an outgrowth of the acquisition of degrees. It must be a manifestation of appropriate knowledge, skills, and attitudes in our day-by-day work in and for organizations. In this sense, I have found the following guidelines helpful:

a. Focus on the problem-solving approach to learning and change; use data, not just hunches.
b. Develop interdependence with others, not dependency.
c. Practice what we preach in the field of our specialized knowledges.
d. Diagnose situations, rather than merely treat symptoms.
e. Understand ourselves so thoroughly that we do not let our personal needs get in the way of helping people and organizations to develop.
f. Communicate on a reality level in an "open" fashion.
g. Admit mistakes and learn from failure.
h. Develop interests and skills so as to be able to work with people in a noncontrolling manner.
i. Be willing to experiment and innovate.
j. Develop a personal philosophy about working and developing people and organizations.
k. Be capable of saying, "I don't know."
l. Be willing to learn and change.

These criteria may not be the most important or only criteria for professional behavior, but they are some I value highly. Unfortunately, I find I am unable to achieve these standards as consistently as I wish. Suffice it to say, that while we want to increase the professionalization of the field of training and development, the real goal is not some acquisition of certain areas of knowledge, but the professional styles of behavior each of us demonstrates in our human resource development responsibility.

In addition, I think we need to perform our task with a clear understanding of the ethical questions related to anyone who is involved in planned change through consulting.

The professional trainer is a person who has responsibility for initiating, designing, and implementing learning efforts that will hopefully change individual, group, organizational, or community performance and behavior. What right does the training and development professional have to try to make others grow, develop and change? On what grounds does he base his values as the professional training and development person?

Recognizing that many words have achieved evaluative weight, it might be well to divorce, for the moment, our necessary value judgments from the processes these words describe. Manipulate, for instance, means the arrangement of conditions so that change in a certain direction may or will take place. The training director who arranges his classroom setting, provides certain selected skill practice sessions, asks certain questions, demands certain self-directed learning experiences, and creates certain motivational drives. You are "manipulating," when you are teaching supervisory skills, technical expertise, or interpersonal effectiveness. From this point of view, each training professional, acting or refusing to act as a learning influence, is under judgment in accordance with his basic beliefs and, stemming from those beliefs, his ethical system.

If we accept this line of reasoning, if we recognize that our commitment to a specific training development responsibility in the organization often makes us potential renewal agents, then I submit that the question usually asked, "What right have I to try to make persons, groups and organizations different than they are?" must be reversed. The basic question which we cannot avoid is "What right have I to withhold myself, my skills and my convictions in a changing situation from helping that change to take place in a direction consistent with my convictions?"

In other words, the training and development professional should be *pro-active* and not just *re-active* in the way he demonstrates certain beliefs and values about the way people learn and change.

Most cultures are based upon a system of values which embrace both individual and social ethics. To apply these ethical standards in consulting with the organization, a group, or an individual is an essential undertaking. As I point out in the book, *Organization Renewal,* it is a challenge to relate these ethical values to individual and organization development. It is important, I think, to understand clearly that there are some underlying assumptions supporting the need for individual and organization renewal[7]:

"1. In today's organizations there are unavoidable human problems which involve varying degrees of interpersonal and intergroup tension and conflict that keep the organization from functioning most effectively.

2. It is better that such human problems be solved than remain unsolved.

3. Deliberate planning of solutions to these problems, which necessarily involve changes in the people, the groups, and institutions concerned, is necessary to a degree that it has not been in the past. Trial and error processes of historical accommodation are no longer adequate to the organizational needs of today.

4. The most promising source from which to derive principles of ethical control in the planning of the changes that we must make is in the system of democratic and scientific values. These values can be translated into norms or principles of *process* which can be used in the guidance and direction of the consulting process, of deciding what changes are needed, and in evaluating the changes that are produced."

Let me identify some ethical guidelines that I feel might be helpful to the training and development professional doing consultation.

The first guideline concerns motivation. A trainer-consultant can be motivated, in part, by such individual needs as status, security, and prestige. One's own awareness of these motivations may clearly demonstrate the professional aspect of his role. The approach to problem-solving consultation should be *task-oriented* rather than self-oriented. The essential concern should be that the new condition achieved is better than the first, not that the person initiating change should receive credit or have an enhanced standing in the eyes of others in the organization.

Secondly, the processes by which individual or organization development is planned should be collaborative; they should involve appropriately the persons affected by the change.

Thirdly, in order for taining specialists to conform to democratic and scientific values, the methods of problem-solving should be *experimental*. An experimental approach means giving any reasonable but novel plan a try; it also means building into the consultation methods of evaluation which will reveal whether the altered practices approach he desired change goals.

Fourthly, the method used for consultation must be *educational and/or therapeutic* for the people involved, leaving them better able to face and control future situations. We are not trying only to solve present problems, but rather to know how better to deal with future problems as they arise. The idea is not to get away from problems, which is to get away from reality, but rather to help people to know how better to confront, diagnose, and solve problems.

Finally, it is my feeling that those of us who are initiating planned change must always be aware that we are *accountable*. In the first place, we are accountable to ourselves. The responsibility rests with us to examine our motivation, the results we desire and the methods we employ, and to see how consistently they correspond with the value response required of a professional. And we are accountable to those who are affected by our efforts. In this it is a help, and further guide, to accept the fact that the training and development specialist is always involved in and affected by the change he produces. We do not stand over and above — a little God who calls the shots and determines the destiny of others. We are involved and affected, whether as an outside consultant or a part of the organization system. We can never dissociate ourselves from the profoundly inextricable relationship we have with our consulting clients in the learning, training and development process.

If we have training professionals as internal consultants with these kinds of value, attitude, and belief we may yet re-institute a confidence in the training specialist as a valued human resource whose help derives from a process that provides mutual growth for both parties, and help to the organizational system in which he functions.

References

1. Lippitt, G., and L. Nadler, "Emerging Roles of Training Directors," *ASTD Journal*, August, 1967.
2. Beckhard, Richard, *Leader Looks at the Consultative Process*, Washington, D.C.: Leadership Resources, Inc., 1961, p. 3.
3. This section was formerly published as a portion of an article entitled "Consulting Process in Action" by Ronald and Gordon Lippitt, *ASTD Journal*, Madison, Wisconsin; May-June 1975.
4. The next section is adapted from a portion of an article by the author entitled "Criteria for Selecting, Evaluating, and Developing Consultants," *ASTD Journal*, August, 1972.
5. Lippitt, G., *Organization Renewal*, Englewood Cliffs, NJ: Prentice-Hall, p. 18.
6. Lippitt, Gordon L., *Visualising Change*, Fairfax, VA: NTL Learning Resources Corp., 1973.
7. Ibid, p. 170.

Gordon L. Lippitt is professor of behavioral science in the School of Business Administration, George Washington University.

The Evolving Role of the Federal Training Consultant

Neal E. Chalofsky

It is no wonder government trainers feel a mixture of envy, cynicism, and fascination with the way federal managers perceive external consultants. The difference between management's oft-held perceptions of external consultants as part guru, part expert, and part confidant and their view of internal trainers as "paper processors" and course instructors has helped perpetuate the belief that trainers cannot function as consultants. I had the occasion to see this belief highlighted in my first government training position. A line-management official asked if I could help him complete the paperwork required for him to hire an outside consultant to facilitate a problem-solving session. He didn't ask me to assist him in their problem-solving session. He didn't ask me to advise him on what kind of consultant or who specifically I could recommend. He asked me to help him process the paperwork. This was a common view of the federal trainer's role as consultant.

Fortunately this view is changing — and for several reasons. First, when managers come to the training department and say they have a problem, get them a training course — trainers are no longer just shopping around for an appropriate training course. They are now starting to question whether training is the answer and whether performance or behavior is the problem. Secondly, trainers are beginning to take the initiative and go to managers, asking if they can be of service. Finally, trainers are slowly developing their consulting skills and increasing their knowledge of consulting theories, concepts, and resources.

Consulting as an Evolving Role

Initially, the federal trainer's primary role was instructing. This quickly expanded to designing and developing courses as well as instructing. At the same time, training began to evolve into a staff function within organizations, as opposed to just one part of a subject matter specialist's or personnelist's job.

The need for administrative and management support functions began to emerge. Training quickly became more than a one-man band. It became a visible organizational unit among the other staff functions such as financial management, procurement, and personnel management.

The early 1950s saw the emergence of the outside management consultant. As consulting became a respected and needed activity, organizations began to demand this type of "service" from their internal staffs.

Internal training staffs began being asked to assume the part of facilitator in problem-solving situations, advisor to line and top management, diagnostician in identifying performance deficiencies, and counselor in career development efforts.

The training client–consultant relationship can also be seen as an evolving series of interactions. Initially, the training consultant was concerned with assisting individual employees or groups of individual employees to improve their skills, to solve performance problems, or to increase interpersonal relationships.

The next level that emerged was to work with groups. The training consultant facilitated group process activities and was involved with intergroup relations.

Training consultants gradually became concerned with management's needs. They helped line management diagnose performance problems and advised on training strategies. As consultants developed more credibility, top management utilized them as advisors and resource persons. Finally, with the advent of the concept of organization development, they began to take a global view of the total organization.

At this point I need to stop the action and explain what may seem to be an obvious contradiction. On one hand I've said that the trainer is seen as a "paper pusher" by management and this perception is only now slowly changing. On the other hand, the evolution of the client–consultant relationship implies that trainers have been consulting for quite some time. Both statements are true. Many federal government trainers have never played the role of consultant, either because of lack of need or because of lack of capability, initiative, or authority. Yet, there are trainers who have proactively perceived one of their roles as an internal consultant, and there are now quite a significant number of practicing training consultants in the federal government. One question that has yet to be answered, however, is how consulting emerged as a viable role for federal trainers.

The Federal Training Consultant

The U.S. Civil Service Commission's Bureau of Training initially became interested in identifying the roles, tasks, and competencies of the federal trainer because of research which indicated that trainers were not meeting the needs of their organizations, especially in the area of consulting. A study designed to uncover the disincentives to effective employee development was conducted by the Bureau of Training.[7] One of the significant conclusions was "the employee development specialist (federal trainer) provides limited counseling and consulting services to the rest of the organization."

One of the data-collection activities was a literature review of the roles of the trainer. This review, based on Nadler's[6] three roles (learning specialist, administrator, and consultant) found that trainers felt they were performing as they thought they should, primarily as consultants and administrators. However, managers felt that trainers were spending too much time as administrators and not enough as consultants. Ackerman[1] discussed the ways in which trainers perceived their role and organizational location. In general, trainers perceived that their role should be:

"...one of providing assistance and advice, etc., to management on employee development and training, determining or aiding in the determination of training needs, administering the employee development program, and specific responsibilities such as evaluating training and arranging for training courses."[1]

The role of the trainer from the point of view of management was discussed in Epstein's study.[4] The purpose of this study was to determine line managers' perceptions and expectations of the operational functions of the trainer in a government research and development organization. Most managers surveyed in Epstein's study perceived the trainer as emphasizing his/her administrative function and as limiting his/her activities as a learning specialist and as an internal consultant.

Another data-collection technique in the Disincentives Study was in-depth case studies of three federal agencies. The three agencies selected represented varied missions, organizational structures, sizes, and occupations. In order to collect data from all levels in the organizations, several vertical slices were identified, each of which consisted of a major unit of the agency, one or more subordinate groups under it, several units under each of those, and so forth, until the employees under the first level supervisor were reached. Questionnaires and interviews were used to obtain individual perceptions. One finding directly related to the consultant role was:

"Employee Development Specialists (trainers) have minimal contact with others in the organization, providing next to nothing in the way of consulting services to top management, managers and supervisors, and individual employees..."[3]

Based on this conclusion, the report recommended that the Bureau of Training conduct a detailed examination of the performance requirements of the trainer in government and business. Furthermore, the Bureau should then develop performance requirements for government trainers.

In 1973, the Bureau of Training assembled a research team to examine the role of the trainer in the federal government.[3] The team developed a list of competencies and surveyed the manager of training in every federal agency. The results were clustered around four roles* and these lists of tasks and competencies were published in U.S. Civil Service Bulletin 410-85. "Improving the Effectiveness of Employee Development Specialists."[8]

The consultant was described as being concerned with research and development and providing management and employees with advice and assistance. The tasks of the consultant's role are to:

— Counsel employees regarding training and developmental opportunities
— Explain training policies and procedures to supervisors and employees
— Counsel management on training implications related to anticipated organizational changes
— Develop and conduct training needs surveys
— Advise management of immediate and long-range training needs of individual employees as they relate to the organization
— Explain training regulations, policies and procedures to management and help insure the execution of provisions of FPM Chapter 410 and appendices, as well as local regulations which apply to training and employee development
— Assist management in analyzing performance problems
— Measure indirect results of training based on posttraining performance on the job to formulate and refine learning objectives
— Measure indirect results of training based on post-training performance on the job to formulate and refine learning objectives
— Assist employees in determining career development
— Conduct manpower planning forecasts

Three of the ten tasks (1, 2, and 9) were clearly counseling activities. Yet, at this time, while career counseling activities were recognized as significant, they were lumped in with the consultant activities. Tasks 3, 5, and 6 represented the subrole of the consultant as advisor to management — the expert who described the potential benefits and problems related to training of a certain organizational change or the expert who explained whether a certain organizational policy was contrary to federal regulations concerning training. Tasks 4 and 10 were activities related to what we now refer to as front-end alyasis.

Task 8 is the most interesting. One activity that the consultant was expected to perform was to be "on the lookout" for unexpected results of a training experience while observing on-the-job performance. Once these unplanned-for behaviors were identified, the consultant was expected to feedback this data to the learning specialist so that he/she could build this information into the learning objectives of the training experience. Task 7 is the only task that directly relates to the consultant assisting in solving organizational problems.

---

*The study team based their role clustering on Nadler's three roles: learning specialist, administrator, and consultant. A fourth role, program manager, emerged during the study, to distinguish between administrative support functions and management functions.

The competency list also seemed to be a conglomeration of different abilities and knowledges that somehow related to the consultant tasks. The consultant must have the ability to:

— Establish rapport with people
— Apply a systematic approach to problem solving
— Predict training needs induced by organizational change and advise management of immediate and long-range training needs
— Assist management in analyzing performance problems
— Determing training needs based on job requirements and level of employee skill
— Explain complex procedures to others
— Apply counseling techniques
— Gauge effectiveness of consultation efforts
— Interface with people within the purview of the consultative strategy
— Conduct cost/benefit analysis

The consultant must have knowledge of:

— The workings and interrelationships of the related personnel functions such as staffing, position classification, salary and wage administration, job analysis, training, labor management relations, performance appraisal, and promotion
— The organization's mission, unit goals, objectives, and work processes
— The formal and informal organizational structure
— Counseling techniques

Some background is needed to provide the proper perspective for considering the above lists. First, this was the first attempt by the federal government (and, for that matter, any other major sector) to identify *specifically* what a trainer does and then categorize the information around certain roles. Secondly, the consultant role, being the newest and most vague of all the roles, was the last to be analyzed. Therefore, several of the tasks were literally "dumped" into this role because they did not fit anywhere else. Notice the mixture of client–consultant relationships. Finally, since this task list reflected more of what trainers actually did rather than what they should be doing, it demonstrated that trainers were not really fulfilling the expectations of management.

Management wanted trainers to operate like outside management consultants; consultants who would help in diagnosing problems, facilitating problem solving and applying consulting interventions aimed at increasing the effectiveness and efficiency of the organization. Trainers, on the other hand, seemed to be groping for the right combination of activities, and what this research captured was the federal training consultant role that was still evolving and had yet to really mature.

After completing Bulletin 410-85, the research team began the next phase of their long-term effort to increase the professionalism of federal trainers.[2] This project called for the development of a competency-based, nonacademic curriculum.[9] Since this curriculum was to be competency-based, a review of 410-85 as the foundation for such a curriculum seemed appropriate. But when the team attempted to match the competencies to their related tasks, it was like trying to put a square peg in a round hole. The competencies were developed separately from the tasks and were clustered around the roles, rather than the tasks.

The team opted to start from scratch in developing new lists, with each task matched with the competencies needed to perform that task. A new literature search was conducted, new data were gathered, and new task and competency lists developed. At this point a fifth role, career counselor, emerged, reflecting an increased emphasis on this set of activities. The team next developed behavioral objectives based on the tasks and competencies and organized these objectives into learning modules.

The consultant role retained the same definition and reduced from ten to eight tasks, but the content and approach totally changed. The consultant's tasks are to:

1. Negotiate with the client to determine the scope of consultation effort. The consultant must have:

   — Ability to determine consultative strategy
   — Conceptual understanding of the subroles of the consultant
   — Ability to construct a detailed plan for a job study specifying the scope and limits of the project, specific objectives, specific steps to meet objectives, time schedules, and staff and task assignments
   — Ability to clarify complex procedures
   — Knowledge of intervention, advisory, and persuasion techniques
   — Ability to apply a cost/benefit analysis
   — Ability to conduct meetings and interviews

2. Gather information on organizational goals, objectives, and work processes. The consultant must have:

   — Ability to learn a variety of specialized vocabularies
   — Ability to determine the formal/informal organizational structure
   — Ability to see the organization in terms of the interrelationships between the organization, its environment, and the groups and individuals composing the organization
   — Ability to gather information through interviews, observation, and research
   — Ability to plan and conduct reliability/validity studies

3. Conduct the data-gathering and problem-identification portions of a performance analysis. The consultant must have:

   — Ability to develop and use information-gathering techniques
   — Ability to determine and measure job performance requirements
   — Ability to determine and measure actual job performance

— Ability to use specialized vocabulary
— Knowledge of the formal/informal organizational structure
— Ability to identify the appropriate problem-finding techniques
— Ability to identify the appropriate problem-solving techniques
— Ability to collect problem indicators
— Ability to determine when to plan and conduct a reliability/validity analysis

4. Select, plan, and/or implement the solution(s) of a performance analysis. The consultant must have:

— Knowledge of training and other solutions
— Ability to apply a cost/benefit analysis

5. Evaluate results of a performance analysis. The consultant must have:

— Ability to determine the effectiveness of an implemented solution
— Ability to apply basic statistical techniques
— Ability to apply a cost/benefit analysis
— Ability to validate the process

6. Determine training implications of proposed changes in mission, technology, and organizational structure. The consultant must have:

— Ability to apply a cost/benefit analysis
— Ability to predict training needs induced by organizational change
— Ability to predict training needs given the plans and goals of the organization

7. Report results of a performance analysis. The consultant must have:

— Ability to advise management of immediate and long-range training needs
— Knowledge of appropriate agency reporting requirements

8. Guide agency personnel in the application of methods and techniques to facilitate the training and development process. The consultant must have:

— Ability to apply specific training methods and techniques to meet desired training and development objectives
— Ability to facilitate decision-making processes to help agency personnel to meet desired training and development objectives
— Ability to transfer to the client the problem-solving skills of the consultant

The tasks now represent a comprehensive role rather than a group of functions sted in a random and seemingly unrelated order. In addition, the competencies ecifically relate to each task and are broader and stronger in scope. There is an nphasis on a process of negotiating a consultation effort, diagnosing the problem, developing solutions, evaluating results, and feeding back to the client. The tasks also clearly reflect a performance-based systems approach to consulting. In addition, the consultant is not just expected to gain expertise, but to transfer skills and knowledge to the client. This consultant role is much more proactive than the 410-85 role. It's important to note that this list of tasks and competencies has yet to be validated. Therefore, it is more representative of what trainers should be doing than what they actually are doing. But it is a vastly more mature, meaningful role than the 410-85 role. Hopefully, it will assist trainers in performing more effectively as consultants in their own organizations.

The Future

This new role description clearly implies a more ideal client–consultant relationship — one based on systematic problem solving, transfer of knowledge and skills from consultant to client, and an OD view of the consulting process.

The consultant role is certainly not static. It will continue to evolve and change. New consulting approaches, new techniques, and new interventions will precipitate changes in the tasks and competencies. Hopefully, the Bureau of Training will encourage periodic research efforts to update the consultant role, as well as the other roles.

The consultant role can help trainers to become involved in their organizations, thus increasing their credibility. Achieving and retaining credibility "... will more and more come to mean advising management, engaging in problem solving, facilitating organizational change, and aiding employees in their career growth."[5]

The consultant role, and the relationships it fosters between trainers and their clients, is one of the most significant stimulants to the professional growth of trainers in the federal government.

References

1. Ackerman, L., "A Study of Selected Employee Development Specialists in the Federal Government: Their Background and Perceptions of Their Role and Organizational Location," doctoral dissertation, The George Washington University, 1967.
2. Chalofsky, N.E., and J.A. Cerio, "Professional Development Program for Federal Government Trainers," *Training and Development Journal* (December 1975).
3. Employee Development Specialist Study Team, *Improving the Qualifications of Employee Development Specialists*. Washington, D.C.: Bureau of Training, January 31, 1975.
4. Epstein, J.H., "Line Managers Perceptions and Expectations of the Operational Functions of an Employee Development Specialist in a Federal Government Research and Development Organization," doctoral dissertation, The George Washington University, 1971.
5. Jorz, J.J., and L.M. Richards, "A Curriculum Plan to Develop Training Professionals," *Training and Development Journal* (October 1977).

6. Nadler, L., *Developing Human Resources*, Houston, TX: Gulf Publishing Company, 1970.
7. U.S. Civil Service Commission, Bureau of Training, *Disincentives to Effective Training and Employee Development*, Washington, D.C.: U.S. Civil Service Commission, 1973.
8. U.S. Civil Service Commission, *Improving the Effectiveness of Employee Development Specialists*, Bulletin 410-85, Washington, D.C.: U.S. Civil Service Commission, July 31, 1975.
9. U.S. Civil Service Commission, Bureau of Training, *The Employee Development Specialist Curriculum Plan: An Outline of Learning Experiences for the Employee Development Specialist*. Washington, D.C.: U.S. Civil Service Commission, November 1976.

Neal E. Chalofsky is a project leader with the Training Leadership Division of the Bureau of Training, U.S. Civil Service Commission.

Part III

<hr>

Entry

A public speaker employs a joke or pleasantry at the beginning of a speech. The gaining of audience attention and interest is only part of the speaker's rationale. Similarly, the old Southern tradition of bringing homemade gifts when visiting a neighbor has more than friendship as its purpose. The white flag in a war zone, a warm-up exercise, and the "Could I get you a cup of coffee?" to an office visitor are other examples that, like the joke and the homemade gifts, might be termed "tools of entry."

Physical and psychological entry of one person into the life space of another carries unique ramifications. The tools of entry indicate that the parties involved are at a minimum intuitively sensitive to the relationship aspects of entry. Some students of behavior point to territoriality as the central variable. Others focus on the dissonance associated with a fear of the unknown. Perhaps the intuitive sensitivity is simply anxious behavior genetically linked to a prehistoric existence.

Whatever the reason, the tools tell the tale; the parties subtly recognize that entry is somehow distinctive from what occurs before and after entry. This distinctiveness resides in the relationship aspects of entry.

The entry phase of the client–consultant relationship generally begins when the client, feeling some need for help, contacts a consultant thought capable of providing that help. Less often, the phase begins when the consultant makes contact with a potential client during a search for new business. Even less frequent is the occasion of entry through a third party. Regardless of how the contact is initiated, the puncturing of one's life space by another surfaces relationship issues which impact the quality and the viability of the client–consultant relationship.

The primary goal of both client and consultant in the entry phase is to find sufficient clues to predict the profitability of the endeavor. Profitability can be defined in the eyes of the seeker; it may or may not be related to monetary gain. Improved performance, increased productivity, broader fame, larger fortune, and psychic satisfaction are but a few of the more popular profits pursued by clients and consultants. It is the search for predictability of profit that makes the entry phase glisten with intrigue and intuition.

Predictability is achieved in the minds of the parties when they have found enough clues to provide satisfactory answers to at least four major questions. The answers are drawn from the universe of information which batters between and around the potential client and potential consultant. While other questions can be fashioned which unlock clues to predictability, the four major questions represent giant steps toward a successful client–consultant relationship during the entry phase of consultation.

Why Am I Here?

Shared by both client and consultant, the "Why am I here?" question might be alternately stated, "What brings me to this moment in time?", "What is the impetus for our encounter and dialogue?" It is the struggle of the client to express the quality and quantity of need; it is the effort of the consultant to feel a kinship with that need and with its source.

A part of the client's attempt to adequately answer the "Why am I here?" question is the definition of the problem in such terms that there is an appropriate unsolved residue remaining. That unsolved residue is the parcel up for bargaining between the parties. Inherent in an adequate problem definition by the client is the justification of why a consultant is needed.

Tantamount to effective consultant assistance is the acceptance by both client and consultant that help is clearly needed. Help is not always helpful; intervention may be interference in sheepskin.

One definition of consultation is "the management of vibes between a helper and a helpee." Part of "vibe management" is a close assessment of the motives of the helper. He or she may seek to create indebtedness, stroke ego by demonstrating superiority, foster dependence, or prove rightness. Likewise, the consultant may want to improve performance, make the client happy, or simply facilitate client growth.

The motives of the helpee-client should likewise be scrutinized. A request for assistance can be a disguised search for a scapegoat. The helpee may be seeking help under duress, that is, pressured to obtain the aid of a consultant by a greater power. The helpee may be attempting to reduce personal guilt or satisfying a need for attention and recognition. Often the client, out of fear of the unknown, is self-induced into being sufficiently open to intrigue the consultant, yet sufficiently vague to maintain control.

The desire for control and the fear of exposure keeps the typical client at attention throughout entry. Most guard their clout and protect their flanks out of a duty both to their ego as well as their domain. The "Why am I here?" dimension of entry affords both parties an opportunity to unlock fears to enable trust to infiltrate the relationship.

The consultant's efforts to answer the "Why am I here?" question lies in determining whether consultant resources match client requests. The consultant is likewise concerned with the accuracy of problem definition by the client. While confidentiality is the badge of most consultants, cases in which the client withholds essential information can lead to dangerous results. Caveat emptor is applicable to both parties in consultation.

Who Are You?

The second question rumbling around in the heads of the potential client and consultant during entry is "Who are you?" The question is not one implying a "name-rank-serial number" answer. Rather, the "Who are you?" question is an inquiry into role definition.

Much has been written on the importance of the client finding the right consultant. Given the marketing side of consultancy, the client seeks to avoid buying the wrong resource. The client is interested in ample expertise, and, likewise, attempts to avoid consultant overkill. The client is interested in a cost–gain ratio that favors gain.

The consultant's first dilemma regarding the "Who are you?" question is to locate the client. The contact (the person asking for help) may not be the client (the person making the decisions about the consultation). Additionally, there may be a sponsor (the person or persons strongly interested in the outcome and who probably is paying the bill). Then there is the client system, the group directly involved in the effort.

For example, the board of directors (sponsor) instructs the president (contact) to find a consultant to help the operations group manager (client) find solutions for reducing turnover in the operations group (client system). Several roles can be played by a single person. The key dilemma for the consultant is "Who is the client?"

Another dilemma is whether the client identified has sufficient power and authority to effectuate the changes which come out of consultation. Too frequently, excellent advice and counsel have been for naught because the client lacked what it took to employ the product of the consultation. Not only is such an outcome frustrating to a results-oriented consultant, but it adversely impacts his or her reputation.

Tightly woven into the "Who are you?" fabric are threads of "Who am I?" The client contemplates self-role in the process to determine if its coupling with the consultant role will result in a complimentary union. Likewise, the consultant examines personal competencies against the demands for problem solution to assess his or her likelihood of effectiveness. Resources available to each are unveiled for inspection by the other.

What Is Likely to Happen?

The entry phase is the ground upon which expectations should be strewn for perusal by client and consultant. Once the problem and roles have been defined to the satisfaction of both parties, there must be clarification of the goal to be achieved and the means of expending energy toward that end.

The "What is likely to happen?" question is particularly pertinent to the client due to a fear of dependency on the consultant. Most client–consultant relationships begin with the client feeling one-down. The client is often fearful his or her momentary vulnerability will contaminate objectivity in consultant selection and contract negotiation. While the "he who pays the piper calls the tune" adage is at work in consultancy, the distance between an excellent piper and a poor tune caller is generally wide enough to make the "keeper of the purse" somewhat powerless.

Bargaining from a position of unequal strength can lead to pride-saving behavior on the part of the client. Such behavior may take the form of the client reporting situations in far more positive terms than really exist. Blaming others and rationalization are further attempts the client may use to ward off dependency on the consultant. Even when entry is around a positive situation (making a good situation better), the client will sometimes attempt to circumvent feelings of self-doubt or incompetence by deliberately or inadvertently altering the description of reality.

The consultant seeks an answer to the "What is likely to happen?" question to find the boundaries of the consultation. Only through boundary clarification can misperceptions be aptly avoided. The management of expectations requires front-end agreement on the norms and conditions of action. Planned renegotiation must be built into the agreement to allow for both reassessment and alterations as the relationship matures throughout the consultation.

Goal clarity and feedback are two crucial ingredients in the consultation contract. Only if expectations are acknowledged by both parties without the intrusion of ambiguity can there be a satisfactory meeting of the minds. A feedback system must be molded into the agreement to insure both client and consultant that consultation progress is on track and proceeding according to plan.

Minimizing organizational goal conflict is also of concern in the relationship. Too frequently, consultation follows the line akin to the familiar adage "the operation was successful but the patient died." It is imperative the goal be sufficiently congruent with other client system values to enhance long-term survival as well as short-run excellence.

What Will Be the Result?

The "What will be the result?" question might be labeled "toll clarification." The clues sought during entry provide the answer to the likely consequences resulting from the consultative effort. Both parties are interested in the toll they are required to pay and whether the relationship will end with a net gain. Unless both parties expect the relationship to result in a profit, they are not likely to invest their energies and time. Answers to the "What will be the result?" question help predict that profitability.

The client is obviously interested in getting the problem solved or the need met at the least cost. Like profit, cost has a broader definition than simply dollars and cents. The consultant is interested in achieving the greatest profit for services rendered.

The negotiation or bargaining between client and consultant typically results in a contract. There are generally two aspects to most contracts. The formal aspect covers time allocation, type and amount of payment, and services expected to be performed. The psychological aspect covers what each party hopes to gain from the relationship.

There are many words used for various types of contracts and fee arrangements. Per diem is a common method of fee setting. Retainer fee implies the client reserves a certain amount of the consultant's time. Cost plus fixed fee is a type of contract specifying that a fixed fee plus specified allowable additional costs will be paid. Cost reimbursable, on the other hand, is a contract issued on the basis of estimated costs; final payment is based on costs actually incurred.

Contract termination is an often overlooked aspect of toll clarification. The manner in which the contract will end holds emotional flavors which spice the relationship from the outset. The client is concerned with improving organizational results, enhancing individual growth, and increasing personal power. The consultant is guardian of much of these outcomes. For the client a challenge during entry is to time the relationship's duration at such a length that the desired outcomes will have occurred.

The consultant has a similar dilemma during entry vis a vis contract termination. Consultative success brings a sense of achievement and the feeling of satisfaction that an associate was made stronger by the relationship. Gauging the end to occur simultaneously with success requires effective planning, open communication, and ceaseless negotiation.

The degree to which the four key questions are answered to the satisfaction of client and consultant determines the success of the entry phase of consulting. Adequate answers increase predictability of profit and create a mental set of cooperation, trust, and openness. The goal is for both client and consultant to perpetually operate with what Chris Argyris calls "free, informed choice." That choices arises out of a cognitive map of where the parties involved wish to travel.

Chapter 8
"The Entry Problem in Consultation"
John C. Glidewell

John Glidewell was one of the first writers to address the predictability issue in the entry phase. His article is a classic in the field of behavioral science consulting. Even though it was written more than 20 years ago, it continues to be relevant and useful. The article is included because it provides an overview of the entry process. The issues raised are addressed in the articles that follow.

Central to the Glidewell focus is the necessity in entry to develop a client–consultant relationship which injects predictability into the perception of the parties. The greater the congruence of both parties in terms of need perception (Why am I here?), role expectations (Who are you?), feelings about control and values (What is likely to happen?), and resource and reward allocation (What will be the result?), the more likely the consultation will succeed.

Chapter 9
"Rate Yourself as a Client"
Antony Jay

The best assurance the client–consultant relationship will yield satisfactory results is for both client and consultant to exercise great care in selecting each other. Antony Jay's pithy article unfolds many pointers useful in choosing and using consultants. Most pointers are aimed at helping the client decide if help is needed and, once decided, how to be a good client.

Of particular use are the techniques identified to define the problem in a way that helps client and consultant come to grips with the "Why am I here?" question. As Jack Gibb, author of a subsequent chapter states, "Problem orientation...is the antithesis of persuasion. When a sender communicates a desire to collaborate in defining a problem...he tends to create the same problem orientation in the listener."

Chapter 10
"How to Get a Good Consultant"
J.P. Frankenhuis

The Frankenhuis article attempts to address three major issues in the entry phase: when to hire a consultant, who to hire, and what to pay.

The issues are not unlike purchasing an automobile. Unless one is the "I trade cars every two years" type, the when-to-buy issue is resolved near the point at which the old car repairs exceed the new car payment. Resolution of the who-to-hire issue is made by reading ads, talking with associates, and interviewing car dealers. What to pay follows proposals ("I'll throw in the power brakes"), test drives, fair market value of trade in, etc.

A major part of the resolution of the "Who are you?" question for the client is the expertise of the consultant and its match with client need. The Frankenhuis article not only provides hints for analyzing consultant expertise but likewise explores the toll clarification issue.

Chapter 11
"Is Help Helpful?"
Jack R. Gibb

Jack Gibb's article slices through the presumption that because a person is in pain, they desire help. The article likewise surfaces the issue that not all help offered by a helper has the helpee's interests at heart. The cataloging of client–consultant orientations that both help and hinder the consultation is a useful tool for relationship clarification during entry.

Gibb's article provides hints on how client and consultant can manage expectations and boundaries. Armed with the proper orientations, the trust potential in the relationship is significantly increased and the likelihood of misuse of power is decreased.

The Entry Problem in Consultation

John C. Glidewell

The aim of this article is to contribute to the definition of a complex problem — the problem faced by a consultant and a client when they first try to enter into a working relationship. It would be presumptuous to propose a solution to such a knotty problem. It seems more appropriate and realistic to limit this article to defining the problem.

The article is based upon the assumption that the entry of the consultant is a special case of a more general problem: the attachment of a new person to an existing social system.

Examples are legion. They might include the introduction into a family of a tutor for a child temporarily unable to attend school, the attachment of a social work consultant to an existing nursing staff, the assignment of a nursing consultant to a teaching staff, or the introduction of a human relations consultant to a corporation board. In each case the members of a functioning social system find that some operations are being initiated and performed by a new person. In this case, the new person, being a consultant, is presumably authoritative, and also, being new, he is relatively unpredictable. The problem is that some relationship to this new person must be developed. Some relationship must be developed so that his performance, and the responses of others to it, can be better predicted. Better prediction will make his performance more amenable to control in the interests of the goals of the system — both substantive achievement goals and affiliative human relations goals.

Limitations on the Problem

For the purposes at hand, a special and limited meaning will be given to the phrase "attachment to a social system." It will be used to refer to the process of development of relationships with a person who is to be only temporarily a member of the system. It will not be used to refer to the process of development of

Reprinted by permission from the *Journal of Social Issues*, Vol. 15, No. 2 (1959), pp. 51–59.

relationships with a person who is to be a permanent member of the system.* It is clearly true that the consultant role is often being established these days as a permanent one, but this permanence involves either the development of a new role and, therefore, a basic structural change, or it involves the socialization of a new person into an existing role. Both are more fundamental processes than can be explored here.

Accordingly, this article is limited to the exploration of the process of initiating a relationship between a client system and a temporary consultant. The consultation functions are to be performed temporarily either because the need is temporary or because the functions can be taken over — after a time — by existing roles.

Consultant vs. Consultant-Trainer

It is important to differentiate those functions which are expected to terminate at the expiration of a short-term need from those which are expected to be taken over and continued by existing roles. The first requires the application of objects, skills, ideas, or feelings which the client need never possess or control (like prescribing medication or greasing an auto). The second requires that the client acquire possession and control of the objects, skills, ideas, or feelings, and it therefore implies learning (like the improvement of a golf swing or the recognition of the proper consistency of a pancake batter). The first relationship involves a consultant role; the second, a consultant–trainer role. This article will be concerned with both roles. The distinction should be kept in mind, however, because the role of the consultant provokes less concern about demands for change in the system than does the consultant–trainer role.

Organizational Attachment and Predictability

It is proposed that a basic criterion of attachment to a social system is predictability. This is a special case of the general proposition that a basic criterion of the existence and nature of relationships is predictability. The statement of lawful relationships takes the form of predicting some aspect of one object or force from a knowledge of other objects or forces.

Any application of this proposition to social relations must take account of the notion that social systems develop ultimate values and immediate goals. For the members of the system, the significant predictability for social roles is the forecast

---

*The term "attachment to a social system" was borrowed from Jules Henry (1959) who uses it to refer to the state of being an integral part of a social system — in no way limited to temporary membership. For present purposes, however, "attachment" seems to carry the implication of a temporary arrangement as intended here. Perhaps the appropriate analogy is the military arrangement by which a person who is "attached" to an organization is only temporarily associated and entitled to only limited support from the organization.

of performance in relation to ultimate values and immediate goals. The kinds of relationships to be developed in the process of attachment to a social system are those which insure, not that one knows just what a member will do in a given situation, but that, whatever he does, it will contribute to ultimate values and immediate goals. If the people in the system set a great store by creativity and invention, it may be important that the exact nature of the performance be *unpredictable* — so long as its goal orientation is assured. To illustrate, it is not too important to predict just what sort of medicine a doctor will give you when you are sick. You may, in fact, feel that if he is a really good doctor, his treatment will be so clearly unique to the time, to you and your illness, that it would be impossible to predict from facts previously known to you. It is quite important, however, to insure that the physician contributes to the ultimate value of survival (that he doesn't kill you) and to the immediate goal of relief from distress and disability.

A Redefinition of the Problem

From the foregoing conceptions, limitations, and distinctions, the entry problem can be redefined as that of initiating the development of relationships to provide a basis for predicting the contribution to ultimate values and immediate goals of a set of functions having certain characteristics, namely:

— They are now needed by the system, although probably to a different degree by different members.
— They either are needed only temporarily or can be taken over by existing roles.
— They are not now available in the system.
— They can be performed expertly by the prospective consultant.

In summary the entry problem becomes more or less difficult, depending upon the goodness of fit between the consultant and the client system with respect to stabilities and change tendencies in terms of perception of need, assignment of values, role expectation, resource and reward allocation, and feelings about the control of dependency. Goodness of fit is intended to imply both congruence (as with values) and complementation (as with roles). The significant dimensions to be fitted can be outlined as follows:

1. Perception of need, in terms of the
   — extent of consensus in the total system that an immediate need exists, and
   — importance of the need as measured against the ultimate values of the total system.
2. Perception of appropriateness of role allocation by those empowered to allocate roles, in terms of the criteria that
   — the needed resources are not available in appropriate persons within the system, and
   — the needed resources are available in the prospective consultant.

3. Perception of the appropriateness of resource distribution by those empowered to distribute resources, in terms of the criteria that
   — the consultant will be available to the different members on an equitable basis, and
   — any new objects, ideas, skills, or feelings developed by the consultation process will be equitably distributed.
4. Perception of the appropriateness of reward distribution by those empowered to distribute rewards, in terms of the criteria that
   — the consultant's fee is appropriate to the need (relative to other needs), and of the quality and quantity of service proposed, and
   — any rewards (income to the system) accruing from the prospective need reduction will be equitably distributed among the members.
5. Perception of the appropriateness of the probable emotional interchange between the consultant and the members of the system, in terms of the criteria that
   — the members do not become so dependent that they will not be able to work without consultative support, and
   — the members do not become so hostile toward or frightened by the dependency involved in the consultation that the consultant cannot be constructively employed.

Each of the five dimensions carries its own dynamic for change. Need perceptions are never entirely satisfactory, and the search for the "real" needs is perpetual. Role allocation can never truly fit the individual differences among people and the ever-changing requirements of the tasks of the system. Both formal and informal role reallocation is continuous, although sometimes painfully slow. Resource distribution can never keep pace with changing needs nor reward distribution with the balance between needs and changing contributions.[15,16] Finally, the exchange of feeling can never be all-supportive. Interdependencies always yield fears of dependency. Deprivation — even relative deprivation — yields apathy or rebellion. Evaluation yields fight and flight. Even support can yield jealousy. Any situation into which the consultant intervenes has its own dynamic for constructive changes and restraints.[11] The task is to find and reduce the restraining forces — liberating the growth potential of the system.

Variations in Optimal Conditions for Entry

The foregoing outline of the significant conditions for entry were cast in terms of perceptions. It might be construed to mean that the optimal conditions for entry are those in which the perceptions of the consultant and those of the power centers of the system are in substantial agreement. Such a construction was not intended — and it seems unlikely that such a situation can ever be found. The entry of the consultant into the system implies more or less change in the system — due in part to success or failure in substantive problem solving and in part to the impact of the attachment of a new role to the old system of role, resource, and reward allocation. The question of optimal entry conditions involves estimates of the extent to which the consultant and the client system may hold congruent, complementary, or conflicting perceptions and change tendencies. Congruence implies almost no change; complementation, slow change; and conflict implies fast change or fast termination of the attachment. The possible combinations of conditions are tremendously large, but it seems likely that most of them have been met somewhere or other in the practice of the helping professions.

Consultation in Conflict. Sometimes a consultant finds himself motivated to attach himself to a social system which disagrees with him in all significant respects: about the existence of the need, about the internal availability of resources, about the consultant's resources, about the basis for role, resource, and reward allocation, and about the feelings appropriate in reaction to the consultant's efforts.

The great tradition of the reformer carries with it the theme of consultation in conflict. The theme has had many variations, but more often than not the reforming consultant and his client system have differed most sharply in their perception of the proper locus of power. For example, Poston's work has been stimulated by a gnawing dissatisfaction with power vested in central control of material resources.

"Human values were lost in a maze of punch cards and number systems which were devoid of flesh and blood. Neighborhood life in any meaningful sense, the environment which had nurtured initiatives, civic integrity, and social responsibility began to grow sterile. The control which men had once exercised over their own lives gradually slipped away into distant offices of a centralized and impersonal society."[18]

It was the intent of the consultant to alter the locus of power in the system, and consequently the distribution of roles, resources, and rewards. The success of the first foray of such a reform movement would appear to depend in part upon the direction of changes already under way in the system and in part upon the availability of a subsystem ready to promote the reform. Taylor's dream of a "third force" of efficiency experts independent of both labor and management lacked a power point of entry — until it sold its independence to either management or labor.[20] Poston[18] seeks his power point of entry in community organization of dormant leadership. His goal is to transfer power from existing "nondemocratic" organizations to the new democratic community organization.

Where resistance to consultation is involved, some consultants have been successful as methodologists who suggest and assist in the conduct of self-surveys or other interpretative appraisals by the client system. Attempts to provide interpretive consultation in conflict have produced some remarkable successes, as with the work of Jacques[9] and the Tavistock Institute, and Lindemann,[12] Klein,[10] and their associates at Wellesley.

One can ask, quite justifiably, whether such change agents as Poston or especially Alinsky[1] were acting in the consultant's role. There is a broad and vague area which separates the consultant group from the assault force, but, differentiated or not, both must select carefully the point in the power structure at which they enter.

Entry in the Dark. As often as not, a consultant is called upon to enter the system without any information about the state of affairs within the system with respect to the dimensions significant to entry. He must gather data as he enters, and he must face the possibility that the need is not seen by the most powerful member (e.g., Poston in Montana); that there is no place for the consultant role in the correct perception of role, resource, and reward allocation; and that the typical emotional reaction to the prospect of the consultant role is one of hostility or fear or both. The entering consultant can assume that, in spite of manifest pleas for help, within the informal channels of communication in the client system, many members are committed — each to a different diagnosis, doctor, and treatment plan. Considering the amount of resistance that consultants regularly encounter, the fact that a consultant will enter in the dark is either a compliment to his courage, a comment on his conceit, or a manifestation of his masochism — or all three.

The Observation Phase. Is there a properly humble posture a prospective consultant can take? Perhaps. He can propose that a provisional relationship be established, enabling him to study the client system and enabling the system to study him. His "entry" is thus confined to the observer role. Observation is threatening to the system, to be sure, but less potent than the active consultant role. And the system is invited to make the observation a two-way activity, so that the consultant withholds no information from any members who could be affected by the problem (so far as he knows). If such a temporary arrangement can be made, data can be collected to provide an estimate of whether any active entry can be made at all, and, if so, at what time and place in the system. Where negative indications are found, a constructive withdrawal is presumably possible.

Congruent Need Perception. A consultant or a client may feel that a minimum requirement for entry is the mutual recognition of the need and its importance. Working on the congruence alone as a base for entry, he will undertake — after an observation phase — a trial period of active consultation. He will propose that the trial period will reveal, first, whether the needed resources are available within the system. If they are found, the relationship can be curtailed and gradually terminated. If they are not found, his own skills can be tested for quality. The distribution of his services among the members of the system can be evaluated from time to time and modified to meet agreed upon requirements for equity. In a like manner the equity of the distribution of other resources and rewards can be insured, with particular attention to the separation of the consultant's and the executive's roles. Finally, the feelings of the members about the consultant's activities can be assessed and, when interpretation seems appropriate, interpreted to the members of the system.

This experimental period is much like the "pilot run" proposed by the Tavistock group,[9] but it differs in that it is seen as a more extensive period of experimentation. It runs through a series of phases, but never really ceases to maintain its experimental orientation, particularly where the consultant–trainer role is required.[21]

The crux of the experimental approach is the initial agreement between the consultant and the power figures of the system on the criteria and the rules of evidence by which the experimental results are to be evaluated. Such an agreement may or may not entail a congruence of ultimate values; it must entail agreement on methods and immediate goals.

In developing mental health consultant–trainer roles in public schools, the St. Louis County group began with observation, used a series of conferences to explore perceptions of needs and definition of roles, and to develop a provisional action plan, with a "built-in" evaluation technique. The results were a program with steady growth but a wide variation in need perception, consultant role definition, and action plans, including, in a few cases, the withdrawal of the consultant.[2, 5, 6]

Congruent Need and Role Perceptions. A less adventurous consultant will want not only an agreed-upon need, but also an authoritative establishment of the need for and acceptability of his role as consultant and the client's role as consultee. Resistance to consultation is often due to the feeling of the executive that he "ought to" be able to solve the problem without consultation. A successful solution by consultation is feared because, in the eyes of the executive, it would discredit his competence. The establishment and acceptance of the complementary consultation roles can neutralize such a source of resistance.

Given the agreement upon need and role allocation as a basis for entry (this assures the rate of the fee if not its cumulative amount), the consultant and the client system will try to agree upon a series of experiments with resources and reward distribution. Again, the necessary time investment must be made to reach initial agreement on experimental methods and evaluative critera.

Bases and Experimentation. A consultant may seek more and more congruence and leave less and less to experimentation, but at least two limits appear.

The consultant who expects fully to insure appropriate and realistic interchange of feelings between himself and the members is asking for some rather unusual advantages. He is asking for valid and reliable data about the feelings of persons, and this is hard to come by. He is also asking that both he and the client system resolve their conflicts about authority and dependency before he enters. Ten years of human relations training and research and experience by the National Training Laboratories has reaffirmed the significance of dependency conflicts, but it has also established the difficulty of resolving them.[19]

A second limit is set by the strength of the value set upon progress and change. At least in western civilization (and certainly in modern India and China) the value set on progress is as strong as the resistance to change. The more the congruence of perception needed by the consultant as a basis for entry, the fewer are the opportunities for change. Most consultants seem to try to strike a balance between an assaultive consultation in conflict and a pedestrian consultation in comfort.

There are, of course, all sorts of possible combinations of agreement and experimentation. Role, resource, and reward distributions often get established before there is an agreement about the nature of the problem. Data collection follows. Sometimes constructive feeling interchanges emerge first and substantive experimentation follows. The situations are as varied as life.

The consultation is often admonished to enter "at the top" of the power structure, but, as has been pointed out[3] in complex organizations there may be many "tops" which will provide points of entry. The combinations and permutations of wholes and parts of a social system present infinite variety.

Experimentation is uncertain, costly in time and work, and provisional even in its outcome. Judgment about entry is a matter of calculated risk. Knowledge of the dimensions of the problem aid in the calculation.

Summary

In summary, it has been suggested that the entry problem can be defined in terms of the goodness of fit (in congruence, complementation, or conflict) between the consultant and the client social system with respect to three principal variables:

— Perception of need
— Perception of prospective equity of role, resource, and reward distribution
— Perception of prospective appropriateness of feeling interchange, with special concern about dependency and counterdependency

References

1. Alinsky, Saul D., *Reveille for Radicals,* Chicago: University of Chicago Press, 1946.
2. Buchmueller, A. D., and H. R. Domke, "The role of the public health department in preventive mental health service," *Children,* Vol 3 (1956), pp. 225–231.
3. Demerath, Nicholas J., "Initiating and maintaining research relations in a military organization," *Journal of Social Issues,* Vol. 8 (1952), pp. 11–23.
4. Festinger, Leon, and Harold H. Kelley, *Changing Attitudes through Social Contact,* Ann Arbor: Research Center for Group Dynamics, University of Michigan, 1951.
5. Gildea, Margaret C. L., "Community mental health research: findings after three years," *American Journal of Psychiatry* Vol. 114, No. 11 (1958), pp. 970–976.
6. Glidewell, John C., "An experimental mental health program in Webster Groves," In *Third Yearbook, American Association Public Schools,* New York: Columbia University, 1955.
7. Henry, Jules, Concepts of Social Structure and Personalization. Unpublished manuscript, Washington University, St. Louis, Mo., 1959.

8. Jacques, Elliott (Ed.) "Social therapy," *Journal of Social Issues*, Vol. 3, No. 2 (1947), pp. 1–66.

9. Jacques, Elliott, *The Changing Culture of a Factory*, New York: Dryden, 1952.

10. Klein, Donald C., and Ann Ross, "Kindergarten entry: a study of the role transition," In Morris Krugman (Ed.), *Orthopsychiatry and the School*, New York: American Orthopsychiatric Association, 1958.

11. Lewin, Kurt, "Frontiers in group dynamics," *Human Relations*, Vol. 1 (1947), pp. 5–41.

12. Lindemann, Elizabeth, Mental health in the classroom: the Wellesley experience. A paper presented at the annual meeting of the American Psychological Association, New York, 1957.

13. Lippitt, Ronald, Jeanne Watson, and Bruce Westley, *The Dynamics of Planned Change*, New York: Harcourt, Brace and Company, 1958.

14. Mann, Floyd C., and Ronald Lippitt, (Eds.), "Social skills in field research," *Journal of Social Issues*, Vol. 8, No. 3 (1952), pp. 1–58.

15. Parsons, Talcott, and Edward A. Shils, (Eds.), *Toward a General Theory of Action*, Cambridge: Harvard University Press, 1952.

16. Parsons, Talcott (Ed.), *Essays in Sociological Theory*, Glencoe, IL: The Free Press, 1954.

17. Poston, Richard W., *Small Town Renaissance*, New York: Harper, 1950.

18. Poston, Richard W., *Democracy is You*, New York: Harper, 1953.

19. Stock, Dorothy, and Herbert A. Thelen, *Emotional Dynamics and Group Culture*, Washington D.C.: National Training Laboratories, 1958.

20. Taylor, Frederick W., *The Principles of Scientific Management*, New York: Harper, 1911.

21. Thelen, Herbert A., *The Dynamics of Groups at Work*, Chicago: University of Chicago Press, 1954.

John C. Glidewell is a professor of education in the Department of Education, University of Chicago.

Rate Yourself as a Client

Antony Jay

It is over fifteen years now since I met my first really dumb multimillionaire, and it made quite an impression on me. Up till then I had thought that you needed brains to make money: I was used to being asked, "If you're so clever, why aren't you rich?" but this was the first I'd ever met someone to whom I could have said, "If you're so rich, why aren't you clever?" At least I myself could not have said it, because I do not have that kind of courage, but it would have been a fair question.

I say it made an impression on me, but what really made the impression was discovering the answer. I ought also to add that the passage of years and brief encounters with a few other millionaires now suggest to me that the original one may not have been quite so dumb as I took him to be: once you are a millionaire, certain social conventions are suspended and you do not have to take the trouble to appear intelligent, interested, alert, or even awake. And he had inherited some of the millions, though he had added many more by his own success. But even so, he was dumb. He had only one of the many qualities that top men are supposed to need, but he had developed it to such a degree of refinement that he did not need any of the others.

That quality almost amounted to genius — a genius for choosing and using professional advisers. Whatever his problem — computers, marketing, works of art, wine, long-range planning, long-range putting — he infallibly found the best man in the world to advise him on the subject and extracted the maximum possible value from the advice. I have since discovered that this skill is widely recognized at the top level, but because I am not a top-level person, it took me many years to make the discovery.

The skill was certainly recognized by one of the richest men in history — Andrew Carnegie's epitaph on himself was said to be, "Here lies a man who knew how to enlist into his service better men than himself." It also explains why the people who come out on top in school and college do not automatically rise to the top in industry and enterprise; the crucial qualification is not to *be* one of the brightest people but to know how to use them.

I came across the same truth from the other direction a few years later, when I was making a television program about the great modern Italian architect Luigi

Nervi. He attributed at least half the credit for one of his most successful buildings (the Pirelli building in Milan) to the fact that his client was as much of a master of the craft of being a client as Nervi himself was of the craft of being an architect.

Few of us, I suspect, have thought of ourselves in terms of how good we are as clients, though when we reflect on it we probably give ourselves pretty good marks. That's half the trouble — it's one of those private activities like selection interviewing or sexual intercourse which, since we never put them on public display or try them out in competition, we can always kid ourselves we're pretty good at. But unlike either of the other subjects, it has not been subjected to extensive and detailed scrutiny, nor has it generated a vast literature describing and analyzing the process and recommending the techniques that are most likely to achieve the desired result.

And yet, as professional skills multiply and the disciplines divide and subdivide, it becomes increasingly difficult for the executive or manager to acquire even the most basic knowledge himself. In addition, it has become increasingly expensive to keep on his payroll professionals of quality in all the disciplines that may at some time or other be relevant to his organization.

The solution, of course, is to hire professional advisers and consultants from outside, and it is a solution that more and more companies are finding, with results that fall fairly evenly along the spectrum from triumph to disaster. But how do you make sure that your own use of advisers and consultants puts you up at the triumphant end and not down with the disasters? Only by acquiring that one professional technique that you can never hire from outside: the technique of choosing and using advisers and consultants.

Twenty-Five Principles and Pitfalls

This technique is not, to be honest, one of the most fully developed in the world of government and management: there is no certificate or diploma, and no organized body of knowledge. But there are some master craftsmen, some directors and executives who over the years have discovered the principles and the pitfalls, and there are some top-class professional advisers who, after a lifetime of dealing with every kind of client, have come to identify very clearly the type of client attitude and behavior that leads to success, and those departures from it that lead to trouble, unhappiness, and failure.

It is the distillation of their wisdom that has led to this first formulation of the rules for the successful use of professional consultants and advisers:

1. Get the habit of asking yourself, whenever you are up against what appears to be a new kind of problem, whether it may not be in essence a problem lots of people have had before. If, for example, you are wondering whether there might not be a more economical way for your fleet of trucks to take the goods from your factories and deliver them to your warehouses or stores, it might occur to you that many others have asked themselves the same question in the past. But, until you learn to

ask yourself that kind of question, you may never even find out that there is something called transport optimization theory, linear programming, or even operations research. The surest way not to find the best professional advice is not to think of looking for it.

2. Before seeking professional advice, however, there is one vital question to which you owe yourself an honest answer: Have you the intention, the resources, and the will to implement the advice when you get it? There is no surer (or commoner) way of wasting money on consultants than by paying for surveys, reports, and recommendations and then doing nothing about them.

3. Once you have decided you need professional advice, give yourself time to choose the right person. Your choice of adviser is far and away the most important single determinant of success or failure, and the most frequent cause of failure is deciding too quickly that this is the person you want. And if there are others in your organization who will be working with him as much as you will, involve them in the selection process too. To foist your personal choice on colleagues or subordinates is asking for trouble.

4. Try to get someone else to make up your list of finalists. It is not just that the job may be tedious, with a lot of phone calls to discover, say, which marketing consultants have experience of international multilingual mailing campaigns, and what their previous and present clients have to say about them; it is also that the one indispensable qualification for success in the advisory field is the ability to impress potential clients and land the business, and you expose yourself to the risk of being charmed too quickly into picking a good person who is not the right person. A preselection by someone else at least ensures you against too grave an error.

5. You will obviously take advice from trusted friends and colleagues — especially those who seem to be experienced and successful with professional advice — but do not be content with client references alone. Clients can only judge part of a professional adviser's skill, and they do not often have a chance to make informed comparisons. A good extra source of advice is the body of people who work for and with many professional advisers: builders will tell you about architects, journalists about public relations companies, publishers about literary agents, insurance houses about brokers, and so forth; and they may give you very different facts and judgments from those of satisfied clients (so long as you don't ask for them in writing). You may also find a consultant network; for example, your lawyers who are accustomed to working with a particular firm of accountants may provide you with a pathway to the right person. Also, if you are going to ask consultants to work together, it helps a lot if they know each other already.

6. There is also the trade press — almost every profession has a journal, and a call to one of the editorial staff will be valuable if you ask the right sort of questions, namely objective and factual questions about the size of the group, how long they have been around, whether they are established or fast-growing, what subdivisions of their professional discipline they specialize in (tax consulting, investment planning, business systems) and what type of clients (government,

industrial, private) they most frequently work for. It is a good idea to avoid asking straight out for a direct assessment — good, mediocre, charlatan — unless you know your informant quite well.

7. It is also worth considering whether the professional advice you need necessarily has to come from a professional firm. If, for example, you want help in establishing a better staff appraisal system, you may find that another company has recently set up a very successful scheme and would be prepared to hire out to you, for two or three days a month, the executive who was responsible for its success. You might even find such skills somewhere within your own organization.

8. Pick someone your own size. An adviser who is in too small a business can be a dangerous risk on a big project — he has so much less at stake than you have. Equally, too large and grand a professional firm may well be unable or unwilling to give your small project the priority and high-level involvement that a smaller and hungrier group would devote to it. And it is also worth taking time to find an adviser who has already worked in your industry; apart from time saved on briefing and familiarization, he is also likely to have useful contacts and perhaps a refreshingly different point of view from yours.

9. Never take on an untried consultant for a project that could make or break the whole organization, or a significant part of it. It is much better to try the adviser out on a smaller and clearly defined project that will not be a great disaster if it fails. You can move on to more ambitious projects when you have discovered if you can work well together. And the experience and lessons of the pilot project will help ensure the success of the main one.

10. If you are personally impressed by a potential adviser, establish clearly, and, if possible, write into the contract how deep his personal involvement in the project is going to be. There was a famous London management consultant in the 1950s whose craggy face, bushy eyebrows, deep perception, and penetrating analysis were almost hypnotically irresistible to the boards of large corporations. But once the corporation was hooked, he was never seen again. For the next 18 months the offices were overrun with hordes of young, fresh-faced business graduates completing their management education at the corporation's expense. The corollary of this is that if the person you first meet admits he will not be doing the work himself, make sure that you meet the people who will be doing it before you decide to go ahead with them.

11. When you talk to potential advisers, get them as quickly as you can off the subject of their brilliant staff, their unrivaled resources, and their tremendous record of successful assignments, and on to the subject of your problem and your needs. Observe how well they listen and pay great attention to the questions they ask. If you are choosing from a list of finalists, ask each consultant to produce for you a brief analysis of your problem as he sees it and lines of approach that he would investigate if hired.

12. When you have appointed your expert, put his job in writing. Better still, get him to do so. He should set down the objectives you have asked him to achieve, the

division of responsibilities between him and you, any special instructions or constraints, the resources he will require from your organization, a provisional time schedule for the various stages and the review meetings, and all details of payment. He may want to add other things, too, but these are musts.

13. Always involve your advisers at the earliest possible stage. This is the single most important piece of advice for those who want value for money. It is an odd fact about large projects that the first few decisions are almost always both the most costly and the most arbitrary. It is at this stage that a good professional can save you millions. I once sat in with two of Britain's leading comedy writers who had been called in to advise on a comedy film that had been two-thirds shot. Their advice was very firm: on no account shoot the other third. But they would have made the same judgment six months earlier simply on the basis of the script, if anyone had shown it to them. Their fee would have been exactly the same, but the producers would have wasted only $800 instead of $80,000.

14. Tell your adviser the basic motivation for the project even if it is confidential or even slightly ignoble. If you have called in a production engineering consultant to give you ammunition for your battle against the board's decision to cut back the reequipment program, it is important that he should be aware of this from the start, even if you do not put it in writing or spell it out in so many words. Equally, it may take him a long time to discover that when you said, "Look at my organization structure," you only meant, "Find a polite way of moving Harry Green sideways."

15. Express the consultant's job in terms of the end result you want to achieve. If you tell the architect you want a three-story office building, that is what he will design for you. But if you explain to him the pressures of staff or the reorganization plan or the diversification policy that led you to the idea of the three-story building, he may see a better solution than you can. Without realizing it you have diagnosed your own complaint and written your own prescription before going to the doctor. So describe your need to your professional adviser in as much detail as possible, but leave it to him to work out the best means of satisfying it. Half the errors in the use of professional advisers spring from what is the equivalent of using a doctor as if he were a druggist.

16. Do not try to teach your adviser his own job — but do not ask him to do yours. The distinction between ends and means is at the heart of your relationship. You are the expert on ends; he is the expert on means. This is a barrier you cross at your peril, and the dangers of crossing it are greatest in areas where the client thinks he can understand what the adviser is doing. Marketing and advertising are minefields, and many a senior agency copywriter has felt his blood pressure rise to the threshold of cardiac arrest to see his granite-chiseled words "improved" by a trainee product-manager from the client company. Do not trespass on the areas of professional skill and professional judgment that you hired your advisers for.

17. An absurdly simple way of getting value from a professional, and one that is overlooked more often than you would believe, is to ask him a few really broad questions in the early stages. It is too easy to stick to limited and precise problems

and never ask him, "What is your view of the basic idea?" "Are we setting about this in the wrong way?" "Can you think of anything else we ought to be doing as well?" "Is any of this unnecessary or extravagant?"

If you do not ask these broad, general questions, he may not feel it is his place to volunteer his view. The higher powered the adviser, the greater his value in these wide, general areas, and it may be worth paying for two or three expensive days of a really top person's time to range over the problem and perhaps guide you toward the right adviser when the proper approach has been identified. One such conversation proved to a senior executive that he did not in fact want a foremen's training program at all, though that was why he sought advice: the fault was in selection of foremen, and it was the selection procedures that needed the urgent attention.

18. Never pretend to understand something out of reluctance to reveal the depth of your ignorance. All professionals slip from time to time into jargon or, even worse, a specialized use of a general term. It is much better to start from the basis that you are slow-witted and ignorant, and that he has to make everything crystal clear. It is nice if you really are well informed, but honest ignorance is a hundred times better than simulated understanding. You and your consultant have to learn to communicate with each other very accurately, which means spending some time in your early meetings constructing a vocabulary; so never hesitate to ask for clarification by example, definition, or synonym.

19. Learn as much as you can about what your expert's skills and abilities are and how his job works. This can be grasped in outline by half an hour's reading but is best filled in over a drink or a lunch. You may discover he is equipped to do many more things than you have required of him. You may find that some things you have kept away from because you thought they were too expensive are in fact very cheap. You may find a simple change in your operation could greatly ease and simplify his work and reduce your costs. But you will never find any of this out unless you talk about his business in a general way as well as talking about the project in a specific way.

20. Try to integrate your adviser into the team working on the project. This is much better than having the professional person bring in his own team, not only because of the problems of teaching a lot of outsiders about your business and its needs, and the dangers of communications difficulties, rivalries, and resentments, but also because he will be spending his skill and knowhow among your people and giving them a short course in his discipline. And at the end of it you have not just a completed project or system but also an educated team. If you do not integrate him, his presence at your side may stimulate suspicion and resistance. And obviously you are heading for disaster if ever you find yourself playing off your outside adviser and internal staff against each other.

21. Never abdicate. This would be too obvious to be worth stating were it not that it has happened so often. The classic years were the 1950s and early 1960s, when every computer horror story turned out to be the story of an abdication by an executive or director to a consultant. Abdication is never the result of any action; it is always a consequence of inaction. The moment you are tempted to leave an

executive decision to your adviser or rubber-stamp his recommendations because the facts and arguments are too complicated for you to follow, you are on the edge of abdication.

You absolutely must stay in firm control of your professional so that you always know what he is doing, why, when it will be done, what its implications for, and repercussions on, the rest of the organization will be, and how much it is going to cost. How he is doing it is another matter. You can expect to understand that only in very broad terms. You are in greater danger of abdication if you have not got absolutely clear in your own mind from the start precisely what the project is intended to achieve, and if you have not built the review points into it from Day 1.

22. One of the reasons for abdication is that the client gets drawn into the adviser's jargon, and then into his assumptions and his world. You have to keep clear to yourself what you are doing in your own words and in your own terms. A good discipline is to imagine you have received a strong memo from your chief executive saying that he has heard you are wasting everyone's time and money on a pointless and self-indulgent exercise: the discipline is to draft your reply, even if only in your own mind. As you work out in clear, straightforward English the reasoned justification of your project, you find yourself redefining your adviser's objectives in a most valuable way.

23. Be enthusiastic if you are pleased. Advisers and consultants (like most other people) blossom in a warm climate, and if they really enjoy the project and feel they are being appreciated, they give much better value. A professional's reputation is like the share price of a company. If he feels that the job he's doing is raising it, he is increasing his market valuation even if he is not actually getting a bigger dividend. The corollary is to tell him clearly and early if you are unhappy with the ways things are going.

24. There is sometimes (especially in England) a certain embarrassment about discussing fees with professional people. The problem is that they are social equals, and in the conventions of polite society money does not change hands between gentlemen except in the payment of gambling debts. To pay someone money for goods or services is to demote him to the category of tradesman or servant, and to argue with him about it is even worse — that reduces him to the status of a stallholder in an Eastern bazaar.

One consequence of this embarrassment has been the monstrosity known as the fee scale, whereby the professional is paid according to a long-established percentage of the total cost of the job. It is a monstrosity because it does not necessarily reflect either the amount of work or the value of the work he does, and because it gives him a pecuniary incentive to inflate the total cost of the work to increase his own fee.

It can often make a great deal of sense to agree to pay the full scale fee and then involve your professional adviser in a cost-cutting exercise that reduces the overall cost of the operation while leaving his personal recompense intact. Other professionals simply charge by the hours they work, and in this case it becomes extremely important to know which activities consume a lot of their time and which do not. Alternatively, you can tell your prospective consultants the budget at the start, and ask them how much they will be able to do for the money.

But whatever method you use, there is no alternative to bringing the question up and laying it on the table. Both the method of payment and the amount have to be got clear and straight before any work begins. If the fee seems too large, you simply have to ask the adviser if you are playing out of your league and ought to go to someone less august and respected, or whether there are ways the project can be modified to reduce the fee to manageable proportions. While there could, of course, never be any question of a professional and a gentleman trying it on in the matter of money, it is sometimes surprising how much the fee can be reduced without any visible diminution of service, so long as there is no direct confrontation with overcharging and exploiting a social relationship for commercial advantage. But whatever else you do, fix an overall sum. Never hand the man a taximeter.

25. Finally, when the project is complete, ask for a report. Not a report on the project, which you presumably will be getting if it is that sort of project, but a report that reviews how the adviser–client relationship worked in practice and what should be avoided or repeated next time. Were there any misunderstandings? Was there information on either side that was not discovered by the other until too late? Did either side cause the other a lot of work or expense that could have been avoided? Were any shortcuts missed? Was the initial formulation of the objective too broad, or too narrow, or too vague?

All these questions have implications for future projects, even if with other advisers and other clients, and putting them on paper helps to focus the mind and activate the memory. You may also want to add an implementation review, perhaps even as much as two years later, to see how it finally worked out in practice and what can be learned from it. A good relationship with a professional adviser improves all the time as you get to know more about each other. Every family doctor or family lawyer knows how much better a job he does through knowing the family over the years and indeed the generations, but the family, too, gets to know how to use the doctor or lawyer. Your professional adviser can therefore do more than complete your project successfully — he can help you to become a more sophisticated client as well.

This then is a first formulation of the rules for using advisers and consultants for your own advantage rather than theirs.

The Seven Deadly Sins of Advisers and Clients

From discussions with a dozen or so top executives and leading professional advisers, one point emerges very clearly: although it takes time to become expert in the use of experts, many of the most serious mistakes can be eliminated as soon as you become aware that you are making them. So, perhaps it is best to end with the seven deadly sins on each side.

Those of the advisers are:

1. Applying tired formulas and book solutions instead of studying the problem with an open mind: adapting the client's problem to fit their expertise instead of adapting their expertise to fit the client's problem.

2. Using a high-powered front man to sell the service and then handing the job over to inexperienced people, inadequately supervised.

3. Using the client's name without permission.

4. Overcommitting themselves, from an emotional inability to turn down offers of work even if accepting means that they will be dangerously overstretched.

5. Privately criticizing and disparaging the client's staff when talking to top executives, and criticizing top executives to the staff.

6. Doing work on fees for the client that could be done just as well, and less expensively, by the client's own staff.

7. Concealing the fact that another company whose products or services they are recommending is giving them a commission or paying them a retainer.

The clients' sins are:

1. Failure to define their requirements clearly to themselves and effectively asking the consultant to find the problem as well as the solution.

2. Changing their minds and altering their decisions on the basis of casual and ill-informed criticism from colleagues or friends.

3. Reacting to criticism from superiors by putting all the blame on the adviser, even though they have approved what the adviser is doing.

4. Not bringing real worries and criticisms out into the open and confronting the adviser with them: terminating the consultant's services without warning, or not having the courage to terminate when they should.

5. Interfering and second-guessing on matters that lie within the adviser's expertise and are outside their own.

6. Blurring responsibility for the consultant's work, so that all those involved try to arrange it so that they take the credit if it succeeds and avoid the blame if it fails.

7. Freeloading, that is, employing an adviser on a small, well-defined project and then trying to milk him "informally" for free advice over a wide range of other, unrelated problems.

Antony Jay is chairman of Video Arts, Ltd., a British film production and distribution company.

How to Get a Good Consultant

Jean Pierre Frankenhuis

Management consultants are generally hired for the wrong reasons. Once hired, they are generally poorly employed and loosely supervised. The result is, more often than not, a final report that decorates an executive's bookshelf with as much usefulness as *The Life and Mores of the Pluvius Aegiptius* would decorate his coffee table — and at considerably more expense.

By no means, of course, do all consulting engagements lead to unsatisfactory results. Satisfactory results are usually due to management's intuitive respect for common sense in making decisions about when to hire consultants, whom to hire, what they are to do, and how they are to do it. The last two decisions can be viewed in the light of objective, logical procedures; it is the subjective aspects of the first two and their importance as a decision-making guide that bear consideration here.

Private and public organizations seek the help of consultants for three reasons: for savings, for an independent view, and for expertise. No one can quarrel with these aims, but their interpretation and use are often debatable.

The assumption that the one-time expenditure for a consultant will be smaller then the salaries and benefits paid to newly hired personnel may be justified for small projects. Obviously, you would not employ a specialist in administrative procedures when you could get a consultant to do the job for $5,000.

Once you reach a certain size, you must weigh the economics of the situation and the side benefits of in-house development against a possible dependency on a consultant. It is well to keep in mind that, unless there is a strong possibility of follow-up work, consultants are masters of the art of vanishing as soon as their fee has been paid.

The second often-used reason for hiring a consultant is to obtain an independent view as a means of settling a dispute at the top level about the solution to a problem. There are, however, three more fundamental reasons for seeking an outsider's viewpoint than executives' indecision: poorly presented solutions; lack of credibility of the persons in charge of recommending the "best" option; and personal issues such as antagonism, political pressure, and jockeying for position in the hierarchy.

Whatever the reasons, the consultant's survival instinct will cause him to side with the seat of power in the organization. Much to his relief, he will find that a number of proposed options can be discarded without endangering his "professional integrity." As for the remainder, they are reasonably sound so that at little risk, for the company or for him, he can choose or reject any of the options.

It becomes a simple matter of redoing the analysis before picking the answer that most closely approaches the opinions of the influential members of management — and incorporating minor variances for good measure that reflect other opinions. So much for independence.

The most common reason for hiring a consultant is to supplement limited in-house capabilities or to handle a project that company personnel lack the time to deal with. If it is understood that a consultant's services are being used on a temporary basis, one cannot argue with this reason. Of course, before the hiring, someone within the company must define the job to be performed and designate a person to supervise the work continually.

While this approach evokes a "mother's helper" image, it is advantageous to both parties, provided that the fee is fair. The client gets the job done, and the consulting firm may have the opportunity of giving staff members on-the-job training at little risk and for an acceptable profit.

The three common reasons that I have considered do not meet the most basic criterion: a management consultant must be a last-resort solution for any project in which he is not merely to assume the passive role of executor. Journeymen consultants are quick to seize on the opportunity for chargeable time, and to them any reason is acceptable. In the context of the three reasons described, however, consulting is hardly descriptive of the work.

When to Hire

It is wise to treat your problem as a difficult sickness. The symptoms are clearly identifiable, the causes are not, and the standard remedies do not work. In short, you should hire a consultant when your organization finds itself beyond the stage of two aspirins and rest for a headache that refuses to go away.

The consultant's usefulness is determined by the results of implementing his recommendations, not by the recommendations themselves. Consequently, if you doubt the quality of the managers and subordinates who must live, day in and day out, with solutions prescribed by nonoperational outsiders, or if you doubt the ability of top and middle management to react to future environmental changes affecting the original recommendations, then you are not ready for a consultant.

Before going on, I should make a distinction between private industry and government entities. Federal, state, and local governments are often obliged to balance necessary projects against restrictive budgets and uncontrolled staff increases. An attempt to hire experts on a permanent basis may run afoul of civil service regulations on salary levels and qualifications, legislative opposition, and public displeasure at the size of the government bureaucracy. It is much simpler to make use of a hidden fund for temporary consulting help, which is seldom contested. Taking this step may be unreasonable, but it is a fact of life.

In private industry, consultants provide two distinct services: specialized advice for the future and imaginative solutions for the present.

Specialized Advice

Most advice provided by consultants relates to future investments or approaches to new developments such as designing a five-year plan for new EDP applications and hardware, defining the needs of a distribution system, establishing the desired characteristics of a new product in a developing market, selecting the site for an overseas production facility, or locating an acquisition candidate. In undertaking such a project, the consultant should possess an extensive background coupled with advanced techniques that the company is unlikely to have now or to want to acquire.

A consultant's effectiveness in such tasks is closely related to the client's ability to express his needs, understand the results, and implement the recommendations. This scope excludes esoteric activities such as long-range planning or long-term economic forecasting.

In the case of long-range planning, it is difficult to comprehend how the same management team that cannot outline its objectives and strategy could implement someone else's plans — not to mention evaluate his worth or reaction to unexpected variances. A new management team, not a surrogate, is needed.

Similarly, a sweeping economic forecast that predicts a glowing future for any country willing to pay for the work or a gloomy forecast for the world to satisfy the latest ecological trend have two traits in common: actual data can be conveniently readjusted in the face of unexpected but frequent incidents such as oil crises, and 20 years from now such forecasts will be as academic as last year's astrology charts.

Imaginative Solutions

The greatest contribution a consultant can make is his experience. He has seen your problem, or a variant thereof, in other situations; he has devised solutions to it or has absorbed solutions implemented by previous clients. He should be a living compendium of case studies.

Thus, the imagination a consultant brings to your problems is not necessarily superior to yours; you are simply taking a shortcut. While the top executives of your company, given a little time, could reinvent the wheel, the use of outside expertise allows you to examine, at a reasonable cost, all the wheels that have been invented.

Of course, you think your wheel has some unique features. Demystification is needed on the subject: with the exception of technical aspects such as manufacturing processes, the same managerial problems repeatedly crop up. In data processing, for instance, the great new theory is "distributed processing." It is no more than a return to the decentralized approach of 15 years ago, with the differences that minicomputers have become extremely powerful, and some centralization is now possible through the accessibility of telecommunications.

A consultant who knew in 1961 how to design interactive production, marketing, and financial systems should do as good a job for you in 1977. All he needs is a computer expert to introduce to the design some technical innovations, if necessary, such as data-base management and teleprocessing.

Whom to Hire

Consultants and consulting organizations can be arbitrarily separated into three categories: individual specialists, small firms with staffs of specialists, and large, multidisciplinary companies. Each presents advantages and drawbacks that you should consider carefully in addition to needs and expectations of your own.

Quality of the Resource

As a rule, in dealing with an individual consultant, you can get a clear picture of his experience, personality, and performance because the person whom you interview is the one who will do the job. You can easily check the references and verify the extent of his or her involvement in previous projects. It is very likely, at any rate, that you singled him out through the recommendation of a business contact, so the references are usually personal.

Much the same is true of a small firm with, say, a half-dozen members; almost certainly you will work with the same people who are selling the job. Generally, such firms are formed to pool resources in order to provide each individual with a steadier, if sometimes lower, income.

Large-and medium-size companies are altogether a different breed. Their duties are often split between the "sellers" and the "doers," between the "managers" and the "operators." Those persons with technical expertise and the ability to sell handle the preliminary talks, define the approach, set the extent of the job, and, most important, establish the size and qualifications of the team that will work on the project. Quite often also, they supervise the work, their involvement depending on the experience of the team.

In regard to that experience, the client must take a stand. In their proposals, management consultants often include a reference list of clients who are either in your industry or whose problems appear to be similar to yours, as well as the names and backgrounds of some of the staff. Such references, intended to influence your choice, may be full of distortions. Here are some of them:

— You have no assurance that the consultants listed will actually form part of the team. Invariably the list includes top officers who are now dedicated to the administration of the company. Precisely because of their technical qualifications, experience, and reputation, they have climbed the hierarchial ladder to a level where they have ceased to be consultants.

— The written backgrounds of staff members often highlight those areas of competence that best suit the needs of the project. This emphasis may not be commensurate with an individual's actual ability or experience.

— The description of a person's work pinpoints neither his other real role nor the extent of his involvement. Words such as "participated in" or "assisted" may conceal his minor role in the project.

— For reasons of confidentiality, clients are described in elliptical terms such as "a major this" or "a leading that." In a brochure there is reason for confidentiality, but you are entitled to a verbal identification of these clients. If your prospective consultant does not trust your discretion, why trust his?

— Work performed for previous clients is often described in as little detail or with as many generalities as the background of the consultants. Consulting firms seldom, if ever, describe the *practical* results of their involvement. Rarely will they commit to paper a bold assertion such as "through this project the client achieved X dollars in savings" or "gained Y% of the market." (Obviously, you will also never read, "The client decided the recommendations were inapplicable and did not implement them.")

— Successful jobs may have been performed by another office of the firm in another part of the world; and, if so, that is where the knowhow for your project will remain.

You should evaluate the firm as you would an individual, regardless of any objections it may raise, on the basis that it will be fully responsible for reaching the established objectives. Moreover, if you are planning to sign the consultant to a fixed-price or fixed-ceiling contract, you should stipulate that the firm will absorb any cost overruns. You should also insist on the inclusion of a penalty for overruns that is severe enough to motivate the consultant to meet the deadlines. There would be little consolation for you in knowing that the financial burden of an overrun or of redoing parts of a poorly executed project lay on the consulting firm; the fact is that other deadlines important to you may have been missed and related scheduled action may have to be delayed.

Apart from the questions of payment and inconvenience to you, you must consider the quality of the work done in the overrun period. It is reasonable to assume that if the consulting firm must work overtime to correct its mistakes at its own expense, the firm's greatest concern will be for speed. The objective is no longer to do the best job but to finish it quickly.

As a prospective client, you are of course entitled to meet the participants scheduled for the assignment — though you may have to overcome objections based on the "firm's policy." Treat these participants as individual parts of a whole, try to evaluate their actual involvement in previous projects, and explore their background and experience — just as you would for an independent consultant.

Obtain the hourly or daily rate and establish whether it is commensurate with the experience and technical knowhow of each participant and the amount of responsibility each will have in the team. If the work to be done lies in a specialized area of your company for which you are not directly responsible and in which the performance of its manager is not in question, include him or her in these discussions.

All this is time-consuming and may seem unjustified, particularly if you are considering one of the well-known management consulting firms. But you do not select a consultant on the basis of a name brand or a fancy brochure. By making the effort now, you can assure yourself that the price you pay for the services will be reflected in the quality of the work done.

Does Size Matter?

Some large consulting firms claim that they offer greater expertise in more fields than their small competitors. When, however, a client holding this expectation contracts with one of the major firms, he often just gets more fields. The successful, respected large firms limit the number of fields in which they seek business and on which they stake their reputations. For the client, it is not a question of putting all his eggs in the same basket but of putting the proper egg in a well-selected basket.

One category of management consultants I have not considered is the "Big Eight" and other large audit firms. Their consulting departments fall in the "supermarket" classification: "you need it, we've got it." Actually, however, they have four undisputed areas of expertise, at least as far as private industry is concerned: finance, EDP, executive search, and employee benefits. These strong points derive from their early role of providing supplementary services to audit clients.

A majority of audit partners in these firms still treat their consulting activities as the frosting on the auditing cake. One can understand that an audit represents repeated income, year after year, and clients seldom switch; that an audit is mandatory for a publicly owned company; and that responsibility, until the recent past at least, is limited.

Consulting projects, on the other hand, are usually one-time affairs; expertise must be sold amid fierce competition; recommendations fully engage those who make them; and mistakes are factual rather than subject to interpretation of accounting standards. In providing consulting services, the auditors are merely cleaning your windshield while continuing to perform their main task of pumping gas.

The question of independence is important. Would the outside auditors criticize weaknesses in your internal controls when the system has been designed by their own consulting department? Can they be truly objective when they highlight the need for new administrative procedures or an inventory control system?

Until this recurring controversy is settled, there is one simple approach to take: never use the same firm for both auditing and management consulting at the same time. You will find that the competitive instincts of accounting firms create a better product in both fields if you keep them separate.

How Much to Pay

Consultants generally calculate and quote their professional fees on an hourly or a daily basis, on the amount of time estimated to be necessary to do the job, and, for their assignment teams, on the number and category of each consultant. Category rates for members of a consulting team are as much a function of their experience as of their salary ranges.

There are two special cases: the "on-call" consultant, whose services are sought on a regular basis but for short periods of time and who charges only for the time spent; and the consultant "on retainer," whom you pay a minimum fee for a certain period whether or not you make use of his services. In both cases, the consultant normally acts more as an adviser on particular matters, such as taxes, than as a problem solver with wider scope.

Rates are usually competitive and depend heavily on reputation, years of experience, and specialization. An individual consultant's fee may strike you as very high, since you know he will be the sole beneficiary of the income and that multiplication of his daily rate by the number of working days in the year probably shows him to be earning far more than you do. The catch, though, is that he will be lucky to work six to eight months of the year; the rest of the time he is prospecting for new jobs.

In the case of a consulting firm, its rate must cover overhead, salaries, benefits, management, and complimentary services, whether or not you are being charged directly for professional staff services.

Factor of Expenses

Traveling expenses are easily identified, estimated, and budgeted. Such is not the case, however, with nontraveling expenses — that is, secretarial help, typing, editing, printing, copying, telephone, and other ancillary services. Their impact should not be ignored, since they are either included in the daily rate structure or billed in addition to the professional fee at an average ceiling of 10 to 15% of the fee.

In its proposal to the prospective client, the consultant should clearly state his policy on nontraveling expenses. If they are included in the rate schedule, you are then in the same situation as a consumer in a store that accepts certain credit cards; the store's prices take into account the commission to be paid to the credit-card issuer, whether or not you use the card. If nontraveling expenses are included in the rate structure, you can do little about it, though you can make it a point of negotiation. But such added costs hardly constitute a prime criterion in selecting a consultant.

Individual consultants must usually pay extra for services such as typing and preparation of audiovisual presentations. Here you have two options: request itemized copies of bills paid by the consultant for services directly related to the job or make as many of these services available to him as your resources permit.

If the cost of nontraveling expenses concerns you when negotiating with a large consulting firm, you have a right to request the rates it applies to administrative services. Don't be surprised to find that they are higher than those of companies whose main business it is to provide these services. While the added cost may not be significant, it says much about the philosophy and efficiency of the consulting firm.

Jean Pierre Frankenhuis is an independent management consultant based in Paris, France.

Is Help Helpful?

Jack R. Gibb

People in the service professions often see themselves as primarily engaged in the job of helping others. Helping becomes both the personal style of life and a core activity that gives meaning and purpose to the life of the professional. The youth worker, the camp director, the counselor, the consultant, the therapist, the teacher, the lawyer — each is a helper.

Helping is a central social process. The den mother, the committee chairman, the parent, the personal friend, the board member, the dance sponsor — each is a helper.

Help, however, is not always helpful. The recipient of the proffered help may not see it as useful. The offering may not lead to greater satisfaction or to better performance. Even less often does the helping process meet a more rigorous criterion — lead to continued growth on the part of the participants.

To begin with, a person may have varied motivations for offering help. He may wish to improve performance of a subordinate, reduce his own guilt, obtain gratitude, make someone happy, or give meaning to his own life. He may wish to demonstrate his superior skill or knowledge, induce indebtedness, control others, establish dependency, punish others, or simply meet a job prescription. These conscious or partially conscious motivations are so intermingled in any act of help that it is impossible for either the helper or the recipient to sort them out.

Depending upon his own needs and upon the way he sees the motives of the helper, the recipient will have varied reactions. He may feel gratitude, resentment, or admiration. He may feel helpless and dependent, or jealous of the helper who has the strength or resources to be in the helper role. He may feel indebted, or pressured to conform to the perceived demands or beliefs of the helper.

We have all noticed that in certain cases the recipient of the help becomes more helpless and dependent, less able to make his own decisions or initiate his own actions, less self-sufficient, more apathetic and passive, less willing to take risks, more concerned about propriety and conformity, and less creative and venture-some. We have also seen circumstances in which, following help, recipients become more creative, less dependent upon helpers, more willing to make risk decisions, more highly motivated to tackle tough problems, less concerned about

Reprinted by permission from the February 1964 issue of the *Forum*, Journal of the Association of Professional Directors of YMCA's in the United States.

Table 11-1
The Helping Relationship

Orientations that help

1. Reciprocal trust (confidence, warmth, acceptance)
2. Cooperative learning (inquiry, exploration, quest)
3. Mutual growth (becoming, actualizing, fulfilling)
4. Reciprocal openness (spontaneity, candor, honesty)
5. Shared problem solving (defining, producing alternatives, testing)
6. Autonomy (freedom, interdependence, equality)
7. Experimentation (play, innovation, provisional try)

Orientations that hinder

1. Distrust (fear, punitiveness, defensiveness)
2. Teaching (training, advice giving, indoctrinating)
3. Evaluating (fixing, correcting, providing a remedy)
4. Strategy (planning *for*, maneuvering, gamesmanship)
5. Modeling (demonstation, information giving, guiding)
6. Coaching (molding, steering, controlling)
7. Patterning (standard, static, fixed)

---

conformity, and more effective at working independently or interdependently. Help may or may not lead to personal growth and organizational health.

Under certain conditions both the giver and the receiver grow and develop. In general, people tend to grow when there is reciprocal dependence —*inter*dependence, joint determination of goals, real communication in depth, and reciprocal trust. To the degree that these conditions are absent, people fail to grow.

Orientations That Help or Hinder

From the standpoint of the organization, help must meet two criteria: the job or program must be done more effectively, and the individual members must grow and develop. These two criteria tend to merge. The program and the organization are effective only as the participants grow. The same conditions that lead to organizational health lead to personal growth. Table 11-1 presents a theory of the helping relationship. Seven parallel sets of orientations are presented. One set of conditions maximize help and a parallel set of conditions minimize help.

Reciprocal Trust. People accept help from those they trust. When the relationship is one of acceptance and trust, offers of help are appreciated, listened to, seen as potentially helpful, and often acted upon. The receiver accepts help from one whose perceived motives are congenial to him. He tends to reject offers from people whose offering is seen as a guise for attempts to control, punish, correct, or gain power. "Help" is most helpful when given in an atmosphere in which people have reciprocal feelings of confidence, warmth, and acceptance. When one feels that his worth as a person is valued, he is able to place himself in psychological readiness to receive aid.

Distrust. When people fear and distrust each other, even well-intended help is resisted, resented, or seen as unhelpful. Offers of help are sometimes given in service of motivations that are unacceptable to the receiver. That is, one offers help in order to place the other person in a dependent position, elicit expressions of gratitude, assert one's superiority, or punish him. In distrust the recipient's guard is up. He is likely to project his distrusts onto the helper and to resist or resent the help.

One often gives help to camouflage or assuage his desire to change another person — change his character, habits, or misconceptions. The desire to change another person is essentially hostile. At a deep level, one who genuinely accepts another person does not wish to change him. A person who is accepted is allowed to be, become, determine his own goals, and follow them at his own pace. The person who genuinely wishes to help offers the help that the recipient wishes. Genuine help is not foisted upon the receiver. Neither the punisher nor the child really believes that the punishment is given "for the good of the child."

Punishment or censure may be given with a conscious desire to help but usually is accompanied by a deep component of retaliation or by a desire to hurt, control, or assert superiority. The giver often speaks of his act as "helpful" in order to rationalize to himself and to the receiver acts that are done for other motivations.

Cooperative Learning. People are helpful to each other when they are engaged in a cooperative quest for learning. The learning atmosphere is one of joint inquiry and exploration. Needs for help and impulses to give help arise out of the demands of the common cooperative task. Help is thus reciprocal. The helper and helpee roles are interchangeable. Each participant has the intent to learn and feels he can learn from the partners and from the common task. The boss and the subordinate, the teacher and the student, the professional worker and the youth — all are most helpful when each member of the pair sees the relationship as a quest with potential learning for each. An effective project team is guided by the task and not by the teacher. It is motivated by the shared potential for learning.

Teaching. When one participant in a project sets out to teach, train, advise, persuade, or indoctrinate the other members or is seen as wanting to do so, the learning of each member is reduced. People cannot be taught. People must learn. People cannot be trained. They grow and develop. The most deeply helpful relationship is one of common inquiry and quest, a relationship between co-learners and co-managers in which each is equally dependent upon the other for significant help and in which each sees and accepts this relationship.

Mutual Growth. The most permanent and significant help occurs in a relationship in which both members are continually growing, becoming, and seeking fulfillment. Each member participates in a mutual assessment of progress, accepts this reality of growth, and participates in a way that will maximize the growth of both participants. In a fundamental sense one can only help himself. The helper can only participate with another in an effort to create a climate in which growth can occur.

Evaluating. Growth is often hindered when one member of the helping team sets out to appraise or remedy the defects in the other member. Help is most effective when it is seen as a force moving toward growth rather than as an effort to remove gaps, remedy defects, or bring another person up to a standard criterion. The limits of growth of any person are extremely difficult to foresee or to assess. The potential for growth is consistently under-estimated by both participants in the helping relationship.

Reciprocal Openness. One of the essential conditions for effective human learning is the opportunity for feedback or knowledge of progress. Feedback is essential in acquiring skills, knowledge, and attitudes. In the areas where professional help is most commonly sought or given, the essential progress in learning and growth is blocked most often by the failure to obtain adequate data on people's feelings and perceptions of each other. In order to do effective work one must know how others feel and how they see things. In the usual situations in which professional helpers find themselves, there are many pressures which camouflage or distort the relevant data necessary for efficient work and best learning. Many factors reduce the availability of the relevant data: differential status, differential perceived power, and fears that one can hurt or be hurt.

Strategy. When some part of the helping process is closed or unavailable to all participants, people are likely to become anxious, resentful, or resistant. Neither participant in the helping process can "use" the other for his own needs. The helping process is most effective when one plans with another, not for another. One is not helped when he is maneuvered into some action which he does not understand. Gamesmanship and gimmicks are antithetical to the helping process.

Shared Problem Solving. The productive helping relationship focuses upon the problem to be solved. Problem solving involves a joint determination of the problem, continual redefinition of the problem as successive insights are gained, joint focus upon possible alternative solutions, joint exploration of the data, and continual reality testing of the alternatives. The expertness and resources of each person are shared. The aspect of the behavior about which help is given is seen as a shared problem — not as a defect to be remedied or as something to be solved by the helper as consultant.

Modeling. A common image of the helping relationship is one where the helper offers a model for the advisee to follow. The expert gives a demonstration of how the recipient may solve his problems. The problem is defined by the expert. Diagnosis is made by the expert. The expert is challenged to offer additional alternatives to the solution of the problem and perhaps even to test the solutions. The process is unidirectional. The limitations of modeling are many. Dependency is increased. The pupil seldom gets better than the model. The worker tries to conform to the image of the supervisor. Growth is limited.

Autonomy. The ideal relationship for helping is an interdependent one in which each person sees the other as both helper and recipient in an exchange among equals. It is essential that each participant preserve his freedom and maintain his autonomous responsibility for guiding himself toward his own learnings, growth, and problem solving. The helper must work himself out of the helping job. The supervisor, youth worker, and counselor must become decreasingly necessary to the people being helped. Psychological weaning, however painful to both helper and recipient, must continue if help is to be truly helpful.

Coaching. The coach molds, steers, or controls the behavior of the recipient, much as a tennis coach or physical education director molds the behavior of the athlete or skill-directed recipient of help. This is another unidirectional process in which the coach is assumed to have special diagnostic and observational powers which he applies in a skilled way to the behavior of the recipient, who puts himself in the hands of the coach. The recipient of help is encouraged to maintain respectful dependency upon the coach, to not challenge his authority or expertness, to put implicit trust in his abilities and powers, and to receive from the coach motivational or inspirational guidance. Both coach and pupil suffer under this pattern. Each may gain in skill. Neither grows as a person.

Experimentation. Tentativeness and innovative experimentation are characteristic of the most productive helping relationship. There is a sense of play, excitement, and fun in the common exploratory quest for new solutions to continually changing problems. The helping process is viewed as a series of provisional trials. Each participant joins in the game and adds to the general excitement. Errors can be made — and are perhaps expected. Help is a search. Finding creative solutions to newly defined problems is a game — full of zest and intrinsic drives that keep the game going.

Patterning. Help is limited when the process is seen as an attempt on the part of one person to help another meet a prescribed standard, come up to a criterion, or reach a goal specified in advance. Helping is a creative synthesis of growth and a continual search for new forms.

"Help" is not always helpful — but it can be. Both the helper and the recipient can grow and learn when help is given in a relationship of trust, joint inquiry, openness, and interdependence. Growth-centered helping processes lead to healthy groups and effective organizations.

Jack R. Gibb is an organizational psychologist and consultant in La Jolla, California.

Diagnosis

"On the morrow Moses sat to judge the people, and the people stood about Moses from morning till evening. When Moses' father-in-law saw all that he was doing for the people, he said, 'What is this that you are doing for the people? Why do you sit alone, and all the people stand about you from morning till evening?' And Moses said, 'Because they come to me to inquire of God; when they have a dispute, they come to me and I decide between a man and his neighbor.' ...Moses' father-in-law said to him, 'You and the people with you will wear yourselves out, for the thing is too heavy for you; you are not able to perform it alone. Listen now to my voice; I will give you counsel.' "

Exodus 18: 13–19

Moses' working relationship with his father-in-law, Jethro, represents one of the earliest references to consultation. The "what" and "why" type inquiry employed by Jethro provided the diagnostic framework for his advising Moses to select competent leaders ("Choose able men who are trustworthy..."), provide training ("...teach them the statues and the decisions..."), and provide an organization structure ("...place such men over the people as rulers of thousands, of hundreds, of fifties, and of tens...").

The power of accurate diagnosis cannot be overstated. As the platform for action, its essence pervades the remaining acts of the consultative drama. The precise beginning and ending of the diagnosis phase is blurred and elusive. While still in entry, the consultant is gathering data which will form a part of diagnosis. At the other end of the diagnosis phase, the data-gathering action is itself a response in that it intervenes into the client culture and precipitates some change. Ask me a question and I am instantly altered by my contemplation of an answer.

What is the relational nature of diagnosis? It is at the outset a bargaining of perceptions — a kind of collusion of reality and truth. There *is* reality and truth. However, the consultant's perception of reality coupled with the consultant's perception of the client's perception is the stuff of which diagnoses are generally made.

The bargaining of perceptions is borne out of client–consultant trust, the greater their trust, the better the bargain for both. "Betterness" for the consultant entails such disclosure on the part of the client that sufficient, quality information is made available. "Betterness" for the client occurs when the consultant gains enough information to intervene usefully, causing minimal pain and disruption in the process.

Client–consultant trust is fostered by joint goal setting, empowering the client and managing client resistance. All three efforts involve consultant initiative; only one involves client initiative. This underscores the fact that diagnosis is primarily consultant lead.

Joint Goal Setting

Diagnosis can be humbling, painful, and humiliating for the client. It can reveal unpleasantries lined with hurt and disappointment. Even on the most positive end of potential outcomes, it is cloaked with the mystery and uncertainty of the unknown.

The first time one of the authors had a physical examination which included use of a proctoscope, the new physician assumed previous experience with the humbling inspection. Needless to say, cooperation was less than enthusiastic. Some explanation of what was to happen and why no doubt would have resulted in a somewhat more trusting subject.

Apprehension can be reduced by actively involving the client in establishing the goals for diagnosis. These goals would include the determination of the type of data required, the manner in which it will be obtained, the persons to be involved, target dates for completion, etc. It is likewise imperative the client play an equal role in ascertaining how the data will be used after accumulation.

The formation and maintenance of a client–consultant trust relationship is enhanced significantly by active client involvement in the joint goal setting process. By-products of the effort include commitment and ownership. Their existence will bolster the relationship and aid the client in functioning as an ally to the undertaking.

Empowering the Client

It goes without saying that part of the end result of consultation is some improvement in the client system. However, in order for that improvement to be maintained, the client must learn from the experience. A major key to a trusting client–consultant relationship occurs by the consultant helping the client to use the consultative experience for personal growth.

Growth comes through undertaking activities one has not perfected. Engaging in such imperfected activities carries risk of embarrassment and decreased power. It is the responsibility of the consultant to provide sufficient emotional support to the client for experimentation to occur despite the risk. Ultimately, increased client growth brings decreased dependency on the consultant.

Diagnosis can be used to empower the client by making data gathering a learning experience. The type and sequence of information can precipitate not only client discovery regarding the content but enhanced skill regarding the process. For instance, joint review of a questionnaire before use and subsequent study of the information generated by the questionnaire can significantly upgrade the diagnostic and problem-solving skills of a client.

Managing Client Resistance

There are activities in diagnosis that are nonreactive or unobtrusive in their impact on the client or client system. Such activities enable the gathering of data without fostering client resistance. Historical data (memos, charts, reports), external data (conversations with suppliers, major stockholders, customers), and observational data exemplify unobtrusive diagnostic activities.

Reactive or obtrusive activities (interviews, surveys, questionnaires) are of such a nature that the potential runs high for the client or client system to exercise some resistance. The potential for pain inherent in the inspection of the unknown necessitates special precautions to anticipate client resistance and take measures to counteract their occurrence.

Resistance management is a highly intuitive skill few consultants completely master. In essence, it involves the consultant disassociating self from actions to assume the self of the client. Much of the time, resistance is due to issues related to the relationship (e.g., telling another what to do) rather than the substance of the diagnosis or action itself.

Central to managing resistance is the consultant's playing his or her role in a manner which gives the client little to resist. By causing the client to experience psychological kinship with the consultant, the need to resist will be reduced.

Diagnosis relates to the acquisition of knowledge, and knowledge is a source of power. The client–consultant relationship can be made productive and positive for all concerned only through the parties managing it with equality of power as a criterion.

Chapter 12
"Surviving as a Messenger: The Client–Consultant Relationship During Diagnosis"
Richard M. Furr

The space between entry and diagnosis is one not known for preciseness. Given that, the Furr article offers us transition by focusing on the use of power as an ingredient required during diagnosis. This article was written for this book and has not previously appeared in any other publication.

While some readers may find the recommendations disquieting, we feel they offer a fresh way of looking at the relational aspects of diagnosis. Unlike other areas of consultation, little has been written about the client–consultant relationship. This is particularly true of the diagnosis phase.

Chapter 13
"Consultants and Detectives"
Fritz Steele

There is editorial danger in lifting a chapter out of a book and presenting it as a separate article. It is somewhat like playing singularly the viola part of a concerto; while it may sound complete as a solo, it misses the breadth of the larger score.

The point of "Consultants and Detectives" is sufficiently provocative to risk losing some of the book's larger message. Taken from the book *Consulting for Organizational Change*, the chapter compares the consultant's diagnosis with the detective's investigation. The persistent forcing of the direct analogy unleashes creative insights into this phase of consulting process. Of particular importance to the client–consultant relationship is the acquisition of credibility without permanent closeness.

Chapter 14
"The Organization as a Micro-Culture"
Leonard Nadler

The vantage point of a cultural anthropologist is a useful perspective for the diagnostician. The anthropological perspective reflects an attempt on the part of those involved in diagnosis (a consultant and/or client) to perceive reality and trust with maximum precision and minimum prejudice. While a value-free inspection of anything "life-ful" is improbable, one moves closer to an egoless inspection as one attempts to acquire the skill of the anthropologist.

The Nadler article provides some of the landmarks along the path to an anthropological perspective. While such dimensions as structure, relationships, communication, and technical-operating systems are typically included in the domains to be perused, the diagnostician less frequently includes time, space, language, and sex in the elements that make up a thorough diagnosis. As Harry Levinson states in his mammoth text *Organization Diagnosis*, "Any fool can tell that a river flows. Only he who understands its cross-currents, its eddies, the variations in its speed, the hidden rocks, and its action in drought and flood is the master of its functioning."

Chapter 15
"How to Market Training Within Your Organization"
Chip R. Bell

The influencing of change toward improved organization health can be viewed as an attempt to market an idea or service to a potential buyer. The Bell article focuses on influencing the outcomes of human resources development decisions by people in senior organizational positions.

Built analogously around the generic marketing functions in an organization — marketing research, marketing planning, advertising, and a direct sales force — the article also provides a strategic model for influencing change. Of particular use in the diagnosis phase of consultation is the concept of marketing research (assessment). Such components as the organization's value system, the personal values of key organizational leaders, the needs of the client system, and the psychological needs of the consultant are critical parts of a comprehensive diagnosis.

Surviving as a Messenger: The Client-Consultant Relationship During Diagnosis

Richard M. Furr

The relationship aspects of the client–consultant engagement are complicated, exciting, and rewarding. A key mechanism for shaping change, the relationship is in fact part of the intervention rather than separate from it.

This article focuses upon the relationship dimensions of the consulting engagement, particularly in the diagnostic stage.

The first part of this article is designed to provide background from which to view the relationship aspects of diagnosis. The components of the relationship and the steps in accomplishing the purposes of diagnosis will then be examined.

The Diagnostic Stage

The diagnostic stage of a consulting engagement is important to both the consultant and the client. To the consultant it is important as a means of learning what he needs to know in order to shape an appropriate response strategy. The diagnostic stage is used as a means for establishing initial awareness and growth in the client as well as influencing the client to feel responsible for ensuring a successful outcome. Change starts with the diagnosis, not after it.

Likewise, the diagnostic stage is important to the client. Here he learns what he needs to understand to achieve the results he wants. It allows the client opportunities to name the game and define how he wants it played in his organization and in the relationship with the consultant.

Perspectives on Diagnosis

There are several perspectives about the diagnostic stage of consultation which warrant attention by the consultant. One simple perspective might be labeled *Multiple Purpose Thinking* and suggests that the consultant proceed with a flexible agenda. This perspective is illustrated by the consultant's thinking, "Given that we are going to do an assessment of some kind, how else can we use it to benefit the client?" Frequently, subpurposes, which can be included efficiently, will become evident.

A second perspective might be called *Evolving Diagnosis*. Such a perspective presumes that diagnosis is not a discrete stage of the engagement but is rather a nearly perpetual enterprise, beginning with the initial client contact and lasting throughout the entire engagement. Everything the consultant does is viewed and managed to further refine the Evolving Diagnosis. Running a seminar at a later stage of the engagement, for example, can be done in a way which allows additional input into the diagnosis.

One further perspective is the distinction between "doing a diagnosis" and *Creating Awareness* or causing the client to arrive at a diagnosis. In the "doing a diagnosis" view the consultant executes the diagnosis and brings the client the results. In the latter view the consultant starts thinking about how to cause the client and key players in the system to see what they need to see in order to achieve the result they want. The key difference is that the consultant focuses on the process of creating awareness rather than the tactic of "doing a diagnosis." This "management of the process" approach tends to keep the client actively and responsibly involved and fosters less client resistance because the consultant is not laying it on him. When performed most effectively, the client may discover things he had never seen before.

Purpose of Diagnostics

As the consultant proceeds through the engagement, his usefulness will be largely a function of energy focused for effectiveness. Rather than energetically charging-up the client and zealously pursuing truth, the consultant must maintain focus assiduously. Focus is manifested in the consultant's commitment and purposefulness. While the former is dependent upon the personal psychological needs of the consultant, the purpose can be defined here.

Concentrating upon the diagnostic stage, we can identify six interrelated aspects of the purpose of diagnosis. The first is to precipitate change itself. Secondly, the diagnosis should provide an assessment of the variables relevant to the change goal. Thirdly, the diagnosis can create an expanded awareness and growth in the client. Fourth, and very specific to the relationship, it should create in the client a personal value out of the relationship separate from his objective organizational purpose. The fifth aspect is to energize momentum toward the change. The sixth is to focus the client's attention on the variables necessary to create the change and to achieve his goal.

The purposefulness of diagnosis is a key relationship consideration. Next, we will look at a relationship model which focuses upon four key operating components.

Figure 12-1. The components shaping the behavior of the client and the consultant.

Components of the Relationship

The client–consultant relationship has four components operating simultaneously to shape the behavior of the client *and* the consultant and, ultimately, the outcome of the relationship. As reflected in Figure 12-1, both the client and the consultant are substantially influenced by their own personality dynamics, their perception of their roles, and their experience of the demands of the organization. The fourth component surrounding, integrating, and interfering with these three is the nature of the communications between the client and consultant. The four components are illustrated below.

Each individual's personality dynamics include their personal needs, self-image, beliefs, feeling, games, and resulting behavior patterns. Compounding these variables, the personal make-up of one individual may be affected by the personal make-up of the other. The client, for example, may be a shy person who is personally intimidated by a consultant who acts very self-assured and assertive.

The second component of the client–consultant relationship is each individual's perception of his own role and the role of the other person. Each individual will most appropriately relate to the other person in a way that conveys respect for role. For instance, the consultant should establish himself as at least a professional peer in the eyes of the client. However, when the client is aloof and generally inaccessible to the consultant, he is probably not being viewed by the client as a professional peer. The result is a consultant having limited access to the power of the client's role.

The third key component is founded in one's experience of the organization — a result of the values, traditions, and norms inherent in the formal organization and the informal organization. From these organizational predispositions, each individual acquires certain expectations. For example, frequently an experience occurs as a result of an institutionalized anticonsultant bias throughout the client's firm. In such cases, the client may perceive that he risks reproach and reprisal from colleagues and as a result may be resistant to taking highly visible and risky actions stemming from the consultation.

The fourth component of the client–consultant relationship is the nature of the communications between them. Like a rapid-fire tennis match, the action–reaction communication sequences shape the perceptions and reactions in each individual. Each person attempts to influence the other by what he initiates as well as by how he responds to what the other communicator initiates. The resulting dialogue shapes the foundation and fabric of the relationship.

With the preceding model of the components of the client–consultant relationship as background, a key to the consulting process becomes the posture or stance the consultant takes in that relationship. A proper consultant stance implies that the consultant functions in a fashion unencumbered by personal dynamics, role influence, organizational influence, or the manipulation attempts of the client. While this describes an idealized stance, the more it can be approximated, the less judgment and action will be influenced by circumstances unrelated to the client situation.

Toward Achievement of the Relationship Objective

While the preceding information is intended to provide a stage, what follows approximates the play. The client–consultant relationship during diagnosis can be viewed as a play with three acts: the shaping of client–consultant agreements necessary to manage the change throughout the diagnosis; the empowering of the client to perform to his fullest capacity; and the handling of resistance.

Shaping Agreements

In shaping the agreements necessary to achieve certain changes, some of the following guidelines and techniques may become appropriate:

— It is important for the client and the consultant to clearly agree on the intention of the diagnosis as it relates to achieving the client's objective. If it becomes necessary for the consultant to be the active agent in obtaining the diagnostic data, the consultant needs to create enough latitude to be able to get the information required. For example, in solving a quality problem it may be important for the consultant to establish broad freedom and trust within the relationship to be able to assess effectively the impact of the leader's behavior on the quality problem.

— The client and consultant need to agree on how the diagnostic information will be handled to meet the client's purpose and to satisfy all ethics criteria.

— The consultant may need to establish a contract with the client regarding the client's implied obligations which may arise as a result of the diagnosis. This is particularly important when a diagnosis involving some of the client's employees raises their hopefulness that something will happen as a result. The client needs to be aware of such expectations and to be committed to taking serious, reasonable steps to follow-up on the implication of the diagnostic results. This also, very positively, reduces resistance at later stages in the consultation.

— Often, it is beneficial for the client to collect his own data. This can be accomplished through a carefully designed process in which the client hears the truth but which provides the necessary protection of others involved. Agreements are formed which establish the respondents' requirements for confidentiality.

— Often, when the consultant must be the one to collect the data, it is very desirable to get the client to ask for it from the followers directly. This practice can speed the data collection and increase the chance of the client learning by direct experience. The client's communication should establish the purpose of the study, the methodology, the ethics, the use to be made of the results, and the value the leader places upon honesty and candor.

Empowering the Client

The second key step in accomplishing the purpose of the consulting engagement through the diagnostic stage is empowering the client. The empowering of the client means helping the client to perform his function to the fullest extent of his ability *and* facilitating his growth as a person in areas which go beyond work.

This is a crucial result of successfully handling the relationship dimensions of the diagnosis and can substantially increase the consultant's value to the client. Likewise, it can enable the client to execute his role in the response phase of consultation. The two issues of empowering — will be addressed separately, though they are clearly interrelated.

Empowering the client to perform excellently involves the consultant looking at those conditions likely to increase the client's *ability,* his *motivation* to act appropriately, and the *organizational* conditions within which the client operates. To increase ability, the consultant will need to work with the client in a manner which increases the client's awareness of what needs to be done *and* increases his own capacity to do it. Additionally, the consultant may need to help the client acquire the necessary skills to do what is required, and the diagnostic process can be one vehicle for doing this.

Increasing the client's motivation to act requires that the consultant arrange positive rewards for acting and entails reducing the self-restraints in the personal make-up of the client. In order to increase motivation positively, the consultant must learn the client's personal needs and arrange positive rewards for taking appropriate steps. The consultant might then arrange feedback to the client from the client system so that the hoped-for reward occurs. An example of empowering the client motivationally occurred when a consultant accurately assessed the client as a person with a need to be seen as progressive and important. The consultant then helped the client view the recommended course of action as progressive and an enhancement to the client's self-esteem.

In addition to empowering the client by causing him to see valued reward from taking action, another technique for empowering the client is to cause the client to see and work through his own immobilizing behavior. What occurs then is a reduction of self-restraints. For example, upon getting the client to see how his decision aversiveness or crippling attention to detail is contributing to the very problem he is trying to solve, an uncomfortable internal conflict is established which the client is motivated to reduce. The consultant can get the client to see the unsolved problem as a risk of even greater proportion which he can avoid by being more decisive and less compulsive about detail.

The third class of conditions which may need to be managed to empower the client is the organizational system. The client may have the ability, vision, skill, and motivation to perform to his fullest capacity, but the organizational variables may be limiting. While these are often used as cop outs which allow the client to disown responsibility, at times the conditions are, in reality, barriers. For example, when roles, goals, and reward systems are in conflict or unclear, they have a limiting effect on the performance of otherwise well-motivated, talented people. One way of empowering the client is for the consultant to assume the role of stimulator, helping the client reduce the drag of these barriers on performance, by clarifying roles, goals, and reward systems. The very process of helping him to act to remove the barriers himself is empowering in the sense of the two earlier conditions. Each success experience builds power.

Handling Resistance

The third key step in accomplishing the purpose of the client engagement through the diagnostic stage is the process of preventing and handling resistance. A major consideration is "Who can resist what?" The resistors could be the client, the client's followers, or the consultant himself. The client or his followers can resist dealing with their beliefs and fears and can resist changing the way they perform their roles. They can also resist changes in the demands the organization makes on them, and can resist the consultant altogether. As for the consultant, we will assume at this point that he is aware of and can manage his own resistance.

A few basic perspectives about resistance may be helpful. One is that resistance is always a motivated behavior on the part of the client, and it makes perfectly good sense to that person to resist. This resistance is often tied to an avoidance of imagined, threatening conditions — a very strong motivation. In such a case it is useful to consider, "What could this person be fearing; what is he attempting to avoid by resisting?"

A second perspective about resistance is that the consultant is far better off proactively managing the relationship to *prevent* or minimize resistance than assuming it will happen and reacting to it after it has built to a peak. From the client's view, the client will typically have many reasons to resent and devalue the consultant who is reactive at this point.

A third perspective about resistance is that the consultant should not play his role in a way that gives the client anything to resist. This is comparable to judo in that the consultant should employ the energy and momentum of the client. Here, a strategy of dominance holds little usefulness since it gives the client much to resist. The key perspective is to operate from the "plain of effectiveness" rather than the "plain of right or wrong."

A fourth perspective in reducing resistance is based on the consultant building a "hopefulness for change" perception and a "seriousness of intent" perception. Both perceptions must be real, with no intent to deceive. In effect the follower's resistance to the diagnosis will be reduced to the extent he (a) feels hopeful that management really wants the truth, and (b) believes management will use the diagnosis responsively.

As in judo, general strategy for managing resistance is to include their purpose in yours rather than argue for your own purpose or against theirs. For example, the president of a company may want his leaders to take the initiative, when they have traditionally avoided doing so. They have already staked themselves out in the position that not taking the initiative is the best way to play the game. On the other hand, they are frustrated by problems which affect their department, and a valued purpose of theirs is to see them solved. If they viewed the consultant's purpose as primarily to get them to take initiative, they may be inclined to resist. However, by incorporating their purpose in his, the consultant can relate what he is doing to something they want done, thus gaining support by providing support.

Several techniques are available for handling the client's or follower's resistance which arises during the diagnostic stage of the engagement. Some are based on the preceding perspectives. Resistance from the client might be managed in the following ways:

— Self-image maintenance is one technique for minimizing resistance. To do this, the consultant learns how the client wants to be viewed by superiors, peers, and followers. The consultant then positions what needs to be done as a means of maintaining or increasing the likelihood the client will be seen that particular way. For example, if a leader wants to be seen as assertive, the consultant might wish to position his recommendations so as to indicate that their implementation clearly demonstrates assertiveness by the client. As the program unfolds, the consultant might arrange honest feedback from superiors, peers, or followers that indicate the perception of assertiveness.

— Another technique which may assist in reducing the client's resistance is creating conformity pressure. In this instance the consultant arranges feedback to the client which results in that client perceiving that the other people he values (those with power, status, popularity, etc.) are doing what the consultant wants the client to do. In order to be identified with them the client will likely want to do it, too.

— Creating a kind of "what if" anxiety is an additional technique. A client who perpetually worries about something going on that he doesn't know about or have under control can be approached from the angle that he would be better off finding out and managing it than remaining in the dark. Or the consultant can arrange a tidbit of feedback that all is not well. The diagnosis in these instances would be positioned as a means for the client to learn what is going on and to re-establish control.

— Another tactic deals with resistance to accepting feedback which indicates that conditions are not what the client expected. Before the data comes in, the consultant needs to establish the perspective with the client that good managers can accept and handle feedback which is not what they thought it would be. This establishes the return of the data as an opportunity for the client to prove his competency.

— When the time or cost of the diagnosis or its potential response is a primary source of resistance, the consultant can bring up awareness of time and money consequences for *not solving* the problem. This awareness can extend to the nonfinancial costs of not solving the problem, such as frustration, tension, and loss of good people. The consultant might also establish the perception in the client that he gets what he pays for.

As mentioned earlier, the views of the client's followers are sometimes sought in the diagnostic process. Their resistance to participating openly and honestly often arises from several sources. These include the fear of repercussions from leaders who might be angered by the data, the expectation that there will not be any response, the reluctance to involve their leader in any kind of trouble, and fear of rejection by peers for participating truthfully.

Techniques for handling the resistance of followers are largely based on the perspectives for handling resistance mentioned earlier. In general, the followers often face a conflict between wanting to tell the complete truth about how they see things and wanting to be sure they remain safe and protected.

— One of the techniques for minimizing follower resistance was alluded to in the discussion about agreements. That is, when there is to be a questioning of followers by the client, by the consultant or through some sort of questionnaire, the consultant should get the leader to state the purpose of the diagnosis, the methodology, how the data will be used, the ethics and the value of their candor. This reduces resistance resulting from some of their uncertainty and it reduces their concern about someone being out to get their leader, since he is indicating he wants their honest views at the outset.

— Clear assurance to the followers that they will be informed of the outcome of the diagnosis is often useful in reducing resistance. This informs followers of management's open and constructive attitude. In reality, the followers do not want to be faced later with data which they know is not representative of the truth, so their inclination is to be honest.

— Follower resistance sometimes occurs due to fear of exposure. Confidentiality and anonymity are frequently key issues. A set of techniques to deal with this would include the consultant emphasizing the value he and the client place on participation, while at the same time making it clear that nonparticipation is okay. In additon, the consultant can waylay some anxiety by visibly putting the interviewee in control of what data goes into the formal study (e.g., "Shall I include that or not?" or "How do you want me to say it?"). The follower, realizing that the consultant is willing to go to some length to protect the anonymity of each respondent, usually decides it must be safe enough to participate openly.

— One kind of follower resistance is the depth of perception. One way the consultant can manage the level of openness is by giving the respondent a bench mark as to what his peers must be saying. For example, having heard about problem X from other sources, or even rumor, the consultant can say "Tell me about X" or "I hear that X...What is your view?" This usually causes the respondent to think to himself, "Oh, people are being *that* open;, well, okay..."

Conclusion

The basic process for managing the client–consultant relationship through diagnosis is that of influence. The responsible consultant must execute those influence attempts which will move the client and followers toward achieving the client's purpose. In reality, the basis of the influence process is that of manipulation. However, all the manipulations are guided by the position of professional ethics and responsibility in accordance with the goal of the engagement. Ultimately, the consultant uses the manipulation process to manage the relationship dynamics so that the client sees what needs to be done, assumes the appropriate responsibility, and is empowered to progress. The client's resistance to doing the appropriate thing at the appropriate time is reduced, and if the consultant has done his job effectively, the client will generally be rewarded by achievement of his goal.

In the days of kings and kingdoms, it was often the case that the messenger who brought bad news to the king was executed. As a consultant, our survival as a messenger, especially during the diagnostic stage of the engagement, is as important to the client's well-being as it is to our own. Our facility in handling the client–consultant relationship during diagnosis is a crucial aspect of our effectiveness and is the foundation on which the total relationship is built.

Richard M. Furr is Vice President of Farr Associates, a management consulting firm in Greensboro, North Carolina.

Consultants and Detectives

Fritz Steele

After years of avidly reading the British detective novels of such authors as Dorothy Sayers, Margery Allingham, Michael Innes, and the like, it occurred to me that the same personal characteristics which draw me to consulting work may determine the form taken by my flight-relaxation behavior. This in turn suggested to me that we may, by examining activities other than those connected with consulting per se, be able to discover some of the more subtle attributes and dilemmas connected with the consultant's role.

In this chapter, I demonstrate this process by comparison of the similarities in the roles of the consultant and the classic British detective. Although I have chosen to focus attention on my interest in British detectives, there are obviously many other attributes which might be looked at: preferences for social gatherings and interpersonal encounters of one sort or another, interest in various sports, activities in the arts, and so on. Many of these might be worth exploring for the same kinds of analogies which will be discussed here.

Comparing the Two Roles

The format will be a rather basic listing and discussion of some of the major similarities which I see between the role of the organizational consultant and the role of the British detective. I should emphasize here a fundamental point: there are obviously many different styles and kinds of organizational consultants, and the analogies I will be making will depend to a great extent on my own personal view of what a consultant does. Also, when I use the term *consultant* here, I am referring to those consultants who are specifically oriented toward changing the structure or behavior of the client system through application of behavioral science knowledge. I do not consider specifically other types of consultants, such as market research firms, which provide services related to the actual tasks of the organization itself.

The Focus on Evidence

Clearly, one of the major activities of the detective is an extensive search for clues and evidence as to what has occurred in a specific situation. Quite often this evidence is fleeting and must be gathered as it passes, as in the following example from Marsh.

> "Alleyn moved forward. He noticed as he did so that Peregrine stationed himself beside Miss Emily Dunne, that there was a glint of fanaticism in the devouring stare that Jeremy Jones bent upon the glove, that Winter Meyer expanded as if he had some proprietary rights over it and that Emily Dunne appeared to unfold a little at the approach of Peregrine."[7]

The detective's reason for wanting evidence may be described as falling into two major categories: one need is to gather clues to help him to *understand* what has occurred in a given criminal situation, and a second need concerns using that understanding to search out more adequate evidence in order to *prove to others* what has occurred and make a case which can stand up in court. Both of these seems to me to be of vital importance to the consultant as well. A consultant who focuses attention on active intervention in an organization must be continually seeking to understand the data with which he comes into contact. And it is of great value to collect and organize these data in such a way as to provide clear, straightforward evidence to the client system supporting the points which he will use in trying to bring about change in the system.

It has been my experience that this building up of a pool of evidence which is clear and can be seen in a relatively undistorted way by the client system is a very important focal point for the consultant who wishes to guide an organization in the direction of greater acceptance of reality. In other words, just *telling* a client system where it ought to go because of a theory which one has about how organizations ought to operate is not really enough. The consultant must be able to present a very good case for where the organization is, what the consequences of its present position are, and some of the major factors which keep it in that particular position. He should also strive to build *within* the client system the capacity and inclination to *continually* collect evidence of what is going on so they can make cases to themselves.

Considering this focus on evidence apart from questions of effective performance, I also recognize in myself a strong emotional attachment to the process of trying to solve challenging puzzles. This is probably one of the clearest of the common attributes which draw me to both the detective novel and the consulting process. I obviously share this love of puzzles with Dickenson's Sir Henry Merrivale:

> "Sudden inspiration seemed to distend H.M.'s cheeks, like an ogre in a pantomime. Breaking open the magazine, which showed the ends of cartridge cases, he plucked out one bullet. He scrutinized it carefully, also weighing it

in his hand. He did this, while Cy's nerves ached, with every bullet in the magazine; and shut it up again.

"So!" he repeated, dropping the revolver on the floor with an echoing clatter of marble. "Don't you see what this place means now?"[5]

As I will discuss below, the love of puzzles for their own sake can at times be a diversion for the consultant from the needs of the client, especially when the consultant gets wrapped up in demonstrating his ability to unravel the puzzle.

Temporary Involvement

Another characteristic of the British detective is his temporary involvement in a system or group of people. He establishes a network of relationships for the duration of the case. He may be quite central to several of these relationships, and they may be very important at the time, but then he generally moves on to a new set. The network of relationships in the detective story implies a sense of impermanence and some psychological distance. The detective acquires a kind of credibility without permanent closeness.* Here is Allingham's Albert Campion settling into a new scene for the first time, a place which will be the locus of a number of startling events.

"Mr. Campion appeared to have been forgotten, and he sat in a little recess in a corner of the hall and looked through the open doorway at the quivering leaves and dancing water without. The old house seemed very quiet after the hullabaloo. It was really amazingly attractive. Like all very old houses it had a certain drowsy elegance that was soothing and comforting in a madly gyrating world."[1]

Campion is at the same time establishing a relationship with the family who lives in the house, and for the duration of the mystery, they and the house are his world.

I find myself strongly drawn toward this temporary kind of involvement with a group of people, and I gather from my contacts with other consultants that many of them do also. This seems to be a seductive characteristic which often intrigues the client system members as well, and they often speak longingly of the consultants' chances to use a variety of settings and engage is a variety of activities day to day. However, this orientation can also have some costs. It may serve as flight from necessary deep involvement in and working through a particular problem, and this may either reduce the clients' willingness to provide important data or impair the consultant's ability to understand the situation. I am sure that there are moments for both the detective and the consultant when each would like to take the earliest opportunity to get out of the system, because things are getting too close or unmanageable. However, as I see it, each has a certain innate basic curiosity or

---

*This is similar to the notion of temporary structures which Bennis sees as being a central characteristic of organizations of the future.[3]

desire to be competent which leads him generally to stay with a particular case or problem or to terminate the relationship because of a prediction of little likelihood of further change (rather than termination simply because of a need to move on).

Another side of the question of involvement concerns the power which a system has over someone who is trying to change it. In the case of a detective the system generally has little or no power over him, including the decision whether he is to be there or not. In the case of the consultant the system has only limited power, chiefly in that area of decisions related to whether the consultant should continue in a relationship with the client (a power which the consultant shares). In this sense, then, a consultant is intermediate (in terms of freedom of action) between the detective and internal members of a system, such as internal agents of change. This in turn suggests that serving as an internal consultant carries with it a need for some important assumptions, such as a willingness to test the degrees of freedom one has, or a willingness to try to increase those degrees of freedom.

Incorporation into the System

One of the forces which is often at work on the British detective is related to his relative independence of a given group. There is usually a series of attempts by the persons with whom he is involved to incorporate him into the group. He is a real threat to that particular group of people, and they attempt to neutralize his threat to them by drawing him inside their boundaries as best they can. Here is another example from Allingham, where Campion's protagonist is attempting to win him over.

> "As he sat down again he [Campion] noticed that the other had undergone a complete change of mood. His bullying vanished and seemed to have decided to become hearty.
>
> 'Well, my boy,' he said, 'So you've come about the papers. Rather good that eh? It sounded interesting. Didn't give anything away. Now, I've been hearing a good deal about you, one way and another, and I've sent for you because I think I can put something your way that may interest you.'
>
> Mr. Campion peered round the corner of his handkerchief.
>
> 'Very nice of you, as long as it isn't a spoke in my wheel,' he murmured idiotically."[1]

The point is that I have had more than one very similar conversation with a company executive at about the time during a project that it began to look as though real change might occur. I believe that the consultant is subject to the same kinds of forces and for the same reasons: he represents a certain threat to the client system, possibly one that has not even been consciously considered by the individuals involved. However, their way of dealing with the threat which he raises is to try to swallow him, if a figurative sense, by making him a permanent part of the system and thereby increasing the system's power over him. Almost every consultant with whom I am associated can call to mind numerous instances of the client system's attempt to incorporate him and make him a permanent resident of that system. One reason for this may relate to his perceived competence and his abilities, which could be of great value for a long term to the group; but I am convinced that at least a large part of this need stems from the threat, which may be unnamed, to the clients themselves. In sociological terms, this is similar to the process of attempted "co-optation" into a system.

Intuition

The British detective often uses intuition as a mode of operation. He generates hypotheses from within, which he then attempts to test by either gathering new data or by sifting through the old data again. He often does not know for a considerable length of time why he is looking at a particular corner of the data pile, but his intuition keeps him there until the connections get made. Consider this description of Gideon from Marric.

> " 'Just tell me what it's all about and I'll tell you what I can.' Gideon did not know why he evaded the question as he did; there was something of a sixth sense in his move, that sense which made him so much more able than most detectives. He knew that Abbott would not interrupt or give him away, and he said: 'She's been missing since Wednesday evening.' "[6]

I think that the intuitive mode is also a very important one for consultants. I find that sometimes I almost stop trying to control *where* I focus my attention and let natural awareness lead me in whatever direction it will. In a sense, I try to stop staring (looking hard without really seeing) at the data and allow the figure and ground relationships to shift around and take on new meanings or new potencies for me. I do not believe that a consultant can do this without some intuition, some way to generate contextual notions so that he can understand what it is he sees as he lets his eye and mind roam over the situation.

One bit of evidence for intuition as an important process for consultants is presented in a study I made.[8] I found that laboratory trainers had a high mean score on the sensation-intuition of the Myers-Briggs Type Indicator. The trainer's mean was 135, compared with 98.7 for a sample from middle management; the higher the score on this scale, the stronger the indication of preference for intuition as a means of becoming aware of things, that is, for generating possibilities from within as well as using data obtained through the senses.

By stressing intuition here, I am not suggesting that the detective and the consultant do not put a very large amount of energy into purposeful plans, logically aimed thinking, or follow-up, but only that a too-quick focusing in on what are "obviously" the major elements in the case or the problem situation may lead to staring. This in turn can create an inability to see new relationships which may, in fact, be more important than the first ones that come to mind.

A Sense of the Dramatic

The British detective likes to be at center stage and to control the timing of events. He often works very carefully to choose just the right time for certain actions, sometimes as much for effect and his own personal centrality as for any other reason connected with accomplishing the case. Agatha Christie's Hercule Poirot is a good example, as are those two rotund rooters-out of crime, Sir Henry Merrivale:

> "H.M., as usual, was basking in the spotlight. In response to the cheers he first bowed, then he lifted both hands above his head and shook hands with himself, like a prize fighter entering the ring."[5]

and Dr. Gideon Fell:

> "Now, then, excuse the old charlatan a moment. I am going to make some telephone calls. Not under torture would I reveal what I intend to do, or where's the fun of mystifying you, hey? Hey! There's no pleasure like mystification, my boy, if you can pull it off..."[4]

I know I can sense within myself at times this same wish to be in the center of an unfolding drama. I suspect that I make more choices to create this situation than I like to think I do. There are times in group settings where I think I do something dramatic, and it is for at least two reasons: one is the perception on my part that confrontation at a particular moment will help to shake up the situation and bring a bit more data to the surface, and the other is that I like the image of myself as one who confronts. I think I like to engage in some behaviors which are seen by the clients as beyond the bounds of what they would do but still within their definition of what is dramatic, unusual, and exciting, with a certain flair.

I am calling attention to this need to be dramatic, because I think there are times when it can get in the way of effective consultation if it is not tested for its value as an intervention. The more dazzling the footwork of the actor, the less the members of the audience are aware of themselves. In consultation, the focus of attention on the consultant may block the clients' awareness of how central *they* must be in the drama of unfolding organizational change, and it may actually decrease self-awareness instead of increase it. It can also lead the clients to a definition of the situation such that most of the responsibility for change, innovation, and creation of excitement lies in the consultant rather than in themselves.

The Expert

Just as the detective–consultant's dramatic *actions* may cause the client's attention to focus too completely on the consultant, the same effect may also be brought about by idealized perceptions of the consultant's *knowledge* in a particular problematical situation. The detective has a tendency to unfold little of his reasoning prior to the climax of a case, and the more he does this, the more likely he is to appear omniscient in the end if he gets the pieces together (for either the right or the wrong reasons). This is another of Sir Henry's favorite tricks:

> " 'Look here,' said Cy, and drank a cup of cold coffee. 'Why in blazes can't you just tell us?... Yes, yes, I know!' he added hastily, as H.M. began to draw himself up, 'you're the old man! We understand that. All the same, can't you give us an idea?'
> 'I told you last night,' H.M. pointed out, 'that Manning's trick was based on the same principle I used myself when I hocussed the subway turnstiles.'
> 'And that tells me a hell of a lot, doesn't it?' "[5]

I think the role of "expert" is a quite seductive one for the consultant; all the more so in behavioral science, since the variables and their relationships are often very fuzzy and complex. It can be quite personally gratifying to have others see me as someone who really "knows" what is going on or what should be done in a given situation. Besides personal gratification on the part of the consultant, another factor pushes him toward the stance of expert: the client's wish to see himself safely in the hands of an expert who is wise and able, so that anxiety over present or future difficulties can be reduced.

Both the consultant's and the client's needs, then, may propel the consultant toward exclusive occupancy of the role of expert in their relationship. This may have some benefits, such as making it more likely that the consultant will be listened to, but it also has some costs. One that is usually mentioned is the potential price in terms of increased dependency of the client on the consultant, a dependency which may keep the client from developing his own strengths and competencies for the diagnosis and solving of problems. A second cost, one which is less often considered, is that a reliance on the consultant as the exclusive expert may often lead to inadequate decisions. The client often has great wisdom (intuitive if not systematic) about many aspects of his own situation, and an overweighting of the value placed on the consultant's knowledge may indeed cause poorer choices to be made than if there was a more balanced view of what each can contribute to the situation.†

Who Are the Suspects?

Another characteristic of the detective's role is the necessity of his considering all possibilities regarding those whom he should suspect in a given case. This means that he tends to consider all people as possible culprits, including both those who seem to be the most innocent and those who seem to be the most guilty. The former category may often include the very people who call the detective onto the

---

†This view of the price paid by ignoring the innate wisdom of the client was clarified for me in a conversation with Edgar Schein.

case in the beginning. Consider this reaction from the member of a theater company being interviewed by Inspector Alleyn after a murder:

" 'Who's going to pitch into me next?' he asked. 'I ought to be getting hospital attention, the shock I've had, and not subjected to what'd bring about an inquiry if I made complaints. I ought to be home in bed getting looked after.'

'So you shall be,' Alleyn said. 'We'll send you home in style when you've just told me quietly what happened.'

'I have told. I've told them others'

'All right. I know you're feeling rotten and it's a damn shame to keep you but you see you're the chap we're looking to for help.'

'Don't you use that yarn to me. I know what the police mean when they talk about help. Next thing it'll be the Usual Bloody Warning.' "[7]

Imagine how much help Alleyn will get from him in his present mood of mistrust. But his feeling is well founded, for at the moment Alleyn needs his help and simultaneously must consider the possibility that he actually is the guilty person masquerading behind his hurt feelings.

In a very similar manner, the consultant must stay open to all possibilities in terms of who may be the "culprits" in a given problem. This means that he considers suspect even those persons who originally invited him into the system. By "suspects," in this instance, I mean people who may contribute in some significant way to difficulties or problem situations. Interestingly enough, the members of the client organization often seem to feel very similiar to the suspects in a detective case, particularly if they do not know exactly what line of thought the consultant is taking. They have a fear of being "caught," even when they do not know at *what* they may be "caught." The analogue in the organization to a crime in the detective novel seems to be being ineffective or doing something which is not seen by the consultant or persons in positions of power as leading to productivity or success in the organization. Using this definition, it has been my experience that almost everyone in a client system seems to feel that the consultant may uncover some "crime" which he has committed in the past or is committing at present. It is no surprise, then, that members of a client system often exhibit many of the same characteristics of uneasiness or mistrust toward a consultant that suspects in a detective case exhibit toward the investigator.

One of the consequences of this mistrust or uneasiness is the withholding or distortion of information which is vital to an understanding of the problem situation. This obviously makes the task of understanding and changing a system just that much more difficult and, at times, impossible. This implies that a key task of the consultant would be to help people stop defining themselves as culprits, that is, to change their view of less-than-perfectly-effective behavior from criminal to human and to redefine change as a continuing process of improvement, rather than a weeding out of antisocial elements.

This redefinition should probably start with the consultant's view of his own process. I think it is all too easy for a consultant to emotionally respond to members of the client system as if they, based on their willingness to change, were two distinct groups, the Goodies and the Baddies, and to treat them so that the Baddies *do* get the impression that they are criminals to be hunted down. This can be very self-defeating behavior on our part if the guilt we induce in the Baddies cannot be dealt with and resolved, and it may also create in the Goodies a sense of having "succeeded" to the point of closing them to an awareness of needed changes in their behavior. In addition, even the Goodies are not outside the limitations of the crime-and-punishment set of assumptions; when a consultant does confront them with some data he feels they should consider, they often feel that a "surprise arrest" has been made when they least expected it, and this can make their resistance to considering the possibility of change just as high as that of the so-called Baddies.

Action Intervention

One characteristic of the style of a number of fictional detectives with whom I am familiar is a precipitation of specific planned events which the detective predicts will produce an imbalance in the situation. This imbalance then causes someone to react, to take further action, which then provides more information about the total situation which the detective is trying to understand. This reaction helps the detective in diagnosing what the major forces are in the problem situation, helps him to understand better the orientations of the other individuals involved, and creates forces for change in the situation. Here for example, is another instance of Albert Campion stirring the pot:

> "But consider, my dear old flag-wagger, how on earth do you imagine this beautiful soul down here [a crook] ever heard about the oak? He heard about it because little Albert sent him a note with 'Look what I've found in the mill loft, Ducky', or words to that effect, neatly written above my usual signature.' "

In this instance, Campion sensed that the best way to find out what the man wanted was to hold out some opportunity for him to get it.

This action–reaction process is very similar to Lewin's suggestion that if you want to understand something, a good approach is to try to change it. It seems to me that one of the reasons why I intervene in a system (such as in confronting someone), as well as affecting that system in some way which I think may be positive, is also just to find out more about the system. In the same way that the detective may obtain some expected or unexpected results from his intervention, I often think that the consultant may gather a large portion of his data by actually doing things: by acting in the system itself. For me, it is this orientation toward action which makes the temporary involvement which I mentioned earlier a palatable one, and this may be true for other consultants as well.

There is another side to this question of action, however. As I thought about it, it dawned on me why I am using British detectives, and not American, as my role comparison. It is because there is less action for action's sake alone in the British detective stories. Rather, there is a mixture of contemplation, detection, and action which I find more appealing than the more violent American novels. The parallel to consulting is clear here: I am suggesting that at times it may be quite important that the consultant *not* engage in action for action's sake, particularly since this often seems to be one part of the clients' value system which is getting them into some of their difficulties. As Argyris[2] has pointed out, engaging in some behavior simply because it fits the clients' expectation or value system may in fact limit the usefulness of the consultant to the client.

Self-Consciousness

A very important characteristic related to taking action in a system is self-consciousness about one's action. This is reflected in the detective's attempts to really step outside himself and look at himself as if he were someone else observing him in action. Here is Alleyn in a "processing session" with himself:

"He could have kicked himself from Whitehall to Blankside. Why, why, why, hadn't he put his foot down about the safe and its silly window and bloody futile combination lock? Why hadn't he said that he would on no account recommend it? He reminded himself that he had given sundry warnings but snapped back at himself that he should have gone further."[7]

The tendency toward self-examination obviously varies with the detectives involved, but I think that it sheds a great light on a key demand of the consultant role.** To me, this self-consciousness needs to be a central characteristic of the consultant's functioning, similar to its importance for the psychoanalyst and psychotherapist. This is because the consultant is serving as a data-gathering instrument (mainly trying to become aware of the data in the situation but also trying to understand how he is "calibrated"), and he himself is also one of the major inputs, causing reactions in the system as he is diagnosing, intervening, et cetera. As such, he must be able to have a sense of who and what he is, what he represents to the client system, what actions he is taking, and whether he can accept them or not.

I find this to be one of the most interesting, most compelling, and most difficult aspects of the role. It requires a great deal of discipline to keep one's self from throwing away three-quarters of the relevant data. By this I mean that so many of the important things having to do with the consultant's own process in a given

---

**The most notable examples with which I am familiar are Tey's Inspector Grant, Simenon's Maigret, and Marric's Commander Gideon.

situation are so close to him and so much a part of him that it is very difficult for him to see them. He therefore has to be willing to take a look at himself in terms of dimensions which he may consider to be almost self-evident, such as the ways he feels when he is about to contact the client, or the method he chooses when he does it. Many of these kinds of data may have important implications for the consultant–client relationship and for needed changes in the consultant's behavior.

Collaboration

Perhaps the above considerations are some of the reasons why most of the British detectives seem to have some sort of partner with whom they can talk, get new ideas and energy, relieve tension, or just speak the same language.†† They are generally people who have worked with the detective in the past, and they often refer to other cases and their similarities to the present one. This may serve as a good advertising mechanism for the author, but in terms of the relationship between the detective and his sidekick, it also seems to signal to each other that they speak a common language, that they understand each other and think along the same dimensions, and that they thereby share a closeness which is lacking in the detective's relationships with others in the case.

It is very important to have an associate in the organizational consulting process. It seems to me that there is a clear need on the part of someone who is dealing with ambiguous data, difficut emotional issues, and a relatively new field, to have someone who speaks his language so that he can discuss problems, issues, and just general feelings of frustration, anxiety, and elation. I know this is true for me, and I also have some sense that this is true for others. For T-group trainers, one major benefit gained from conducting a laboratory is having intensive contact with other trainers. As another example, I served for some time as a consultant to an internal consultant in a company, and one of my major functions was simply to be an available professional who spoke his language. I provided someone to whom he could let off steam and talk about things in a relatively unguarded way that would be understood. In essence, I am saying here that it really is very difficult for a consultant to try to go the whole route alone; he could probably go just so far without some chance to connect with others who are concerned with similar issues in the field or organizational change.

The mirror image of this process is also important: the conflict and competition which can develop between detectives (and consultants) who interact for mainly collaborative purposes. When collaboration occurs under the stress of a crisis situation, whether it be a crime or an interpersonal crisis within the organization, the outside professionals involved are also likely to experience a rise in their own

††For instance, Sherlock Holmes has Watson, Sir Henry Merrivale has Inspector Masters, and Roderick Alleyn has Inspector Fox.

emotionality, and hence the likelihood that they may create difficulties for each other. Here is an example of Commander Gideon with a colleague:

> "The manner in which the words were uttered annoyed Gideon, and for the first time, he thought: *I'm going to have to watch him.* He stared into Cox's very bright dark-blue eyes, and read the defiance in them. If he used the wrong tactics now he might make co-operation extremely difficult, and he had plenty to do without adding a kind of departmental feud."[6]

Consultants are likely to create similar problems for one another, particularly when feelings run high, and it is difficult to know whether or not you are being truly effective with the client. A consulting colleague offers an easier, safer target for pent-up feelings. This release can be useful *if* there is enough open processing to keep it manageable, as noted in chapter seven.

Sequential and Parallel Cases

One final dimension of the detective and consulting roles was suggested to me by the *differences* among detectives rather than by a basic pattern common to all of them. This is the question of whether the detective works on cases one at a time; in sequence; or on several cases at once, in parallel. Most of the detectives whom I have read about tend to work on the sequential model, but J. J. Marric's George Gideon is a notable exception to this rule. In fact, one of the main attractions of his books to me is the number of different cases in which he is involved at once, and the ways in which his thinking about one case produces ideas or new directions for another which is continuing at the same time.

I think this same variation exists in terms of the consultant's process. Working on several cases in parallel can lead to many conflicts in terms of time and energy and in terms of emotional commitment to several systems. On the other hand, I seem to be drawn toward these kinds of conflicts, and I apparently like having to make those kinds of choices. I find that working on several cases in parallel leads to getting more ideas about each than I would if I were working in one client system at a time. My experiences in one setting seem to trigger off new ideas or new ways of looking at the experiences that I am having in another, and I feel that they build upon each other in a way that they couldn't if they were taken over more extended periods or separated times.

It is not clear to me that there is really a "best" position for a consultant on this particular dimension. I can also see advantages to working in sequence, because it does cut down on the demands in terms of output of conflicting time and inputs of energy, and also because it provides one with a chance to stop and think a bit about the previous case before moving on to another. This may lead to better planning than would have occurred if both were happening at the same time. The choice of sequential versus parallel cases should probably depend on several factors, such as the personality and stage of development of the consultant, the needs of a particular phase in a client system, and other demands which life makes on the consultant.

Conclusions

At this point, I should like to summarize very briefly what has been written and sketch out one or two patterns which seem to emerge. I have looked at the attributes of the role of the fictional British detectives and tried articulate points where it seemed to me to be analogous to that of the behavioral science oriented organizational change consultant. One major theme was that both roles seemed to have several attributes which I find to be emotionally satisfying and which I am guessing may also be a positive force on other consultants: the temporary nature of involvement in a system, the concentration on gathering evidence and trying to solve the puzzles which it represents, the potential for "dramatics," the potential for action and the excitement it contains, the stance of "expert" in behavioral science, and the stimulation of working on several cases at once. It was suggested that each of these satisfactions, while important, carried potential dangers in terms of making it more difficult to reach the major task goal of the consulting process, which is to improve the capabilities and functioning of the client system. Several other demands of the consultant role were described, and these might be seen as ways of keeping the above satisfactions from getting out of hand: promoting consciousness of self; avoiding incorporation into the client system; arranging for some collaborator or sounding board with whom to check perceptions, ideas, and feelings; using intuition as one means of generating ways to understand the situation; and being wary of the tendency to lump people into the over-simplified categories of "good" and "bad."

There are also two general questions relating to consulting which seemed to come up again and again as I thought about the above categories. The first one is well known: How does a consultant facilitate the obtaining of *informational inputs* to his "detection" process? How does he get valid information from the organization and its members, ideas they may have about problem solutions, useful ideas from behavioral science in general, outside views of his own operation, and new ways of his own for looking at the situation? Several means have been suggested, such as an intuitive stance, parallel cases, action intervention, a focus on evidence, self-consciousness, and collaboration (both with clients and with external professionals). One implication of this chapter is that there are some tensions among these various means of getting inputs. For instance, an active step (such as immediate feedback to a working group) which is too threatening may lead to the clients defining themselves as "suspects" and consequently cause them to eliminate or distort the information they communicate to the consultant. This suggests the obvious point that the degree of *trust* between the client and the consultant will be an important determinant of the consultant's success at being able to accurately perceive reality in a given consulting situation.§

Less obvious, perhaps, is the notion that the consultant's trust of *himself* is also a factor in this search for useful definitions of the situation. He needs this trust in order to be willing to look at the data which his own self-consciousness will generate. He also needs it in order that his own anxiety about getting a viable view of the situation not block him from obtaining new views through following events wherever they lead, that is, to look at the client system for some period with an intuitive stance requires some confidence on the consultant's part that something *will* come out of this free period, that a total blank will not be drawn. This may seem like an unnecessary elaboration of a simple point, but I think that this lack of trust in self may be at least part of the reason why some consultants tend to go into an organization with a relatively solidified view of what they will find; a view which sometimes proves not to be very useful but can be held to very tenaciously.

This brings me to the second general question which is relevant here: How does the consultant balance his professional needs with his other personal needs? For example, how does he get satisfaction in terms of feeling competent, being active, being central, being held in high esteem by the clients, et cetera, without blocking or overshadowing the clients' view of themselves and thereby limiting possibilities for growth in the client system? I have suggested that the consultant can strive for self-awareness and getting data from others as ways of testing why he is doing something at a given moment. This does not mean that he should discard some behavior just because it is personally gratifying to him; that would be removing many of the very reasons why the consultant has chosen to play this particular role. Rather, it suggests trying to choose based on a view of integrating both the professional and the personal, a process that I think is quite possible given the high motivation toward professional competence of many of the consultants with whom I am acquainted.

Finally, there is an interesting similarity in role structure between detective and consultant which the writing of this chapter has clarified for me. Expressed simply, the detective (consultant) is able to develop a certain amount of credibility and connectedness with those involved in a mystery (the particular members of an organizational unit) because of his structural position. At least for the amateur detectives, they represent some general societal values, such as truth and justice (effectiveness, organizational and individual health) without being an official member of the governmental hierarchy, for example, the police department (or the

---

§I had originally assumed that the question of trust was a point (like many others not discussed in this article due to limitation of space) where the analogy between the detective and the consultant was not relevant. It became clear, however, that although the detective often starts out operating on a model of *mistrust,* the costs to him are the same as to the consultant: it becomes much more difficult to get accurate data from participants in the situation or help in solving the mystery.

top management of the organization.) Both the detective and the consultant then, tend to be seen as not having a particular vested interest to uphold other than getting at the truth of a situation. When this disinterest is doubted, each has a much more difficult task, usually because of interference from those most concerned.§§

In terms of the process of this chapter, I would also like to repeat my beginning suggestion: as a part of the continuing search for better understanding of the organizational change consultant and his process, one useful strategy seems to me to look at the interests and peripheral characteristics of those who are drawn to consulting. Not, as in the case of much of the early leadership literature, only to see what makes a "good" consultant, but rather to discover and articulate new dimensions of the consultant's role.

References

1. Allingham, M., *Sweet Danger,* Harmondsworth, Middlesex, England: Penguin, 1950.
2. Argyris, C., "Explorations in Consulting-Client Relationships," *Human Organization,* Vol. 20 (1961), pp. 121–133.
3. Bennis, W., *Changing Organizations,* New York: McGraw-Hill, 1966.
4. Carr, J.D.., *The Blind Barber,* New York: Collier, 1962.
5. Dickson, C., *A Graveyard to Let,* New York: William Morrow, 1951.
6. Marric, J.J., *Gideon's March,* New York: Berkeley, 1963.
7. Marsh, N., *Killer Dolphin,* London: Ngaio Marsh, 1966.
8. Steele, F., "Personality and the Laboratory Style," *Journal of Applied Behavioral Science,* Vol. 4 (1968), pp. 25–45.

Fritz Steele, formerly a professor at Yale University, is a consultant in Boston, Massachusetts.

§§The vested interests of the police are partly created by the government agency most concerned about public opinion, while the stockholders' opinion is the threat in many organizations. Both these groups of people are usually very far removed from the actual facts of a case and therefore call for mainly image projection rather than effectiveness.

The Organization as a Micro-Culture

Leonard Nadler

We have all walked into a room where there are people who are dressed differently. We recognize there are differences and adjust our behavior accordingly. When we look at people who might be the same as we are, but who then begin talking a different language, we receive a signal that they are different and we therefore modify our behavior. In both cases we have experienced obvious differences which are cultural. The different language and the different dress are automatic signals.

In our daily life we often see signals from different cultures but since they may not be highlighted by dress or an obviously different language, we are sometimes unable to see or hear the signals and therefore behave inappropriately. If this is so, is it possible that there are aspects of our behavior within our work organizations which are likewise the result of a cultural orientation? It is possible that some of the training activities for which we have responsibility — particularly organizational development — should give adequate recognition to the various cultures which we embrace.

One of the more obvious examples of people crossing cultures is seen in the waves of migration which came to our shores during the nineteenth and early twentieth century.* This gave rise to a concept of the United States as a melting pot. It was thought that through a process of assimilation and acculturation all the children of the immigrants would now be the same. History has since taught us that the result was not the melting pot but a pluralistic society in which each cultural group has retained some of its own habits and customs.†

Volumes have been written on the organization man in his many aspects. Still, we notice differences within organizations and we wonder if a large organization is not more likely to be a pluralistic society rather than a melting pot. Each organiza-

---

*In his book *The Uprooted,* Oscar Handlin explores the cultural implications of the great migrations, New York: Grosset & Dunlap, 1951.

†In a follow-up volume entitled *Children of the Uprooted,* Oscar Handlin has brought together a book of the writings of the second generation which indicates that they did not become one indistinguishable mass, New York: George Braziller, 1966.

---

tion has a culture of its own which is unique, and within a large organization it is possible to identify more than one culture as we move from one unit to another.

In the above paragraphs, the word "culture" has been used many times without definition. It could be wasteful to engage in a long discourse on the appropriate definition of this provocative word. Rather, let us look at two definitions which are offered by writers in the field and which will satisfy our needs. One definition is "common and more or less standardized ideas, attitudes, and habits which have evolved with respect to man's recurrent and continuous needs."*

Another way to look at culture is to see it as "the cumulative ways of mankind, of the capacities the human animal has developed to tame or cope with the world of nature and the world of his own kind."†

A definition I have evolved and found useful in introducing this topic to managers is "culture can be viewed as the habits and customs that people develop to cope with changing conditions." This definition, which is not seen as being in conflict with most of the accepted definitions of the word, is the one which will be used in this article.

"Habits and customs" are usually based on tradition, which is sometimes defined as "anything that has been done twice!" It is amazing how rapidly traditions develop.**

Habits and customs, for purposes of studying culture, do not include those which have been codified by law or regulations, for once a habit or custom is written, it is no longer cultural behavior but legal behavior. This does not mean that everybody obeys it, but at least it is written and identified and available for everybody to see. We are more concerned with those habits and customs which "everybody knows," yet nobody can point to a written or common source which can be used as the basis for everybody knowing it.

A second part of the definition is "people develop." Cultural behavior is constantly developing. It is what people do to themselves rather than something that is imposed from the outside. There have been times in history when a conqueror has tried to impose a new cultural behavior, and in the world of business we see similar practices as acquisitions have become part of our current economic behavior. Basically, no matter what the conqueror or parent organization does, the people affected will develop their own cultural pattern to deal with the situation. It is usually not planned behavior, but behavior which develops and evolves.

The third part of the definition is to "cope with changing conditions." Conditions are constantly changing and, therefore, to cope effectively it becomes

---

Sociology by Kimball Young, New York: American Book Co., 1942, p. 35.
†*Personality and Social Life* by Robert Endelman, New York: Random House, 1967, p. 4.
**Where do traditions come from? In the hit play, "Fiddler on the Roof," one of the opening songs is about tradition. The actor steps to the front of the stage to explain to the audience how tradition gets started. He looks at the audience, shrugs his shoulders, and says, "I don't know."

necessary for people to change their habits and customs. We are concerned here with those changes which are not planned, but which merely develop as people try to cope with the changing world around them. Sometimes, a change in a law or regulation induces a cultural change so that people can cope with the new legal behavior which is expected of them.

Micro-Culture

The common term that is used to identify a culture which is part of something larger is the term "subculture." However, I have found that there appears to be an implication in using the prefix "sub." From the viewpoint of an exact definition one would probably find that the use of this prefix is perfectly in order. But in terms of the reactions of various groups and individuals, the experience has been that the term "sub" connotes something which is less than or under. It contains the implication that it is not as good as something else. Therefore, in order to avoid any value judgments let us use the term "micro-culture." There are instances of others concerned with this area who have also begun to use the term to mean one of the many cultures to which all of us belong.

In behavioral science terms it has frequently been said that we hold membership cards in many organizations. Likewise, we hold membership in many micro-cultural groups. For each of us, these will be different and might include the company we work for, the community in which we live, the religious group to which we belong, the kind of recreation we seek, and our racial group. The list could be much longer. By reviewing the various micro-cultures to which we belong, it can be seen that as we move from one micro-cultural group to another, we modify our behavior accordingly. The habits and customs we practice in a religious institution are different from those we use in our work organization.

This does not address itself to ethical values but to the specific form of behavior such as the appropriate dress for each situation. However, if we were to change our religious affiliation, we might find that some new forms of behavior would be required beyond that which is contained in the ritual of the new religious group. We would find this modification of behavior equally valid as a move from one job to another, from one business organization to another. Might not the new organization have cultural patterns which are unknown to us and a source of difficulty until we have been able to identify them? Bell has commented on "the tendency of employees reared in a given culture to carry values consistent with that culture into other organizations and occupations in which they participate."*

We are constantly seeking to identify the behavior that a particular micro-culture expects of us so that we can behave in the accepted ways. Even those who believe they are in revolt against the existing cultural patterns (by being part of the hippie

---

*Organization and Human Behavior, edited by Gerald D. Bell. Englewood Cliffs: Prentice-Hall, 1967, p. 11.

movement, for example) find that they, too, must accept the norms of that particular new micro-culture or risk being expelled.

Why Look at Culture?

In our early years we go through a constant process of acculturation in order to make us more effective members of a particular group.† Sometimes, this behavior is fairly obvious and we come to it almost spontaneously. At other times we need additional help in understanding the behavior expected of us in a particular micro-culture. Then training becomes not only appropriate but mandatory.

Knowing the accepted culturally directed behavior can be extremely helpful. It can help us avoid making mistakes (i.e., coming into conflict with the accepted cultural behavior). It can signal ways in which we can make the most effective use of human resources in a particular micro-cultural group. If we violate the expectations within our particular micro-cultural group, we may find ourselves ignored, pushed outside the group, and blocked for reasons which we have been unable to identify. Those of our population whom we now classify as the subemployed** are faced with just this problem of not knowing the cultural signals of the system they have been trying to enter. They have not been able to learn the appropriate cultural behavior to give them entry, acceptance, and success in the micro-cultures of business and industry.

Each of us carries with him his own cultural baggage. It is not necessary to describe the baggage as we move from one micro-culture to another in the course of a day, but it is necessary to understand what behavior is appropriate for each of the micro-cultures. It is amazing how rapidly we are able to modify our behavior as we receive cultural signals.

Our own cultural baggage can impose limits on our creativity. Too strong an identification with a particular micro-culture may deny us the possibility of changes which new experiences in new cultures can demand. Cultural baggage of which we are not aware may produce tunnel vision, which prevents us from seeing the world except through a very narrow peephole.

The behavior of individuals within any micro-culture can be identified in many dimensions. For purposes of this article, only four of these will be discussed. They are space, time, language, and sex. There is no implication that these are the only manifestations of micro-culture behavior, nor are they necessarily the most significant. However, in the years that I have been using this topic in training sessions, I have found that these four areas are the ones which have proven the most

---

†Endelman, *op. cit.* See chapter 2 ("Socialization: the Family and Its Alternatives") and Chapter 3 ("Socialization: Some Problems in Large-scale Societies.").

**For more on the sub-employed see "The Concept of the Sub-employed" in *Manpower Report of the President,* Washington, D.C.: U.S. Government Printing Office, 1968, p. 34.

recognizable to the trainees and most easily identifiable within their own organizations. If we can deal effectively with at least these four, we may be on the way to understanding much more of our own behavior which is culturally biased.

Space

There are many aspects to the use of space. One of these is the concept known as the "territorial imperative."* In one sense this tells us that certain functions are performed in specific places by particular groups and that it is helpful to learn which functions are performed where. The child is taught one aspect of cultural behavior in his early years and we call it toilet training. For the adult in the work situation we assume that toilet training is no problem, but we do give keys to the Executive Washroom to some and not to others. Presumably, certain space can only be used by selected individuals, although they perform like functions.

In how many places do we have Executive Dining Rooms? Sometimes it is specifically stated as to who can or cannot eat in the Executive Dining Room, but in other situations the actual break in the executive line, as to who can eat in the Executive Dining Room and who must eat in the general cafeteria, may not be clearly stated as much as generally understood. It then becomes a manifestation of cultural behavior for that organization.

Another concept related to space is that of the "space bubble."† This says that each of us has a need for a certain amount of space around us. At certain points we feel we are being crowded or invaded and respond accordingly. Hall's work in measuring this space should be of importance to those who are engaged in international operations.** Its implications should not be overlooked, however, for those working within the United States or even within a single organization. How is individual space allocated in your organization?

It is also possible that this use of space must be considered when selecting training techniques. Today, we are offered the possibilities of individual study carrells with individual space clearly defined. At the other end of the spectrum is the new work being done in the body-contact training programs where individual space is purposely invaded. Might it not be desirable for us to have some research or at least some sophisticated exploration of the implications of each of these training techniques as they relate to cultural behavior?

---

*The Territorial Imperative by Robert Ardrey, New York: Atheneum, 1966. The reader should be alert that the book is based on research with animals, not with people.

†A brief version of the concept can be found in William Kolman, "E.T. Hall and the Human Space Bubble," Horizon, Autumn, 1967, pp. 42-47.

**See Edward T. Hall, The Hidden Dimension. (New York: Doubleday and Co., 1966), pages 118-119 for an interesting table listing some of the distance involved between people.

The use of space within organizations raises some questions such as, where should meetings be held? Sometimes it is fairly obvious, since a conference room may be specifically designated for this activity. There are some kinds of training which, by their very nature, indicate the particular space which is required. This may not be directly related to the quality of the physical facility as much as how it is viewed within the organization as being a status or nonstatus site for training. The use of "off-the-ranch" training facilities with certain status implications is an example of culturally identified space. Even our use of the words "cultural island" for certain kinds of training indicated our desire to create a different use of space and a new culture with its attendant culturally oriented behavior.

What about performance appraisal? Does it make any difference whether the appraisal is held in the supervisor's office, at the employee's work station, or at some neutral territory?

Time

There are those of us who see time as being something which is broken into small segments, or the instrument which is used to mark off the segments. If you are engaged in international operations, you have experienced the concept of time which varies from one country to another. In some countries it is absolutely necessary to keep an appointment at the specific time designated; whereas in others, when a meeting is called for a definite time, it will not start for at least one hour after the time agreed on. It is almost impossible to find these time perceptions written down, although occasionally a sensitive social scientist will be able to reduce some of this to writing.*

How else can time be conceptualized? The examples are endless, yet we seem to deal with time as if everybody knows its dimensions and expressions.† For those who have not developed a sensitivity to cross-cultural implications there may be difficulty in appreciating the wide divergence in the cultural use of time when it occurs quite close to home. For example, the subemployed probably have a different concept of time and deferred gratification in their micro-cultural behavior than the cultural norm required in business and industry.

---

*One description tells of a dinner invitation for 8:00 p.m. Those who have accepted because they want the food will arrive at the exact time, and never earlier. The more courteous guest will arrive anytime between 9:00 and 11:00 p.m. (In Cultural Patterns in Ethiopia as employees of the Agency for International Development, 1959, p. 5.)

†Very few books have dealt with this aspect of cultural behavior as well as Edward T. Hall in The Silent Language, Garden City, NY: Doubleday, 1959. See particularly Chapter 9 ("Time Talks: American Accents").

You and I have not had this difficulty. If we had, I probably would not be writing this article and you probably would not be reading it. We have absorbed the cultural concept which signifies that there are many kinds of activities which need not produce any immediate results, but are engaged in for their long-range contribution to our growth and welfare. Some of our citizens have difficulty with this, for there is little in their previous experience to indicate that building for the future produces any rewards.

Within organizations time can vary from unit to unit as easily as from organization to organization. For example, what is the length of the work day? Where there is union agreement, a management directive, a time clock, or some physical manifestation, the length of the day as well as the starting and stopping time may be fairly exact. But what happens where the micro-cultural practices have not been agreed upon or reduced to writing? The experience of organizations with "washup time" has provided the basis for many a grievance hearing.

What constitutes coming in late? If there is no directive, then culturally directed behavior becomes the norm. In your organization, what is "late"? Is it one minute after some agreed upon starting time? Is it ten minutes, or is it half an hour? In some organizations there is no regulation and yet the standards have evolved within that particular micro-culture. A new person entering the organization will not be privy to this information with the result that his/her standards may appear to not conform to the accepted practices. In such a situation, we usually penalize the newcomer until somehow he learns the appropriate cultural behavior or leaves the organization.

One of the more obvious conflicts in time occurs in the use of time for coffee breaks. It appears that many organizations try to avoid the legitimization of the coffee break by not specifying the behavioral rules involved. Other organizations have identified periods of time, but in still others there are some implied agreements such as a ten-minute limit. In the latter situation it is not unknown for the coffee break to go to thirty minutes! The length of break for the individual or a unit may be related to status within the organization or some other cultural component which an outsider may have difficulty identifying.

Even where the time has been specified by some directive, it does not mean that all will adhere to it. A mutual unwritten understanding as to how it will be interpreted for different units within the same organization may arise, and then it once again becomes micro-cultural behavior.

The same cultural conflicts can apply to the length of the work day, rest periods, lunch period, and other activities where time is a factor. It may include practices such as the appropriate time to utilize certain services of the organization which are based on cultural understandings rather than specific planning and directives.

In the field of training and development, what is the appropriate length of a training session? Is there still the tendency to design a two hour session? Historically, we conducted sessions for two hours a day for fifteen weeks. This was probably related to the source of our instructors, in those days college professors, who had organized themselves in the typical college pattern of the two 1-hour-15-minute session which made a semester of learning.

With the advent of programmed instruction and the movement towards some kind of individual learning, we had hoped to see some breakdown in traditions. As we would expect, however, cultural practices have rapidly evolved and now we find teaching machines being scheduled in half hour blocks of time. There is little in the way of research to reinforce this practice, but a folklore has evolved and crystallized into cultural behavior. I have observed organizations using teaching machines where there is an actual schedule established in thirty-minute blocks. This is institutionalization of cultural behavior, and change becomes difficult. Notice how rapidly cultural behavior can become institutionalized. The very element which was introduced to bring about change becomes an element which blocks change.

Language

Language as cultural behavior should be easy to identify but we use so much of it we do not remain sufficiently sensitive. The sociologists tell us that language is a manifestation of culture. Language is one mechanism whereby we transmit our cultural behavior to others. If a particular practice does not exist in our micro-culture, we will not have words to express the practice for we have no need for such words.

An example of language manifesting culture may be found in the word "snow." In most parts of the northern United States the word snow is fairly obvious and communicates to the listener who has had similar cultural experiences. To the person from the tropics, snow is a meaningless term until it is described to him and even then he can only surmise what it is and may not be able to identify it when presented with the real thing. It is doubtful if his language will even have a word for this natural phenomenon if it is not part of the changing conditions with which he must cope.

For the Eskimo, the snow is so significant that it is estimated that there are more than twenty different words to describe this aspect of his changing conditions. There is no one word which can adequately describe the condition. To survive, the Eskimo must know a great deal about snow, so his language has words which tell when it fell, its thickness, quality, tendency to drift, etc. To those of us living in the temperate zone these distinctions are meaningless and we cannot include them in our cultural behavior. To an Eskimo, either he learns this extensive vocabulary concerning snow or he does not survive.

Within organizations in business and industry, language may not be a matter of life and death, but the result of not knowing the culturally oriented language can mean the difference between effective utilization of manpower or the waste of this valuable resource. Each of our organizations has specialized language which an outsider cannot possibly understand. The more physically oriented the work, the more likely it is that a specialized kind of vocabulary or speech pattern may emerge. Frequently, there is no glossary which is formally written to capture these micro-cultural differences, but some nationwide organizations have found it necessary to develop such a glossary.

Given the number of new plant startups in which many of our organizations are involved, it would seem that this problem of language becomes acute. People from different sections of the country, even if part of the same national organization, may be using different language to describe different functions or products within the organization. Until these culturally variant vocabularies have been reconciled, communication may be difficult.

In most countries of the world, social status is significant and different vocabularies and speech patterns emerge as part of the cultural behavior. The child may not be taught the differences in any organized way, but he learns them as he grows up and moves from one micro-cultural group to another.

In the United States we have prided ourselves on being a classless society. Yet, do we use exactly the same language to the person who is below us in the hierarchy as to the person above? It is not a question of being polite — it is something more and very difficult to define and identify. It is culturally oriented behavior. Taking just one example, when is a first name used or when is a title used within the particular organization with which you are familiar?

Our movie films have captured this for us in innumerable pictures about the military. Custom says (and it may even be written down somewhere) that military personnel usually address each other by rank. When the individuals involved use their respective first names, it is a signal that a comradeship had developed which supersedes the regulations. As the movie proceeds to the climax the actors reach an emotional point when they are in conflict and then each reverts to using the rank in addressing his colleague. What has happened? In our cultural framework the audience now knows that they are signalling a new aspect of their previous relationship. Culturally, through the use of language, the film has communicated much more to us than the spoken word.

Sex

The drive towards equal opportunity has highlighted discrimination based on sex in our society. Some of this is based on the realities (how real?) of the nature of the jobs to be performed and the need for the worker to have certain physical attributes. Some jobs, then, are classified as either male or female — or at least they have become culturally classified.

In the course of business a phone call is made and a female voice responds on the other end of the line. The immediate assumption is that this is the secretary. How embarrassing it becomes when one discovers that the "C.T. Jones" who left a call-back message is not Charlie but Carolyn! And, Carolyn is not a secretary but an executive!

As our practices change is it possible that the male voice on the phone is the secretary and his boss (female) is the executive? At this moment in our cultural evolvement, this could be extremely disquieting and yet there is little that keeps this state of affairs from becoming reality. The prevalent cultural practice is not having a man work for a woman, not having a woman executive, not having a male secretary — yet all of these are perfectly acceptable and do happen in some micro-cultures all around us.

Cultural behavior which discriminates against sex prevents us from using many of those in our population who have positive contributions to offer. The shortage of nurses in our hospitals might be alleviated if our traditional picture of the female nurse could be changed. The cultural bias might then be altered to an affirmative one for the male nurse, allowing and encouraging many more men to enter this noble and short-staffed profession.

Conclusion

This article has endeavored to look at the influence of micro-cultural behavior on organizations and individuals. Only four of the many dimensions were identified, namely time, space, language, and sex. Much more profitable work could be done in exploring these four elements as they relate to organizational development, organizational renewal, career development, and other aspects of our efforts to more effectively utilize our human resources.

Cultural behavior can be changed if this is necessary and desirable. There will always be culturally determined behavior. The need is to explore how behavior, which is the result of a particular micro-culture, might be adapted without doing an injustice to the individual and the culture involved.

At the outset, cultural behavior must be identified and recognized. It must be differentiated from behavior which is organizationally determined and directed by rules and regulations. Next is the recognition that culturally determined behavior cannot be eliminated. There will always remain the need for individuals and groups to develop new habits and customs as conditions change.

When the need exists, a new cultural behavior will rapidly emerge if the micro-cultural group is not thrown into chaos. In the process of forming new cultural behavior, it is possible for the sensitive behavioral scientist and the trained manager to recognize those areas in which the group is to be allowed to develop their own customs, as contrasted with those areas in which the organization must exert some influence through rules and regulations. To the degree the group-induced behavior does not correspond with the organizationally-directed behavior, we produce cultural conflict within our own organizations.

Each of us carries his own cultural baggage. We must not presume that the cultural baggage we carry is similar to that of other members of our organization. Each man belongs to many micro-cultural groups and he carries some behavior from one group to another.

It is hoped that we can begin doing much more work in identifying micro-cultural behavior. This does not relate only to the introduction of the hard-core unemployed into our organizations, where the cultural conflicts may be obvious, but also to the cross-cultural problems created by new plant startup, acquisitions, the recruitment of large numbers of college graduates, and similar situations where micro-cultural groups can be expected to impact.

Today, there is a healthy movement towards organization development and renewal. Such activities can be expected to disturb the cultural practices which crept into our organization and training program which have therefore inhibited our tendency to explore change and new behavior.

The exploration and identification of micro-cultural behavior can prove exciting and rewarding to the trainer. He may need to seek out his own areas of competence in recognizing such behavior, or he may need to identify those competencies which he must further develop as he serves his organization.

Leonard Nadler is a professor of human resource development and adult education in the School of Education, George Washington University.

How to Market Training Within Your Organization

Chip R. Bell

A friend once told me that all human resources development managers would do well to have either marketing experience or a marketing planner on their HRD staff. At the time, I mentally labeled the comment an "egotistical pearl of wisdom"; my friend was a marketing planner. But considering recent demands for results in our adversary economy, I know my marketing friend was on the right track: The successful HRD manager should be able to think in marketing.

Training pros have for years recognized the need to be able to sell their ideas, proposals, budgets, and requests for additional human and material resources to decision makers. While the words selling and marketing are both cut from the same cloth, they involve different activities and, more importantly, different ways of viewing the act of influencing an outcome. Philosophically, selling is like a solo played by a violinist, while marketing is more like a symphony performed by an orchestra.

The model (Figure 15-1) includes four phases in the marketing of the training process — assessment, marketing strategy, presentation, and decision. Effective marketing requires awareness of each phase, and skill in managing the forces incumbent in each phase. Contained in the explanations that follow are questions designed to help tailor the model to the users' needs. All the component parts may not be appropriate to all situations; parts not explored in this article may occur to the reader just in the process of experiencing the concept. In a sense, the model represents a penciled beginning rather than an engraved capstone.

Assessment Phase

A fellow HRD manager had an outstanding training proposal shot down in the boardroom because he failed to assess that the company was on the verge of reorganization. His proposal referred only to the existing organization when it could have been subtly arranged to provide a transition into the emerging structure.

Reprinted with permission from *Training: The Magazine of Human Resources Development,* February 1977.

Figure 15-1. The four phases in the marketing of the training process.

The assessment phase incorporates research and analysis and is analogous to preparatory work in the generic marketing function. Assessment includes a comprehensive diagnosis of the major elements in the marketing situation — the buyer (decision maker), the seller (HRD manager), the setting (organization), and the user (learner). Each of these elements holds characteristics which restrain and assist the ultimate decision. Minimizing the restraining characteristics and optimizing the assisting characteristics requires accurate assessment and adroit action by the HRD manager.

What appears to be the top concern at the moment among decision makers? Will there be a near-term shift in objectives, markets, products, services, people? Why should a decision maker do something differently? Why should a training program be proposed? Assessing the needs of the organization should be a critical event in the development of all training programs. This same assessment done for design can be used again when the HRD proposal is placed on the docket for vote by decision makers.

Ultimately, decisions regarding a training proposal will be "business decisions" which reflect the value system of the organization. The organizational value system, reflecting the degrees to which form and substance factors are appreciated — like long run, short run, aggregation, integration, proaction, reaction — are by-products of the sum influence produced by key clout people. Thus, the needs of the organization (and concomitantly, the organizational response and direction) are in part shaped by the personal psychological needs and values of major decision makers.

Knowledge of the decision makers and their psychological needs can be vital when anticipating the reaction to the training proposal and when structuring the proposal presentation — its promotional form and HRD substance. Frequently, effective sales people size up the potential buyer during the opening of a sales presentation.[1] The HRD manager has an advantage over the outside salesperson — sizing up can be done before the pitch, thereby tailoring it in advance to a tune to which the buyer enjoys dancing.

How does the HRD manager assess the personality makeup of the decision makers? All people act out certain psychological needs. While we each have basically the same needs, they have different weights or priorities in different people. My high need to be liked may be only a moderate need of yours; your high need to achieve may be a low need of mine. Since people tend to act (behave) to satisfy the high needs, diagnosis can occur by observing the chosen actions in a given situation and hypothesizing what high need precipitated a certain action. If a person has a high need for power, even a small opportunity for power will likely evoke action toward that opportunity.

Think of the actions or behaviors you have seen or heard a decision maker emitting. Ask yourself, what sort of need would cause a person to engage in those actions? For instance, the decision maker who requires lots of documentation might be operating out of a high need for order, control, or power. This could provide a clue about how to structure your proposal presentation.

Coupled with diagnosis of the decision makers' needs is what one might call personal psych-out — assessing the psychological needs of the HRD manager. We are all guilty of occasionally letting our own needs get in the way of our effectiveness. Our intense need to win, for example, might cause us to choke on the road to victory. Our need to be liked may cause us to delay following up with an associate because the follow-up might include negative evaluation — a risk we are unwilling to introduce into the relationship. And our need to be perfect might cause us to fail to meet deadlines while continuing the pursuit of "perfection." The point is, our own needs can doom a training proposal to a negative decision unless we recognize that possibility and take steps to counteract it.

If your training proposal is for a program which has occurred successfully in the past, either in your organization or another organization to which you have access, the previous users' responses could represent a valuable resource to marketing assessment efforts. User response may be in the form of pre-test post-test measurement, post-workshop reaction sheets, observable behavior change, improved productivity, and reduced turnover — each credibly linked to the training program.

We have all been bored with those repetitious user-response advertisements which tell us why Ms. Anita Break from Muddywater, MT, swears by a certain brand. Despite their vanilla quality, these ads are reinforcing; buyers gain some measure of confidence in knowing that others found the product satisfactory. The confidence produces new customers and at the same time increases brand loyalty among old customers.

The possession of hard, irrefutable proof that the proposed training program worked elsewhere in a similar setting can sometimes mean the difference between a go and no-go decision. As will be explored in the next phase of the model, previous users can also be helpful when designing the marketing strategy, personally influencing individual advocates or decision makers, and providing supporting data useful in the presentation of the training proposal.

Marketing Strategy Phase

The development of the marketing strategy starts with analyzing the marketing situation defined in the assessment phase in order to derive certain assumptions. These assumptions are further scrutinized and ultimately lead to tactics or maneuvers for obtaining specific results (in this case, a favorable decision). The creativity required of the marketing planning unit in a generic marketing function is typically rivaled only by the advertising unit which communicates the result.

The accompanying conceptual model includes four activities for formulation and implementation of the strategy for marketing a training proposal — generating and selecting proposal attributes for marketing, winning individual advocates prior to the proposal presentation, assembling supporting data, and structuring the proposal presentation. From the standpoint of creativity, attribute generation and selection is likely to be the most taxing of the four activities. This activity requires viewing the proposal from a variety of perspectives in order to generate attribute alternatives responsibly. The knowledge acquired in the assessment phase then becomes the criteria for ultimate attribute selection.

Why generate and select proposal attributes for marketing? Shouldn't the pure, ostensive altruism of the proposal be sufficient? In some cases it may be. But as Theodore Levitt stated in *Marketing for Business Growth*, "It is not so much the basic central thing we are selling that counts, but the whole cluster of value satisfactions with which we surround it. It does little or no good to make a better mousetrap when 'betterness' now has a new, more subtle meaning."[2] In clothing, it is not dresses or suits one sells, but fashion; it is not cosmetics, but hope. People buy quarter-inch drill bits, not because they want drill bits, but because they want quarter-inch holes.[3]

The task of attribute generation is accomplished by multiplying perspective; the task of attribute selection is accomplished by matching the attributes with the assessment. The process is useful for escaping from the thought-pattern prisons of conventionality. By defining the training proposal differently than one traditionally defines it, it is possible to "see" new aspects — opportunities — which could be useful for internal marketing. The railroads failed to do this and almost stopped growing because they assumed they were in the railroad business rather than the transportation business; the movie industry was practically overrun by television because Hollywood defined their business as movies rather than entertainment.[4] HRD could be perceived as "programs to produce behavior change." It could also be seen as "an experience to facilitate learning how to learn." As you plan the marketing strategy for your training proposal, think of at least four different ways of perceiving or defining the proposal.

Another activity in the marketing strategy phase is the winning of individual advocates. Advocates are important influence allies. We have all heard the line, "it's not *what* you know, but *who* you know that counts."

Are there individuals you can influence who could in turn influence the decision makers? Are there previous program participants or colleagues who could be persuaded to put in a good word? Once advocates have been solicited and signed, the HRD manager can tap the advocate's knowledge of and experience with the decision makers and/or channel the advocate to influence the decision makers. A training manager I know is convinced her proposal was approved by top management because she had her friend, the dean of the local university business school, review the training proposal and then favorably mention it to the company president at a cocktail party. Secretaries can also be highly effective downfield blockers! Their ability to manage the timing and exposure of correspondence regarding the proposal can enhance the development of a positive proposal image.

Once proposal attributes for marketing have been selected and individual advocates influenced, the HRD manager is now in a position to structure the proposal presentation.

Another key point to remember in structuring the presentation, whether it is a formal "event" with a group or an informal dialogue with a single decision maker, is to couch the request in the language and style appropriate to the buyer and setting. Many excellent proposals have been disapproved because the presenter failed to accurately assess and deliver the form and substance which the decision makers preferred. Sellers have oversold, undersold, used figures and graphs before a nonfigures-oriented audience, used excessive buzz words and technical language, and used dog-and-pony showmanship when it wasn't showtime. What supporting data might be expected by the decision makers? What and how the buyers need to see and hear can be as important as what the buyers needs to know — a subtle distinction which can turn the tide in the affairs of the seller!

The critical issues in need of pre-presentation resolution can be distilled. Here are some suggestions to increase the chances of covering all the bases:

1. Anticipate resistance and then plan the necessary steps ahead to ensure success. There are risks involved with most proposal presentations. To assume tacitly your proposal will be approved is foolhardy.
2. Analyze the successes and failures which you and others experienced in the past to determine why they occurred.
3. Consider coupling your proposal with another proposal which you know to be a sure winner.
4. Plan a fall back or compromise position. Consider recommending a longer program, a shorter program, a more expensive program, a less expensive program, et al.
5. Consider selling to decision makers individually rather than as a group. Decision makers rarely enjoy surprises.
6. Consider changing the principal presenter.
7. Consider selecting a different time, place, or method to make the proposal presentation.
8. Consider the organization's budgeting methodology and its impact on the proposal. Would a zero-base approach be more appropriate? Could the proposal be financed in a different manner (e.g., a grant, marketing the program externally, budgets from other units, going over budget, changing the rules)?
9. Consider changing the program methodology, length, materials, timing, instructor(s), target market.
10. Consider whether risking a disapproval on this proposal will start a chain of events which multiplies the loss to the HRD unit. Better to lose a battle — win the war!

Before leaving this section, take an HRD proposal which was not approved at some time in the past. Using your present knowledge of the needs and values of the decision makers, the presenter, the organization, and the ten considerations listed above, try to figure out why the proposal failed to be approved. Done inclusively, this is a productive way to develop advocate involvement. Now think of a training proposal you plan to present some time in the future. What supporting data should you collect which might be expected by the potential buyer? Like saving canceled checks for that 1-in-100 chance of a tax audit, consider every training program and activity as someday requiring cost justification to top management.

Presentation and Decision Phases

I once heard a highly effective marketing executive say, "When it comes to selling, if you've done your homework, the final exam is a piece of cake!" Admittedly overstated, it holds a measure of truth. If the HRD manager has mapped the mental terrain of the decision makers, maintained cognizance of his/her own needs and those of the organization, and constructed a marketing strategy with the assessment as mortar between the bricks, the actual presentation or promotion should include few surprises. Trump cards may be represented by advocates who are members of the decision-making body — stacking the deck in favor of approval. One should remember, however, that advocates represent reserve power, not core power. They are rarely kamikaze pilots. Unless the proposal is itself meritorious, when the curtain is drawn the HRD manager may find the audience devoid of supporters.

Keep in mind that the approval decision will occur only if the majority of the decision makers perceive (consciously or subconsciously) some direct or indirect personal benefit. The presentation should be made around the diagnosed personal needs of the audience. As the presentation proceeds, ask yourself, "What can I say or do to assist Mr./Ms. X in feeling that approval will be to their advantage?" Maintain awareness of where you stand or sit, how you dress, the words you use, the material you present, and how each might be perceived by those present.

The marketing process continues beyond the achievement of a favorable decision. The HRD manager should "romance the sale" — selling advocates and the decision makers on the correctness of their decision. This prevents the onslaught of "buyers' blues." A way to nurture the process is to have those affected by the decision — the learners — voice favorable reaction in a way which filters to the top. Individual advocates should be continually won. Periodic status reports, while in some cases a requirement, can also serve to intensify decision correctness.

Each success brings greater likelihood of subsequent approval decisions; nothing breeds success like success. And perhaps nothing facilitates success more than awareness. Formal and informal feedback will serve to identify problems and opportunities for the HRD manager. A post-process critique of the marketing effort — assessment through decision — is critical for improved future endeavors. Objective appraisal of ongoing programs will help in making proposal changes which enhance the credibility of the entire HRD function.[5]

References

1. Bell, Chip R., Selling: Persuasion or Manipulation? *Xchange* (Xerox Learning Systems). 1976, No. 3 p. 5.
2. Levitt, Theodore, *Marketing for Business Growth,* New York: McGraw-Hill, 1974, p. 47.
3. Ibid, p. 8.
4. Levitt, Theodore, "Marketing Myopia," *Harvard Business Review,* (Sept.-Oct. 1975), p. 26.
5. Appreciation is expressed to Bruce W. Fritch, Director of Marketing Planning, NCNB Corporation, for his editorial suggestions.

Chip R. Bell is vice president and director of management development and training for NCNB Corporation headquartered in Charlotte, North Carolina.

Response

The response phase of the consulting process is often seen as the most crucial. Relying heavily on what has come before, it represents the focal point or main event of consultation. It is in response that the most obvious action takes place. Variously termed "intervention" or "strategic and tactical planning," response is the time when both client and consultant begin to see the possibililty of successfully completing their relationship and meeting their mutual expectations.

The response phase must be girded by the diagnosis phase. At the end of diagnosis, the consultant is typically in a position to present the client with a variety of alternatives which the client may have helped to generate. The alternative ultimately selected may be a hybrid alternative produced either by combining alternatives or creating one out of the substance of the discussions. This collabora-tive process can be enormously beneficial. Synergistic client–consultant relationships enhance creative action planning.

The range of possible responses appears to be endless. Some writers have even developed helpful systems to categorize the input and indicate the appropriate answer. Response in a can! The listing can be misleading for it implies comprehensiveness when we are continually evolving new interventions. There is likewise a temptation, particularly for new consultants, to look for the kind of list which indicates that for Diagnosis A one should use Response B. The field has yet to reach such a level of research and practice which precipitates clean choices of action.

Among consultants there exists a wide range of expertise, despite the use of the label identifying an individual with a specific background and experience. This imposes limits on the response phase: the consultant can legitimately focus on those responses which are clearly within the realm of personal expertise. If the consultant lacks the knowledge and skills for a particular response alternative, it may be time to secure the assistance of another consultant or terminate the existing client–consultant relationship.

This conflict often arises when the consultant uses "training" as a response. (In this context, training is defined as a learning experience, usually in a group situation.) When a person designs and conducts a learning experience, he or she is assumed to have competencies as a learning specialist. While it is likely there are consultants who can function as learning specialists, it is doubtful all consultants have such ability. Therefore, while training can be an appropriate response alternative, it is not one every consultant can employ without obtaining additional assistance.

Similarly, not every learning specialist can function as a consultant. Learning specialist and consultant entail specific kinds of behavior requiring different skills, knowledge, and experience.

If the chosen response is a plan, the consultant should devise a plan which the *client* can successfully implement. If additional resources are needed to implement the plan, the consultant should be certain these are carefully and clearly specified.

A common error among clients and consultants is to view the response phase as the only action phase and to proceed with desperate vigor for a "win." Organization development efforts are commonly burdened with this distortion — inappropriately amplifying the consultant's importance. If the consultant becomes too directly involved in carrying out the plan, it is easy for the consultant to become the change manager. Here, the consultant's role will have been altered so significantly that the usual consultant behaviors are no longer effective. The consultant and client should recognize that if this happens, the former can no longer effectively function as a consultant but has in reality become a part of the system. This role change can also occur when the consultant has a retainer arrangement and therefore can be called upon readily and frequently. The consultant can easily cross the line to become a part of the client system, thus diminishing consultative effectiveness.

An ethical consideration arises when the plan calls for the use of an external resource and the consultant appears to fill that requirement. While there are times this is unquestionably logical and appropriate, there are other situations where the consultant-produced plan specified that only that consultant can bring the effort to a successful conclusion. For example, in the U.S. government an initial, small contract is often given for consulting. The end product is to be a plan arrived at through a feasibility study or by actually producing a plan of action. The contractor is then awarded a "sole source" contract, or the original contract gets an "add on." There are times when such action by the contracting and/or project officer is clearly in the best interests of the government. There are other times, however, when the contractor knows this process beforehand and takes the initial consulting contract at a ridiculously low fee knowing the pay-out will come in the subsequent contract to implement the plan.

In the private sector this occurs less frequently. Consultants have, however, assumed contracts which would produce a plan, knowing full well the plan will be something which only that consultant can carry out, or which will definitely require the consultant's help. The client has some responsibility for being familiar enough with the consultant and the plan to avoid such ethical dilemmas. An important consideration is the timing and the response. It is obviously desirable to bring the client and consultant's time expectations to the surface as early as possible. Developing a plan as a response can usually be completed in a short period of time. It is unusual, but possible, for this to extend over a period of several months. An action response — actually conducting those activities which will result in a desired change — can easily extend from several months to several years.

Organizations and people generally change slowly, and in the process new factors may arise to modify the situation. There are times when the client is given the impression that a particular response by the consultant will cause the desired change to occur with lightning speed, followed by a thunderous clap of the door closing as the client exits with finality. Instead, the relationship is extended over a longer period and the solution process is prolonged. Gaps in expectations about timing can cause the relationship to terminate prematurely, ultimately because insufficient funds will have been provided for the long-range relationship needed to implement the action.

By the end of the response phase, it will be possible for the client and the consultant to see how the objectives of their relationship will be met. Some formative evaluation (i.e., during the consultation) is usually built into the relationship, making it possible to determine if the objectives can be met by successfully concluding the response phase. The final evaluation usually takes place in a later phase.

Chapter 16
"Choosing the Depth of Organizational Intervention"
by Roger Harrison

Harrison makes an important point in his article which might too easily be by-passed. He says, "...an intervention strategy can focus on instrumentality or it can focus on interpersonal relationships, and that there are important consequences of this difference in depth of intervention."

He defines instrumentality as "change work behavior and working relationships" but sees interpersonal relationships as a deeper level where "...the focus is on feelings, attitudes, and perceptions which organization members have about each other." He helps focus on the need for relating the interventions to the appropriate need. The selection of strategies is value laden — the values of the client as well as the values of the consultant must be considered.

Chapter 17
"Planned Renegotiation: A Norm-Setting OD Intervention"
by John J. Sherwood and John C. Glidewell

At what point can a consultant intervene? This is always a delicate matter since the best intervention or strategy at the wrong time can be worse than useless. Sherwood and Glidewell present a model for looking at interpersonal relationships and the roles which evolve. They indicate how it is possible to identify the point at which individuals can renegotiate their roles and relationships. The sensing of relational conflicts (called a pinch) is more likely when both parties at the outset agree such sensing (and the subsequent confrontation) is appropriate for either party.

Chapter 18
"Primary Target for Change: The Manager or the Organization?
by W. Warner Burke and Warren H. Schmidt

This article deals with several points at the heart of consultation and organization development. There are times when it is desirable to facilitate individual change through learning and other times when the organization work setting must be changed. The authors contrast the possibilities for both individual and organizational change. The reader is not asked to select one or the other, but rather to experience the alternatives in an effort to recognized which target is most appropriate, given a thorough situational diagnosis.

Choosing the Depth of Organizational Intervention*

Roger Harrison

Since World War II there has been a great proliferation of behavioral science-based methods by which consultants seek to facilitate growth and change in individuals, groups, and organizations. The methods range from operations analysis and manipulation of the organization chart, through the use of Grid Laboratories, T Groups, and nonverbal techniques. As was true in the development of clinical psychology and psychotherapy, the early stages of this developmental process tend to be accompanied by considerable competition, criticism, and argument about the relative merits of various approaches. It is my conviction that controversy over the relative goodness or badness, effectiveness or ineffectiveness, of various change strategies really accomplishes very little in the way of increased knowledge or unification of behavioral science. As long as we are arguing about what method is better than another, we tend to learn very little about how various approaches fit together or complement one another, and we certainly make more difficult and ambiguous the task of bringing these competing points of view within one overarching system of knowledge about human processes.

As our knowledge increases, it begins to be apparent that these competing change strategies are not really different ways of doing the same thing — some more effective and some less effective — but rather that they are different ways of doing *different* things. They touch the individual, the group, or the organization in different aspects of their functioning. They require differing kinds and amounts of commitment on the part of the client for them to be successful, and they demand different varieties and levels of skills, and abilities on the part of the practitioner.

I believe that there is a real need for conceptual models which differentiate intervention strategies from one another in a way which permits rational matching

*A revised version of a paper presented at the International Congress of Group Psychotherapy, Vienna, Austria, September 16, 1968.

of strategies to organizational change problems. The purpose of this article is to present a modest beginning which I have made toward a conceptualization of strategies, and to derive from this conceptualization some criteria for choosing appropriate methods of intervention in particular applications.

The point of view of this article is that the depth of individual emotional involvement in the change process can be a central concept for differentiating change strategies. In focusing on this dimension, we are concerned with the extent to which core areas of the personality or self are the focus of the change attempt. Strategies which touch the more deep, personal, private, and central aspects of the individual or his relationships with others fall toward the deeper end of this continuum. Strategies which deal with more external aspects of the individual and which focus upon the more formal and public aspects of role behavior tend to fall toward the surface end of the depth dimension. This dimension has the advantage that it is relatively easy to rank change strategies upon it and to get fairly close consensus as to the ranking. It is a widely discussed dimension of difference which has meaning and relevance to practitioners and their clients. I hope in this article to promote greater flexibility and rationality in choosing appropriate depths of intervention. I shall approach this task by examining the effects of interventions at various depths. I shall also explore the ways in which two important organizational processes tend to make demands and to set limits upon the depth of intervention which can produce effective change in organizational functioning. These two processes are the autonomy of organization members and their own perception of their needs for help.

Before illustrating the concept by ranking five common intervention strategies along the dimension of depth, I should like to define the dimension somewhat more precisely. We are concerned essentially with how private, individual, and hidden are the issues and processes about which the consultant attempts directly to obtain information and which he seeks to influence. If the consultant seeks information about relatively public and observable aspects of behavior and relationship and if he tries to influence directly only these relatively surface characteristics and processes, we would then categorize his intervention strategy as being closer to the surface. If, on the other hand, the consultant seeks information about very deep and private perceptions, attitudes, or feelings and if he intervenes in a way which directly affects these processes, then we would classify his intervention strategy as one of considerable depth. To illustrate the surface end of the dimension, let us look first at operations research or operations analysis. This strategy is concerned with the roles and functions to be performed within the organization, generally with little regard to the individual characteristics of persons occupying the roles. The change strategy is to manipulate role relationships; in other words, to redistribute the tasks, the resources, and the relative power attached to various roles in the organization. This is essentially a process of rational analysis in which the tasks which need to be performed are determined and specified and then sliced up into role definitions for persons and groups in the organization. The operations analyst does not ordinarily need to know much about particular people. Indeed, his function is to design the organization in such a way that its successful operation does not depend too heavily upon any uniquely individual skills, abilities, values, or attitudes of persons in various roles. He may perform this function adequately without knowing in advance who the people are who will fill these slots. Persons are assumed to be moderately interchangeable, and in order to make this approach work it is necessary to design the organization so that the capacities, needs, and values of the individual which are relevant to role performance are relatively public and observable, and are possessed by a fairly large proportion of the population from which organization members are drawn. The approach is certainly one of very modest depth.

Somewhat deeper are those strategies which are based upon evaluating individual performance and attempting to manipulate it directly. Included in this approach is much of the industrial psychologist's work in selection, placement, appraisal, and counseling of employees. The intervener is concerned with what the individual is able and likely to do and achieve rather than with processes internal to the individual. Direct attempts to influence performance may be made through the application of rewards and punishments such as promotions, salary increases, or transfers within the organization. An excellent illustration of this focus on end results is the practice of management by objectives. The intervention process is focused on establishing mutually agreed-upon goals for performance between the individual and his supervisor. The practice is considered to be particularly advantageous because it permits the supervisor to avoid a focus on personal characteristics of the subordinate, particularly those deeper, more central characteristics which managers generally have difficulty in discussing with those who work under their supervision. The process is designed to limit information exchange to that which is public and observable, such as the setting of performance goals and the success or failure of the individual in attaining them.

Because of its focus on end results, rather than on the process by which those results are achieved, management by objectives must be considered less deep than the broad area of concern with work style which I shall term instrumental process analysis. We are concerned here not only with performance but with the processes by which that performance is achieved. However, we are primarily concerned with styles and processes of work rather than with the processes of interpersonal relationships which I would classify as being deeper on the basic dimension.

In instrumental process analysis we are concerned with how a person likes to organize and conduct his work and with the impact which this style of work has on others in the organization. Principally, we are concerned with how a person perceives his role, what he values and disvalues in it, and with what he works hard on and what he chooses to ignore. We are also interested in the instrumental acts which the individual directs toward others: delegating authority or reserving decisions to himself, communicating or withholding information, collaborating or competing with others on work-related issues. The focus on instrumentality means that we are interested in the person primarily as a doer of work or a performer of functions related to the goals of the organization. We are interested in what facilitates or inhibits his effective task performance.

We are not interested per se in whether his relationships with others are happy or unhappy, whether they perceive him as too warm or too cold, too authoritarian or too laissez faire, or any other of the many interpersonal relationships which arise as people associate in organizations. However, I do not mean to imply that the line between instrumental relationships and interpersonal ones is an easy one to draw in action and practice, or even that it is desirable that this be done.

What I am saying is that an intervention strategy can focus on instrumentality or it can focus on interpersonal relationships, and that there are important consequences of this difference in depth of intervention.

When we intervene at the level of instrumentality, it is to change work behavior and working relationships. Frequently this involves the process of bargaining or negotiation between groups and individuals. Diagnoses are made of the satisfactions or dissatisfactions of organization members with one another's work behavior. Reciprocal adjustments, bargains, and trade-offs can then be arranged in which each party gets some modification in the behavior of the other at the cost to him or some reciprocal accommodation. Much of the intervention strategy which has been developed around Blake's concept of the Managerial Grid is at this level and involves bargaining and negotiation of role behavior as an important change process.

At the deeper level of interpersonal relationships the focus is on feelings, attitudes, and perceptions which organization members have about others. At this level we are concerned with the quality of human relationships within the organization, with warmth and coldness of members to one another, and with the experiences of acceptance and rejection, love and hate, trust and suspicion among groups and individuals. At this level the consultant probes for normally hidden feelings, attitudes, and perceptions. He works to create relationships of openness about feelings and to help members to develop mutual understanding of one another as persons. Interventions are directed toward helping organization members to be more comfortable in being authentically themselves with one another, and the degree of mutual caring and concern is expected to increase. Sensitivity training using T Groups is a basic intervention strategy at this level. T-Group educators emphasize increased personalization of relationships, the development of trust and openness, and the exchange of feelings. Interventions at this level deal directly and intensively with interpersonal emotionality. This is the first intervention strategy we have examined which is at a depth were the feelings of organization members about one another as persons are a direct focus of the intervention strategy. At the other levels, such feelings certainly exist and may be expressed, but they are not a direct concern of the intervention. The transition from the task orientation of instrumental process analysis to the feeling orientation of interpersonal process analysis seems, as I shall suggest later, to be a critical one for many organization members.

The deepest level of intervention which will be considered in this article is that of intrapersonal analysis. Here the consultant used a variety of methods to reveal the individual's deeper attitudes, values, and conflicts regarding his own functioning, identity, and existence. The focus is generally on increasing the range of experiences which the individual can bring into awareness and cope with. The material may be dealt with at the fantasy or symbolic level, and the intervention strategies include many which are noninterpersonal and nonverbal. Some examples of this approach are the use of marathon T-Group sessions, the creative risk-taking laboratory approach of Byrd,[1] and some aspects of the task group therapy approach of Clark.[2] These approaches all tend to bring into focus very deep and intense feelings about one's own identity and one's relationships with significant others.

Although I have characterized deeper interventions as dealing increasingly with the individual's affective life, I do not imply that issues at less deep levels may not be emotionally charged. Issues of role differentiation, reward distribution, ability and performance evaluation, for example, are frequently invested with strong feelings. The concept of depth is concerned more with the *accessibility* and *individuality* of attitudes, values, and perceptions than it is with their strength. This narrowing of the common usage of the term "depth" is necessary to avoid the contradictions which occur when strength and inaccessibility are confused. For instance, passionate value confrontation and bitter conflict have frequently occurred between labor and managment over economic issues which are surely toward the surface end of my concept of depth.

In order to understand the importance of the concept of depth for choosing interventions in organizations, let us consider the effects upon organization members of working at different levels.

The first of the important concomitants of depth is the degree of dependence of the client on the special competence of the change agent. At the surface end of the depth dimension, the methods of intervention are easily communicated and made public. The client may reasonably expect to learn something of the change agent's skills to improve his own practice. At the deeper levels, such as interpersonal and intrapersonal process analyses, it is more difficult for the client to understand the methods of intervention. The change agent is more likely to be seen as a person of special and unusual powers not found in ordinary men. Skills of intervention and change are less frequently learned by organization members, and the change process may tend to become personalized around the change agent as leader. Programs of change which are so dependent upon personal relationships and individual expertise are difficult to institutionalize. When the change agent leaves the system, he may not only take his expertise with him but the entire change process as well.

A second aspect of the change process which varies with depth is the extent to which the benefits of an intervention are transferable to members of the organization not originally participating in the change process. At surface levels of operations analysis and performance evaluation, the effects are institutionalized in the form of procedures, policies, and practices of the organization which may have considerable permanence beyond the tenure of individuals. At the level of instrumental behavior, the continuing effects of intervention are more likely to reside in the informal norms of groups within the organization regarding such matters as delegation, communication, decision making, competition and collaboration, and conflict resolution.

At the deepest levels of intervention, the target of change is the individual's inner life; and if the intervention is successful, the permanence of individual change should be greatest. There are indeed dramatic reports of cases in which persons have changed their careers and life goals as a result of such interventions, and the persistence of such change appears to be relatively high.

One consequence, then, of the level of intervention is that with greater depth of focus the individual increasingly becomes both the target and the carrier of change. In the light of this analysis, it is not surprising to observe that deeper levels of intervention are increasingly being used at higher organizational levels and in scientific and service organizations where the contribution of the individual has greatest impact.

An important concomitant of depth is that as the level of intervention becomes deeper, the information needed to intervene effectively becomes less available. At the less personal level of operations analysis, the information is often a matter of record. At the level of performance evaluation, it is a matter of observation. On the other hand, reactions of others to a person's work style are less likely to be discussed freely, and the more personal responses to his interpersonal style are even less likely to be readily given. At the deepest levels, important information may not be available to the individual himself. Thus, as we go deeper the consultant must use more of his time and skill uncovering information which is ordinarily private and hidden. This is one reason for the greater cost of interventions at deeper levels of focus.

Another aspect of the change process which varies with the depth of intervention is the personal risk and unpredictability of outcome for the individual. At deeper levels we deal with aspects of the individual's view of himself and his relationships with others which are relatively untested by exposure to the evaluations and emotional reactions of others. If in the change process the individual's self-perceptions are strongly disconfirmed, the resulting imbalance in internal forces may produce sudden changes in behavior, attitudes, and personality integration.

Because of the private and hidden nature of the processes into which we intervene at deeper levels, it is difficult to predict the individual impact of the change process in advance. The need for clinical sensitivity and skill on the part of the practitioner thus increases, since he must be prepared to diagnose and deal with developing situations involving considerable stress upon individuals.

The foregoing analysis suggests a criterion by which to match intervention strategies to particular organizational problems. It is *to intervene at a level no deeper than that required to produce enduring solutions to the problems at hand.* This criterion derives directly from the observations above. The cost, skill demands, client dependency, and variability of outcome all increase with depth of intervention. Further, as the depth of intervention increases, the effects tend to locate more in the individual and less in the organization. The danger of losing the organization's investment in the change with the departure of the individual becomes a significant consideration.

While this general criterion is simple and straightforward, its application is not. In particular, although the criterion should operate in the direction of less depth of intervention, there is a general trend in modern organizational life which tends to push the intervention level ever deeper. This trend is toward increased self-direction of organization members and increased independence of external pressures and incentives. I believe that there is a direct relationship between the autonomy of individuals and the depth of intervention needed to effect organizational change.

Before going on to discuss this relationship, I shall acknowledge freely that I cannot prove the existence of a trend toward a general increase in freedom of individuals within organizations. I intend only to assert the great importance of the degree of individual autonomy in determining the level of intervention which will be effective.

In order to understand the relationship between autonomy and depth of intervention, it is necessary to conceptualize a dimension which parallels and is implied by the depth dimension we have been discussing. This is the dimension of predictability and variability among persons in their responses to the different kinds of incentives which may be used to influence behavior in the organization. The key assumption in this analysis is that the more unpredictable and unique is the individual's response to the particular kinds of controls and incentives one can bring to bear upon him, the more one must know about that person in order to influence his behavior.

Most predictable and least individual is the response of the person to economic and bureaucratic controls when his needs for economic income and security are high. It is not necessary to delve very deeply into a person's inner processes in order to influence his behavior if we know that he badly needs his income and his position and if we are in a position to control his access to these rewards. Responses to economic and bureaucratic controls tend to be relatively simple and on the surface.

If for any reason organization members become relatively uninfluenceable through the manipulation of their income and economic security, the management of performance becomes strikingly more complex; and the need for more personal information about the individual increases. Except very generally, we do not know automatically or in advance what styles of instrumental or interpersonal interaction will be responded to as negative or positive incentives by the individual. One person may appreciate close supervision and direction; another may value independence of direction. One may prefer to work alone; another may function best when he is in close communication with others. One may thrive in close, intimate, personal interaction, while others are made uncomfortable by any but cool and distant relationships with colleagues.

What I am saying is that when bureaucratic and economic incentives lose their force for whatever reason, the improvement of performance *must* involve linking organizational goals to the individual's attempts to meet his own needs for satisfying instrumental activities and interpersonal relationships. It is for this reason that I make the assertion that increases in personal autonomy dictate change interventions at deeper and more personal levels. In order to obtain the information necessary to link organizational needs to individual goals, one must probe fairly deeply into the attitudes, values, and emotions of the organization members.

If the need for deeper personal information becomes great when we intervene at the instrumental and interpersonal levels, it becomes even greater when one is dealing with organization members who are motivated less through their transactions with the environment and more in response to internal values and standards. An example is the researcher, engineer, or technical specialist whose work behavior may be influenced more by his own values and standards of creativity or professional excellence than by his relationships with others. The deepest organizational interventions at the intrapersonal level may be required in order to effect change when working with persons who are highly self-directed.

Let me summarize my position about the relationship among autonomy, influence, and level of intervention. As the individual becomes less subject to economic and bureaucratic pressures, he tends to seek more intangible rewards in the organization which come from both the instrumental and interpersonal aspects of the system. I view this as a shift from greater external to more internal control and as an increase in autonomy. Further shifts in this direction may involve increased independence of rewards and punishments mediated by others, in favor of operation in accordance with internal values and standards.

I view organizations as systems of reciprocal influence. Achievement of organization goals is facilitated when individuals can seek their own satisfactions through activity which promotes the goals of the organization. As the satisfactions which are of most value to the individual change, so must the reciprocal influence systems, if the organization goals are to continue to be met.

If the individual changes are in the direction of increased independence of external incentives, then the influence systems must change to provide opportunities for individuals to achieve more intangible, self-determined satisfactions in their work. However, people are more differentiated, complex, and unique in their intangible goals and values than in their economic needs. In order to create systems which offer a wide variety of intangible satisfactions, much more private information about individuals is needed than is required to create and maintain systems based chiefly on economic and bureaucratic controls. For this reason, deeper interventions are called for when the system which they would attempt to change contains a high proportion of relatively autonomous individuals.

There are a number of factors promoting autonomy, all tending to free the individual from dependence upon economic and bureaucratic controls, which I have observed in my work with organizations. Wherever a number of these factors obtain, it is probably an indication that deeper levels of intervention are required to effect lasting improvements in organizational functioning. I shall simply list these indicators briefly in categories to show what kinds of things might signify to the practitioner that deeper levels of intervention may be appropriate.

The first category includes anything which makes the evaluation of individual performance difficult:

— A long time span between the individual's actions and the results by which effectiveness of performance is to be judged.
— Nonrepetitive, unique tasks which cannot be evaluated by reference to the performance of others on similar tasks.
— Specialized skills and abilities possessed by an individual which cannot be evaluated by a supervisor who does not possess the skills or knowledge himself.

The second category concerns economic conditions:

— Arrangements which secure the job tenure and/or income of the individual.
— A market permitting easy transfer from one organization to another (e.g., engineers in the United States aerospace industry).
— Unique skills and knowledge of the individual which make him difficult to replace.

The third category includes characteristics of the system or its environment which lead to independence of the parts of the organization and decentralization of authority such as:

— An organization which works on a project basis instead of producing a standard line of products.
— An organization in which subparts must be given latitude to deal rapidly and flexibly with frequent environmental change.

I should like to conclude the discussion of this criterion for depth of intervention with a brief reference to the ethics of intervention, a problem which merits considerably more thorough treatment than I can give it here.

There is considerable concern in the United States about invasion of privacy by behavioral scientists. I would agree that such invasion of privacy is an actual as well as a fantasied concomitant of the use of organizational change strategies of greater depth. The recourse by organizations to such strategies has been widely viewed as an indication of greater organizational control over the most personal and private aspects of the lives of the members. The present analysis suggests, however, that recourse to these deeper interventions actually reflects the greater *freedom* of organization members from traditionally crude and impersonal means of organizational control. There is no reason to be concerned about man's attitudes or values or interpersonal relationships when his job performance can be controlled by brute force, by economic coercion, or by bureaucratic rules and regulations. The "invasion of privacy" becomes worth the cost, bother, and uncertainty of outcome only when the individual has achieved relative independence from control by other means. Put another way, it makes organizational sense to try to get a man to *want* to do something only if you cannot *make* him do it. And regardless of what intervention strategy is used, the individual still retains considerably greater control over his own behavior than he had when he could be manipulated more crudely. As long as we can maintain a high degree of voluntarism regarding the nature and extent of an individual's participation in the deeper organizational change strategies, these strategies can work toward adapting the organization to the individual quite as much as they work the other way around. Only when an individual's participation in one of the deeper change strategies is coerced by economic or bureaucratic pressures do I feel that the ethics of the intervention clearly run counter to the values of a democratic society.

So far our attention to the choice of level of intervention has focused upon locating the depth at which the information exists which must be exchanged to facilitate system improvement. Unfortunately, the choice of an intervention strategy cannot practically be made with reference to this criterion alone. Even if a correct diagnosis is made of the level at which the relevant information lies, we may not be able to work effectively at the desired depth because of client norms, values, resistances, and fears.

In an attempt to develop a second criterion for depth of intervention which takes such dispositions on the part of the client into account, I have considered two approaches which represent polarized orientations to the problem. One approach is based upon analyzing and overcoming client resistance; the other is based upon discovering and joining forces with the self-articulated wants or "felt needs" of the client.

There are several ways of characterizing these approaches. To me, the simplest is to point out that when the change agent is resistance-oriented he tends to lead or influence the client to work at a depth greater than that at which the latter feels comfortable. When resistance-oriented, the change agent tends to mistrust the client's statement of his problems and of the areas where he wants help. He suspects the client's presentation of being a smoke screen or defense against admission of his "real" problems and needs. The consultant works to expose the underlying processes and concerns and to influence the client to work at a deeper level. The resistance-oriented approach grows out of the work of clinicians and psychotherapists, and it characterizes much of the work of organizational consultants who specialize in sensitivity training and deeper intervention strategies.

On the other hand, change agents may be oriented to the self-articulated needs of clients. When so oriented, the consultant tends more to follow and facilitate the client in working at whatever level the latter sets for himself. He may assist the client in defining problems and needs and in working on solutions, but he is inclined to try to anchor his work in the norms, values, and accepted standards of behavior of the organization.

I believe that there is a tendency for change agents working at the interpersonal and deeper levels to adopt a rather consistent resistance-oriented approach. Consultants so oriented seem to take a certain quixotic pride in dramatically and self-consciously violating organizational norms. Various techniques have been developed for pressuring or seducing organization members into departing from organizational norms in the service of change. The "marathon" T Group is a case in point, where the increased irritability and fatigue of prolonged contact and lack of sleep move participants to deal with one another more emotionally, personally, and spontaneously than they would normally be willing to do.

I suspect that unless such norm-violating intervention efforts actually succeed in changing organizational norms, their effects are relatively short-lived, because the social structures and interpersonal linkages have not been created which can utilize for day-to-day problem solving the deeper information produced by the intervention. It is true that the consultant may succeed in producing information, but he is less likely to succeed in creating social structures which can continue to work in his absence. The problem is directly analogous to that of the community developer who succeeds by virtue of his personal influence in getting villagers to build a school or a community center which falls into disuse as soon as he leaves because of the lack of any integration of these achievements into the social structure and day-to-day needs and desires of the community. Community developers have had to learn through bitter failure and frustration that ignoring or subverting the standards and norms of a social system often results in temporary success followed by a reactionary increase in resistance to the influence of the change agent. On the other hand, felt needs embody those problems, issues, and difficulties which have a high conscious priority on the part of community or organization members. We can expect individuals and groups to be ready to invest time, energy, and resources in dealing with their felt needs, while they will be relatively passive or even resistant toward those who attempt to help them with externally defined needs. Community developers have found that attempts to help with felt needs are met with greater receptivity, support, and integration within the structure and life of the community than are intervention attempts which rely primarily upon the developer's value system for setting need priorities.

The emphasis of many organizational change agents on confronting and working through resistances was developed originally in the practice of individual psychoanalysis and psychotherapy, and it is also a central concept in the conduct of therapy groups and sensitivity training laboratories. In all of these situations, the change agent hás a high degree of environmental control and is at least temporarily in a high status position with respect to the client. To a degree that is frequently underestimated by practitioners, we manage to create a situation in which it is more unpleasant for the client to leave than it is to stay and submit to the pressure to confront and work through resistances. I believe that the tendency is for behavioral scientists to overplay their hands when they move from the clinical and training situations where they have environmental control to the organizational consulting situation, where their control is sharply attenuated.

This attenuation derives only partially from the relative ease with which the client can terminate the relationship. Even if this most drastic step is not taken, the consultant can be tolerated, misled, and deceived in ways which are relatively difficult in the therapeutic or human relations training situations. He can also be openly defied and blocked if he runs afoul of strongly shared group norms; whereas when the consultant is dealing with a group of strangers, he can often utilize differences among the members to overcome this kind of resistance. I suspect that, in general, behavioral scientists underestimate their power in working with individuals and groups of strangers, and overestimate it when working with individuals and groups in organizations. I emphasize this point because I believe that a good many potentially fruitful and mutually satisfying consulting relationships are terminated early because of the consultant's taking the role of overcomer of resistance to change rather than that of collaborator in the client's attempts at solving his problems. It is these considerations which lead me to suggest my second criterion for the choice of organization intervention strategy: *to intervene at a level no deeper than that at which the energy and resources of the client can be committed to problem solving and to change*. These energies and resources can be mobilized through obtaining legitmation for the intervention in the norms of the organization and through devising intervention strategies which have clear relevance to consciously felt needs on the part of the organization members.

Unfortunately, it is doubtless true that the forces which influence the conditions we desire to change often exist at deeper levels than can be dealt with by adhering to the criterion of working within organization norms and meeting felt needs. The level at which an individual or group is willing and ready to invest energy and resources is probably always determined partly by a realistic assessment of the problems and partly by a defensive need to avoid confrontation and significant change. It is thus not likely that our two criteria for selection of intervention depth will result in the same decisions when practically applied. It is not the same to intervene at the level where behavior-determining forces are most potent as it is to work on felt needs as they are articulated by the client. This, it seems to me, is the consultant's dilemma. It always has been. We are continually faced with the choice between leading the client into areas which are threatening, unfamiliar, and dependency-provoking for him (and where our own expertise shows up to best advantage) or, on the other hand, being guided by the client's own understanding of his problems and his willingness to invest resources in particular kinds of relatively familiar and nonthreatening strategies.

When time permits, this dilemma is ideally dealt with by intervening first at a level where there is good support from the norms, power structure, and felt needs of organizational members. The consultant can then, over a period of time, develop trust, sophistication, and support within the organization to explore deeper levels at which particularly important forces may be operating. This would probably be agreed to, at least in principle, by most organizational consultants. The point at which I feel I differ from a significant number of workers in this field is that I would advocate that interventions should *always* be limited to the depth of the client's felt needs and readiness to legitimize intervention. I believe we should always avoid moving deeper at a pace which outstrips a client system's willingness to subject itself to exposure, dependency, and threat. What I am saying is that if the dominant response of organization members indicates that an intervention violates system norms regarding exposure, privacy, and confrontation, then one has intervened too deeply and should pull back to a level at which organization members are more ready to invest their own energy in the change process. This point of view is thus in opposition to that which sees negative reactions primarily as indications of resistances which are to be brought out into the open, confronted, and worked through as a central part of the intervention process. I believe that behavioral scientists acting as organizational consultants have tended to place overmuch emphasis on the overcoming of resistance to change and have underemphasized the importance of enlisting in the service of change the energies and resources which the client can consciously direct and willingly devote to problem solving.

What is advocated here is that we in general accept the client's felt needs or the problems he presents as real and that we work on them at a level at which he can serve as a competent and willing collaborator. This position is in opposition to one which sees the presenting problem as more or less a smoke screen or barrier. I am not advocating this point of view because I value the right to privacy of organization members more highly than I value their growth and development or the solution of organizational problems. (This is an issue which concerns me, but it is enormously more complex than the ones with which I am dealing in this article.) Rather, I place first priority on collaboration with the client, because I do not think we are frequently successful consultants without it.

In my own practice I have observed that the change in client response is frequently quite striking when I move from a resistance-oriented approach to an acceptance of the client's norms and definitions of his own needs. With quite a few organizational clients in the United States, the line of legitimacy seems to lie somewhere between interventions at the instrumental level and those focused on interpersonal relationships. Members who exhibit hostility, passivity, and dependence when I initiate intervention at the interpersonal level may become dramatically more active, collaborative, and involved when I shift the focus to the instrumental level.

If I intervene directly at the level of interpersonal relationships, I can be sure that at least some members, and often the whole group, will react with anxiety, passive resistance, and low or negative commitment to the change process. Furthermore, they express their resistance in terms of norms and values regarding the appropriateness or legitimacy of dealing at this level. They say things like, "It isn't right to force people's feelings about one another out into the open"; "I don't see what this has to do with improving organizational effectiveness"; "People are being encouraged to say things which are better left unsaid."

If I then switch to a strategy which focuses on decision making, delegation of authority, information exchange, and other instrumental questions, these complaints about illegitimacy and the inappropriateness of the intervention are usually sharply reduced. This does not mean that the clients are necessarily comfortable or free from anxiety in the discussions, nor does it mean that strong feelings may not be expressed about one another's behavior. What is different is that the clients are more likely to *work with* instead of *against* me, to feel and express some sense of ownership in the change process, and to see many more possibilities for carrying it on among themselves in the absence of the consultant.

What I have found is that when I am resistance-oriented in my approach to the client, I am apt to feel rather uncomfortable in "letting sleeping dogs lie." When, on the other hand, I orient myself to the client's own assessment of his needs, I am uncomfortable when I feel I am leading or pushing the client to operate very far outside the shared norms of the organization. I have tried to indicate why I believe the latter orientation is more appropriate. I realize of course that many highly sophisticated and talented practitioners will not agree with me.

In summary, I have tried to show in this article that the dimension of depth should be central to the conceptualization of intervention strategies. I have presented what I believe are the major consequences of intervening at greater or lesser depths, and from these consequences I have suggested two criteria for choosing the appropriate depth of intervention: first, *to intervene at a level no deeper than that required to produce enduring solutions to the problems at hand;* and second, *to intervene at a level no deeper than that at which the energy and resources of the client can be committed to problem solving and to change.*

I have analyzed the tendency for increases in individual autonomy in organizations to push the appropriate level of intervention deeper when the first criterion is followed. Opposed to this is the countervailing influence of the second criterion to work closer to the surface in order to enlist the energy and support of organization members in the change process. Arguments have been presented for resolving this dilemma in favor of the second.

The dilemma remains, of course. The continuing tension under which the change agent works is between the desire to lead and push, or to collaborate and follow. The middle ground is never very stable, and I suspect we show our values and preferences by which criterion we choose to maximize when we are under the stress of difficult and ambiguous client-consultant relationships.

References

1. Byrd, R. E., "Training in a Non-group," *Journal of Humanistic Psychology,* Vol. 7, No. 1 (1967), pp. 18–27.
2. Clark, J. V., Task group therapy. Unpublished manuscript, University of California, Los Angeles, 1966.

Roger Harrison is a principal with Situation Management Systems, Inc., in Berkeley, California.

Planned Renegotiation: A Norm-Setting OD Intervention

John J. Sherwood

John C. Glidewell

Organization development has been described as "an educational process by which human resources are continuously identified, allocated, and expanded in ways that make these resources more available to the organization, and therefore, improve the organization's problem-solving capabilities."[18] The concept of planned renegotiation describes a procedure by which controlled change can enter an organization in such a way that resources become more available to the organization. It is derived from a clear and simple theory of how roles are established and changed.[5]

The theory itself is a norm-setting intervention because it is intended to become part of the normative structure of an organization, and as such to become part of the language, rhetoric, and expectations of members of the organization. Furthermore, the use of these concepts in successful problem-solving leads to the learning of behavioral skills by insight, reinforcement, and imitation. As we often like to hear Lewin[14] say, there is nothing as practical as a good theory. Where the concept of planned re-negotiation becomes part of the norms of an organization, it can constitute the heart of an OD effort.

The Model

The model describes how social systems — that is, relations between persons and relations between groups — are established and become stabilized so that work can get done, and how change can enter the system. The model is cyclical and it includes four phases:

Reprinted by permission of the authors, *New Technologies in Organization Development*, Vol. 1, W. Warner Burke (Ed.), University Associates Press, La Jolla, California, 1975. Copyright © 1971 by John J. Sherwood and John C. Glidewell.

(1) Sharing Information and Negotiating Expectations. When persons begin to establish a relationship which they expect may endure over some period of time — as brief as as a preemployment interview or as long-lasting as a marriage or an appointment to the U.S. Supreme Court — they first exchange information. They share information about themselves and they exchange expectations, which are usually implicit and unspecified, about how each is to behave with the other(s). They are essentially trading information and establishing expectations about how a "member" of this relationship, or a member of this group, is going to behave (see Goffman, 1956, p. 162, 1961, pp. 105–132; Thibaut & Kelley, 1959, pp. 21–25; Blau, 1960).

Once a sufficient exchange of information occurs, so that uncertainty is reduced to an acceptable level and the behaviors of the parties are more or less predictable, and if the relationship is seen as enduring sometime into the future, then commitment to these shared expectations takes place.

(2) Commitment. Once commitment to a set of shared expectations takes place, then each member knows for the most part what is expected of him and for the most part what he can expect from the others. The strength of each individual's commitment and the range of his behavior encompassed by his role are both measures of the importance or centrality to him of this particular relationship. The more important the relationship, the more evidence of commitment is required and the more behaviors — including attitudes, values, and perceptions — are embraced by the role expectations. With commitment comes stability.

(3) Stability and Productivity. When there is commitment to a set of shared expectations, these expectations govern the behavior of group members and provide stability within the relationships — that is, for the most part you do what I expect of you and for the most part I do what you expect of me. This stability in the relationships leads to the possibility that work can now get done. While stability does not guarantee productivity, it is necessary for productive work to occur. The energy of the principals is now available for other things, since their relationships are sufficiently predictable that they no longer required sustained attention. Commitment to a set of shared expectations then governs behavior during a period of stability — but invariably, sooner or later, disruption occurs.[2, 10]

(4) Disruption. Disruption occurs because of a violation of expectations by the principals or because of external intrusion into the system. It is assumed that disruption is inevitable, only the duration of the period of stability varies, because (a) information is never completely shared during the initial period when expectations are negotiated; and (b) individuals, groups, and organizations are viewed as open systems[11] — i.e., they change as a consequence of transactions with their environment.[5]

Disruptions may be external in origin, such as a new person assigned to a work group, a loss of personnel, an assignment of a new task or higher quota, a budgetary cut and reallocation of resources, or reorganization of personnel and subsequent reassignment of duties. The first child born into a marriage is an example of a new input into the relationship which is likely to lead to the violation of previously established expectations. Disruptions may also be internal in origin, such as the sharing of information which was not made available earlier when expectations were being negotiated. Persons also change as a consequence of new experiences, training, and education. When the changed person returns to the unchanged role, expectations may be violated, leading to a disruption of the relationship.

It is at the point of disruption that change can enter the system, for it is at this time that expectations are no longer fixed. New information can now enter the system, and the renegotiation of expectations can occur. Once again the system recycles through: (1) sharing information and renegotiating expectations, then (2) commitment to a set of expectations, which governs behavior during a period (3) of stability and productivity, when, for the most part, you do what I expect of you and I do what you expect of me, until (4) disruption once again occurs, because of a violation of expectations by the principals or because of external intrusion into the system. With disruption, change can once again enter the system, as it cycles from renegotiation through disruption, and yet another opportunity for renegotiation (see Figure 17-1).

The paradox is that the very moment the system is most open to change there are strong inhibiting forces working to return things "to the way they used to be," because of anxiety accompanying the uncertainty which characterizes the system at the time it is in a state of disruption.[13,12]

When a disruption of expectations occurs, uncertainty follows — because I can no longer depend on your doing what I expect of you, and my own role is also unclear to me — and with uncertainty the principals become anxious. The anxiety is uncomfortable. The quickest and surest way to reduce that anxiety is for the relationship to return once again "to the way things used to be." This is often a ritualized commitment to prior expectations, such as a perfunctory apology, handshake, or embrace, without admitting the new information into the system, which is now available since it gave rise to the disruption. This new information would form the basis for renegotiating the expectations governing the relationship. The relationship remains closed to change, when the parties deal with the uncertainty and anxiety produced by disruption by returning to the original level of sharing expectations without renegotiation — for example, the pledge, "it won't happen again," or the admonition, "don't let it happen again," or the reaffirmation of the way things used to be, "let's be gentlemen" or "I'm sorry, I was wrong, everything is now okay...nothing is changed!"[16,9]

It is during the period of disruption, when the parties are uncertain about their roles and the future of the relationship and are therefore anxious, that the system must be held open if change is to enter. If new information is allowed to enter the

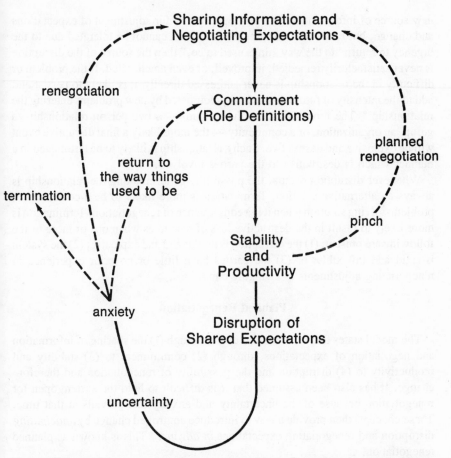

Figure 17-1. Possible sequences of transactions due to disruptions in negotiations.

relationship and is treated in a problem-solving way, it can provide the basis for renegotiating the expectations governing the relationship. The newly renegotiated expectations are therefore more likely to be in line with the current realities of the situation, and once commitment occurs, the period of stability is likely to be more enduring before the next ensuing disruption.

If the parties share this model as a part of their language and their mutual expectations, these concepts are likely to help them by increasing their tolerance for the uncertainty and the accompanying anxiety which surround their relationship while expectations are held open during renegotiation. Through continued use of these concepts, the behavioral skills of the parties also increase, thereby facilitating the renegotiation process.

The theory predicts that disruption without renegotiation leads to an increasing frequency and intensity of disruptions. When each disruption is not treated as a new source of information and a new opportunity for adjustment of expectations and change, but rather as a disagreeable state that cannot be tolerated due to the urgency to return "to the way things used to be," then the source of the disruption is never satisfactorily remedied, improved, or even ameliorated. If the problem or difficulty in the relationship is never addressed directly, it is likely to persist and add to the intensity of future disruptions precipitated by new problems entering the relationship.* The more inflexible the system — a two-person relationship, a group, an organization, or a community — the more likely a final disruptive event will be explosive and destructive. Such a relationship is likely to be terminated in a manner which is destructive to the parties involved.

Whenever disruption occurs, the possibility of terminating the relationship is always an alternative solution. Termination is more likely to be a constructive, problem-solving solution when it is a consequence of renegotiation. Termination is more likely to result in the destructive loss of resources when one or more of the following are present: (1) the disruption is unplanned and explosive; (2) the system is rigid and inflexible; or (3) the parties have little or no prior experience in renegotiating adjustments to changing conditions.

Planned Renegotiation

The model states that relationships cycle through (1) the sharing of information and negotiation of expectations, through (2) commitment to (3) stability and productivity to (4) disruption and the possibility of renegotiation and therefore change. It has also been assumed that it is difficult to hold the system open for renegotiation because of the uncertainty and anxiety that prevails at that time. These concepts then provide a way to introduce controlled change by *anticipating* disruption and renegotiating expectations *in advance*. This is known as planned renegotiation.

Where this simple model of how roles are established and how they change is available to the parties, and where they have skills in sharing their reactions, feelings, and perceptions about their relationship, change can be introduced in a controlled and systematic way through planned renegotiation. This is less stressful than renegotiation under conditions of disruption. Both the model and the concept of planned renegotiation thus become parts of the relationship — so that "whenever I feel a pinch," that pinch is shared and the possibility of renegotiation is raised. A *pinch* is a signal of the possibility of an impending disruption and it describes a sense of loss of freedom within one's current role (see Figure 17-1). The

---

*The intensity of future disruptions is not likely to be increased where problems or difficulties in a relationship are handled by reducing commitment to the relationship. In this case, an apparent "return to the way things used to be" is actually a withdrawal of commitment. Over time such a strategy leads to an atrophied relationship. (In the *Marriage Grid* by Mouton and Blake, this is a 1,1 orientation, e.g., "Home is where I eat, sleep, and keep my things.")

felt loss of freedom may be due to a sense of expanded resources or to subtle constriction of expectations by others. In either case, there is the possibility of resources lost to the system.

Some examples of pinches which raise the possibility of renegotiation are:

—"I think I am now ready to go to New York on a buying trip without you."

— "I find that I am defensive with you, because you judge others so harshly. I don't want you judging me that way."

— "While I will continue to do all the drafting work, I would like to do some engineering work on this project."

— "I think that I somehow have to know all the answers, because no one in this group ever admits that they don't know something. I therefore bluff my way along."

— "We are always talking about how bright we all are, and as a consequence I am becoming more and more cautious about the ideas I choose to share lest they appear but brilliant."

— "I have to begin saying, 'no' to you or you have to stop adding to my workload. I will be unable to meet the commitments I have already made unless something is changed."

— "I like you a lot, and I suddenly realize that I am very hesitant to disagree with you for fear that you will then dislike me."

When the question of renegotiation of expectations is raised "when I feel a pinch," the parties have more *choice* and more control over change. They are subject to fewer negotiations "under fire," and they are less often victims of crises and pressures to return to the way things used to be.

Implications and Discussion

Planned renegotiation is likely to be a successful norm-setting intervention in an organization where there is some prior commitment in an organization development, so that persons are neither so closed that differences are ignored and inappropriately smoothed over, nor so competitive that differences are exploited by subversive rivalry.

On the other hand, people need concepts to guide their behavior. Organization development efforts often involve skill training in interpersonal relations, or process consultation, or prescriptions to do things differently — such as "be open" — with training in interpersonal skills, but without an adequate theoretical framework that provides concepts to guide behavior. The tools of Gestalt therapy help people expand their own awareness of themselves and make more data available to the system. But what to do with data once it becomes more available? The planned renegotiation model supplies a framework for building more productive working relationships with information generated through organization development efforts.

Similarly, participative management systems need more information from all levels of supervision in order to function effectively. But once the information is generated, how is it to be handled? The planned renegotiation model provides a framework for allowing new information to change the system, where such change is agreeable to all parties involved.

The theory underlying the concept of planned renegotiation is clear and simple and straightforward. Theoretical elaborations have been purposedly avoided. It is intended that the concepts become part of the language of organizational life. Persons can be trained in the skills of planned renegotiation. It is important that people learn to detect pinches before disruptions develop. A pinch is felt by an individual, whereas a disruption is experienced by all parties involved in the relationship. It is therefore incumbent upon an individual who feels a pinch also to take responsibility for raising the question of renegotiation with the other(s), rather than asserting that it is someone else's problem or responsibility. At the same time, it is important he understand that when he experiences a pinch, this is going to make him anxious. When a pinch is shared and renegotiation considered, then others become anxious as well. People get anxious both because of the uncertainty which is introduced into the relationship, and because they are never sure whether they will personally be better off after the renegotiation is completed than they were before. When people work with this model, they learn that anxiety becomes controlled and tolerable, when there is a commitment to problem-solving. There remains nevertheless a risk each time the relationship is opened for examination and renegotiation.

In the first few attempts at renegotiation within the model, people are simultaneously working on two problems: (1) trying out a problem-solving model and developing skills and procedures for its use; and (2) working on the pinch that gave rise to the renegotiation. Over time both skills and procedures develop, as does confirmation of the model and its usefulness to the parties involved (or its lack of usefulness).

Based on the assumption that "most people in organizations prefer a fair negotiated settlement to a state of unresolved conflict," Harrison[8] has developed a very sound procedure for changing role relationships. It should be useful to those who would like to try planned renegotiation in a formally structured and specifically programmed way. Harrison calls his procedure "role negotiation." It is a detailed program for exchanging expectations and demands for the behavior of others in terms of what each wants others (a) to do more or do better, (b) to do less, or (c) to remain unchanged. These expectations are written so as to be clearly understood by both sender and receiver. When one person makes a request or demand for changed behavior on the part of another, he must specify a *quid pro quo* he is willing to give in order to get what he wants. The process is complete when an agreement is written which specifies the agreed-upon changes in behavior and makes clear what each party is expected to give in return, including a discussion of possible sanctions for noncompliance. The procedures are clear and simple, if a bit mechanical, and they require a consultant in the early stages to establish the rules and to moderate their use.

There are various other ways organizations might make use of the concept of planned renegotiation. An organization might design a "renegotiating arena," where the principals commit themselves not to leave the field until a satisfactory set of mutual expectations is established.† A skilled third-party consultant might be available to them.[20]

The question is sometimes raised, if planned renegotiation is encouraged, won't this lead to the termination of some relationships that would not otherwise terminate? Yes, it probably will. Where relationships are terminated by choice, this is likely to be an outcome which is more healthy for the individuals and more productive for the organization over the long run, than to retain members who are essentially "captive."

While the theory of how roles are established and changed seems to be interpersonal in focus and appears to concentrate on the modification of behavior in one-to-one situations, the concepts also describe the relation of a person to a group and the relations of all members of a group to one another — e.g., task group, committee, subordinates reporting to one supervisor, family, etc. Relations between groups are also subject to disruption and renegotiation as well — e.g., relations between departments, branch offices, or project teams.**

Rather than a theory of interpersonal affairs, the theory is better described as a description of the establishment and change of *relations* between elements of a social system — persons or groups. The theory is more encompassing than it first might seem; it can include some of the major realities of organizational life, such as the power of economics and legitimate authority and the competition between persons or groups for scarce resources. A subordinate can certainly raise the question of renegotiation with his supervisor, and can help his supervisor learn to use the model. Issues of authority can be subjects of renegotiation. Where individuals or groups are highly competitive, renegotiation can take the form of more open bargaining rather than secretive, and sometimes subversive, rivalry.

While all of us need concepts to guide our behavior, it would seem that the model of how roles are established and changed and the concept of planned renegotiation would be particularly useful for those who frequently enter and work

---

†The method, "Meeting for Two" in Fordyce & Weil (1971, pp. 114-116), is a highly structured session designed to provide the opportunity to renegotiate expectations in a two-person relationship without the benefit of a theoretical model. While a third party is not required, the procedure is so highly structured that the presence of a third person seems almost essential.

**Several persons have reported that this model is also useful for negotiating change in the behavior of a single person (intrapersonal change). Persons have talked to themselves about themselves and held dialogues in a Gestalt fashion between "how I am now" and "how I would like to be," followed by commitment to a new set of expectations, stability, disruption, and renegotiation.

with temporary systems.[1] The more fluid and changing the system, the more important it is to be able to develop means of producing information rapidly which then permits people to appropriately influence one another and to accept appropriate influence. Furthermore, working within this model even within an enduring and established relationship is likely to help a person develop those behavioral skills which are effective in life in temporary systems. These concepts are also probably useful to those who play a mediating role as a third-party consultant to others in conflict.

Summary

This article is based on the assumption that people need concepts to guide their behavior. A clear and simple model of how roles are established and changed is presented — relationships cycle through (1) the sharing of information and the negotiation of expectations, then (2) commitment to a set of expectations, which governs behavior during a period (3) of stability and productivity, when, for the most part you do what I expect of you and I do what you expect of me, until (4) disruption occurs and the possibility of change enters the system. This theory itself is a norm-setting intervention into an organization when it becomes a part of the normative structure, language, and expectations of members of the organization.

The concept of planned renegotiation is derived from this model and represents a procedure by which controlled change can enter an organization, thereby freeing and expanding resources for problem-solving. This enhances an organization's internal flexibility which is one important criterion of organizational effectiveness.[17]

With a statement such as planned renegotiation, people have more choice in their lives and are less likely to be victims "of the way things used to be..."

References

1. Bennis, W.G., and P.E. Slater, *The Temporary Society*, New York: Harper, 1968.
2. Blau, P.M., *Exchange and Power in Social Life*, New York: Wiley, 1967.
3. Blau, P.M., "A Theory of Social Integration," *American Journal of Sociology*, Vol. 65 (1960), pp. 550 – 553.
4. Fordyce, J.K., and R. Weil, *Managing with People: a Manager's Handbook of Organization Development Methods*, Reading, MA: Addison-Wesley, 1971.
5. Glidewell, J.C., "System Linkage and Distress at School," in M.J. Feldman (Ed.), *Studies in Psychotherapy and Behavior Change*, Buffalo, NY: State University of New York at Buffalo, 1971, pp. 25 – 44.
6. Goffman, E., *The Presentation of Self in Everyday Life*, Edinburgh, Scotland: University of Edinburgh, 1956.
7. Goffman, E., *Encounters*, Indianapolis, IN: Bobbs-Merrill, 1961.
8. Harrison, R., "Role Negotiation: A Tough-minded Approach to Team Development," in W.W. Burke and H.A. Hornstein (Eds.), *The Social Technology of Organization Development*, Washington, D.C.: NTL Learning Resources Corporation, 1972.

9. Hermann, C.F., "Some Consequences of Crisis which Limit the Viability of Organizations," *Administrative Science Quarterly*, Vol. 8 (1963), pp. 61 – 82.
10. Homans, G.C., *Social Behavior: Its Elementary Forms*, New York: Harcourt, Brace and World, 1961.
11. Katz, D., and R.L. Kahn, *The Social Psychology of Organizations*, New York: Wiley, 1966.
12. Korchin, S.J., et al., "Visual Discrimination and the Decision Process in Anxiety," *AMA Archives of Neurology and Psychiatry*, Vol. 78 (1957), pp. 424 – 438.
13. Lanzetta, J.T., "Group Behavior under Stress," *Human Relations*, Vol. 8 (1955), pp. 29 – 52.
14. Lewin, K., *Field Theory in Social Science*, D. Cartwright (Ed.), New York: Harper, 1951.
15. Mouton, J.S., and R.R. Blake, *The Marriage Grid*, New York: McGraw-Hill, 1971.
16. Postman, L., and J.S. Bruner, "Perception under Stress," *Psychological Review*, Vol. 55, (1948), pp. 314 – 323.
17. Schein, E.H., *Organizational Psychology*, Englewood Cliffs, NJ: Prentice-Hall, 1965.
18. Sherwood, J.J., An introduction to organization development, *Experimental Publication System*, Washington, D.C.: American Psychological Association, No. 11 (April 1971), Ms. No. 396-1. Also appears in J.W. Pfeiffer and J.E. Jones (Eds.), *1972 Annual Handbook for Group Facilitators*, Iowa City, IA: University Associates Press, 1972.
19. Thibaut, J.W., and H.H. Kelley, *Social Psychology of Groups*, New York: Wiley, 1959.
20. Walton, R.E., *Interpersonal Peacemaking: Confrontations and Third Party Consultation*, Reading, MA: Addison-Wesley, 1969.

John J. Sherwood is professor of administrative science in the Krannert Graduate School of Management, Purdue University.
John C. Glidewell is professor of education in the Department of Education, University of Chicago.

Primary Target for Change: The Manager or the Organization?

W. Warner Burke
Warren H. Schmidt

This article's purpose is to present a way of comparing two basic approaches to the improvement of managerial effectiveness within an organization: (1) management development — the educational development of *individual* managers; and (2) organization development (OD) — the development of the *organizational* units of people. During the past 20 years, the concept of "management development" has received wide acceptance. Management development involves a variety of activities — such things as training, counseling, job rotation, coaching, sabbatical leaves, and career planning. In this article we are discussing management development primarily as an educational and training endeavor. Organization development is a concept of recent origin — but has already received significant interest and attention.

Underlying both approaches is the assumption that the most effective manager or specialist is a learning person — one who is capable of continually improving his insight, knowledge, and skill. A beginning question might be: Under what conditions can he best learn the information, concepts, or skills he needs in order to be most effective in his job? What can the manager (or staff specialist) best learn by being *removed* from the job context — away from the problems and people making up his world of work? What can the manager (or staff specialist) best learn *in association with* his work colleagues — by grappling with the same problems and people he must deal with day after day?

Work units — task forces, departments, divisions — must continually confront questions which parallel those asked by an individual manager or staff specialist: Under what conditions can we best learn the information and skills required in order to be an effective working unit? How can we as a collection of individuals learn to work together most effectively as a team — to learn to use the full resources we represent, to learn to communicate with one another more accurately, to learn to make team decisions which lead to individual commitment and responsibility? What can we as a team best learn by spending a weekend together away from the job — or should be attempt to learn team skills during the week "on the job"? How can our work unit relate most effectively to other work units to achieve overall organization goals most efficiently?

To date, the development of managers has typically been done on an individual basis. For example, executives leave their jobs to attend a management seminar or a sensitivity-training laboratory that might last a few days or two weeks; staff specialists attend seminars or workshops in their area of expertise; managers sign up for extension courses or night school.

What happens as a result? Often some individual change occurs. People learn to communicate more effectively, or some improvement in decision making is realized. Frequently, however, others respond to these changes with questions like, "What has happened to this guy, anyway?" Sometimes, subordinates will say to one another, "We learned to live with this boss of ours the way he was; now, since his return from this management training program, he expects us to adjust to his new way of doing things. Well, I guess we'll just have to straighten him out!"

In other words, when persons gain some new insights into their behavior, they may find it difficult to use these new behaviors on the job. They may fear that people around them "won't understand"; so it's easier to continue in old ways to conform to expectations. As Campbell and Dunnette[1] have pointed out in their review of the research literature concerning the effects of T-group training, individual change may occur as a result of the training, but there is little evidence to support the contention that the training facilitates organization change. Findings like this may account for the current notion of "training the system" in addition to training the individual.

If an individual's colleagues understand how he wants to change, they can support his efforts, and the training is put into action with more discernible benefits to the organization. For individuals to make personal changes on the job, there must be an organizational climate which supports these changes. Otherwise, training the individual will have little or no impact on the organization. "Training the system" to support needed individual change is a basic part of organization development.

Beyond increasing the impact of training on individuals, however, "training the system" involves building more effective interpersonal relationships among members of a working unit. For example, the team may become a more efficient, responsive, flexible, and creative part of the organization. This approach — that is, team building — lies at the heart of organization development, but organizational effectiveness requires more than smooth-functioning teams. In this next section we shall explore the broader meaning of organization development.

A Definition of Organization Development (OD)

Using knowledge and techniques from the behavioral sciences, organization development (OD) is a *process* which attempts to increase organizational effectiveness by integrating individual desires for growth and and development with organizational goals. Typically, this process is a planned change effort which involves a total system over a period of time, and these change efforts are related to the organization's mission. Key terms in this rather broad definition are: *process, planned change, total system,* and *organizational mission.*

While an OD project involves planning deliberate changes, it is not a "program" or "project" as such but rather a process. The terms program or project imply that the effort is limited, especially in a temporal sense. While OD has a beginning, it does not necessarily have an ending. It is a *continuing process.* This process may involve (1) certain projects, for example, planning and implementing a change in the organization's structure, or (2) specific programs such as a training conference in appraisal interviewing. But the overall effort consists of *a continuing attempt to develop better procedures and a supporting climate for dealing with organizational problems.*

Technological change in industry is usually *planned* in great detail and implemented with considerable care to deal with the consequences of the change. Organizational change — for example, modifying some part of the organization's structure or implementing a new work process for people — on the other hand, is often not as deliberately planned. These kinds of changes, and particularly the consequences of them, may be planned in part, but more often than not they occur more haphazardly than technological changes do. Planning, implementing, and evaluating these organizational changes is OD. Although it may be implied in the statements above, OD is not exclusively involved in changes which are non-technological in nature. For example, when a new computer is introduced in the organization, developing a strategy for handling the consequences of this change with respect to such things as how people will now relate to each other or make decisions is a part of OD.

OD involves a *total system.* When the term "total system" is used, we probably think of the total organization. Indeed OD can and, to be most effective, probably should, encompass an entire corporation, university, or governmental agency. But a "total system" does not have to mean every subpart of the organization. Generally speaking, a system is a relatively autonomous unit which has the responsibility for, and performs the basic requirement of, a specific work process. Taken at the extremes, a system may include only three persons who among them assemble a transistor radio, or the thousands of people who constitute AT&T or the University of California. Commonly, however, OD involves such systems as a particular plant within a corporation, a major division of a diversified industry, the "Department of Social Services" of a state government, or the University of California at Los Angeles.

For best results, OD must take a "systems" approach because the process not only promotes such activities as collaboration, the sharing of power, and the building of interpersonal trust, but has as its core the planning and implementing of change. And, as most students of change know, any change involving a part of a system affects — either directly or indirectly — all other parts of the system. By the same token, a change within System A affects System B, provided the two systems have any reason to be interdependent.

The last term in our rather broad definition of OD is *organizational mission*. Unless OD efforts are congruent with whatever the organization is trying to accomplish, the process is likely to be irrelevant and a waste of time and money. If the organization's mission is to produce and sell gadgets, then OD concentrates on how the organization can produce more gadgets of a high quality by more fully utilizing the human resources available to the organization. This last phrase, "by more fully utilizing the human resources...," has not been mentioned earlier and may not seem directly relevant to organizational mission; however, a fundamental effort in OD is to integrate individual needs and goals with the goals of the organization. Thus, *the way* the organization can realize greater productivity and generally be more effective in reaching its goals is to make maximum use of its human resources. Furthermore, the integration of individual and organizational goals can be facilitated when the organization pays strict attention to the talents of its personnel by creating conditions whereby a person can feel relatively free to actualize his known abilities as well as his unknown potential.

OD, then concentrates on the development of people in such a way that development of the organization is insured and vice versa.

The basic assumption underlying these statements is that if a work climate is one in which a person can utilize his talents, feel responsibility for what he does, and be appropriately rewarded for his efforts, his individual needs and goals are likely to be more congruent with the organization's goals. This assumption and the statements above are not original with us. In part, they paraphrase McGregor's Theory Y of management, which underlies a substantial portion of OD.

A Comparison of Management Development and OD

The concept and scope of OD can be more sharply defined by comparing it with the more traditional forms of management development along several critical dimensions:

— Typical goals
— Reasons for and difficulties in initiating management development or OD
— Strategies and interventions for producing change
— Time frame
— Staff requirements
— Common problems and criticisms

Each of these dimensions will now be discussed in order to identify similarities and differences between management development and OD. A summary of these comparisons is presented in Table 18-1.

Typical Goals. Although management development and OD efforts are concerned with such issues as communication, motivation, and coordination, the goals of these two strategies are stated quite differently. For example, one large U.S. corporation's management development program has as its objectives the following:

— To transmit the philosophy and values of the company as expressed through a review of the organization's principles, policies, and practices.
— To provide practice in those management skills which will improve organizational performance and cooperation.
— To increase ability to plan, coordinate, measure, and control the efforts of company units.
— To improve skills in problem analysis and decision making.
— To develop a greater awareness of the company's functional and divisional organizations and their interrelationships.

These objectives cover all three of the areas that most management development programs stress: knowledge, skill, and attitudes; and, as can be seen, the emphasis is on the individual manager.

When the *organization* "goes to school," however, the goals are likely to be stated as follows:

1. To create an open, problem-solving climate throughout the organization.
2. To supplement authority associated with role or status with authority of knowledge and competence.
3. To locate decision-making and problem solving responsibilities as close to the information sources as possible.
4. To build trust among individuals and groups throughout the organization.
5. To make competition more relevant to work goals and to maximize collaborative efforts.
6. To develop a reward system which supports achievement of the organization's mission as well as individual efforts toward personal development and achievement.
7. To have organizational objectives "owned" by the entire work force.
8. To help managers to manage according to relevant needs and objectives rather than according to "past practices."
9. To increase self-control and self-direction for people within the organization.
10. To develop a process for continuing organizational self-renewal.[2]

Table 18-1
A Comparison of Management Development and Organization Development

Category/Dimension	Management Development	Organization Development
Typical Goals	Teach manager new skills Expand manager's conceptual understanding Upgrade and/or update manager's present knowledge and skills	Facilitate problem-solving on the job Plan and implement changes more systematically Increase sense of "ownership" of organization objectives throughout work force Create conditions where conflict is managed rather than handled indirectly Create conditions so that decisions are made on the basis of competence rather than organizational role
Reasons for Initiating	Something wrong with the manager Managers do not know company policy or philosophy Managers do not have a needed skill	Something wrong with the system Problems with a recent merger Present organization structure and roles within it are not efficient Competition hurting more than helping Managers do not understand company policy or philosophy
Difficulties in Initiating	Individual resistance and feelings of threat Making training relevant	High risk Support from many persons, especially top management, is needed Strong need for long-term commitment to change efforts

(Table continued on next page)

Table 18-1 (continued)
A Comparison of Management Development and
Organization Development

Category/Dimension	Management Development	Organization Development
Strategies and Interventions for Producing Change	Send manager to some educational program Job rotation of managers Courses and/or conferences Specialized training "packages" Reading books and/or articles	Treatment is usually on the job; learning while problem-solving and solving problems while learning Team building Techno-structural intervention Action research Certain training programs Survey feedback Intergroup interfaces for problem-solving
Time Frame	Short, intense	Prolonged
Staff Requirements	Teacher/trainer Program manager Designer of training programs	Diagnostician Catalyst/facilitator Consultant/helper Knowledge and skill in planned change Experience in laboratory training
Common Problems and Criticisms	Lack of continuity, follow-up, reinforcement on the job to transfer of learning Usually middle managers only Dependence on experts Lip service given but little transfer Difficult to make training relevant to manager's everyday problems	May become "another program" Top management must be perceived as supportive Requires considerable risk-taking on the part of management

From these two examples of goals, it can be seen that the emphasis in management development is different from that of OD. Management development strives toward developing managers who will be able to contribute more to the organization, and OD attempts to create conditions in which the manager can make these contributions. Even though this latter statement points out an obvious difference of emphasis, it also states that the two areas of development have objectives which dovetail with one another. Furthermore, both are attempts at improving the management of an organization and, at times, both may concentrate on changing the managerial strategy in the organization. The point is that while both areas of development have different objectives, these two sets of goals are not incompatible but rather complementary.

Reasons for and Difficulties in Initiating Management Development or OD. A common reason for beginning a program in management development is that top management or the personnel department has determined that some inadequacy exists or improvement is needed for individual managers. For example, new supervisors may need to learn something about "handling people." Or, staff personnel who have moved to a line position may know very little about the basic principles of management. Or, several managers may lack some particular skill, for example, interviewing, developing budgets, and so on. Such inadequacies or needs clearly suggest training programs for the individuals to increase their competence in their managerial positions.

Participating in a training program, by definition, provides the opportunity for individual as well as organizational change. Whenever this type of change interrupts a manager's routine, he may respond with resistance. When a boss or someone from personnel suggests to a manager that he might like to attend a conference or take a course, it is not uncommon for him to feel threatened, wondering whether he is doing a poor job. (Why else would he be "asked" to go to some program?)

Often, resistance can be reduced if the potential participant somehow becomes involved in deciding which programs will be offered. As one approach toward involvement, some personnel departments spend considerable time interviewing a cross section of managers to determine which kinds of training programs should be planned.

The reasons for starting OD are more varied than those for management development. The problems which call for OD are more broadly based than is a single individual's inadequacy. Some typical reasons for initiating OD are as follows: (1) lack of cooperation between two departments or divisions, for example, manufacturing and sales, or finance and research, or production and maintenance; (2) ambiguous lines of responsibility and authority as a result of a merger; (3) perennial labor–management disputes; (4) dull and ineffective staff meetings; or (5) a project team or task force which needs some work on their internal interpersonal relationships.

Even though a definite need for some OD effort may be called for, getting started may prove difficult. To decide on OD is to agree to a process which not only requires total system involvement but commitment to a long-term renewal effort as well. Although a part of OD may involve a certain project which has a beginning and an ending, it is not a one-shot, ad hoc program geared toward accomplishing a single task. OD is, rather, an all-out effort toward more effective organizational functioning which involves all members. As such, the risk is greater than it is for management development.

Strategies and Interventions for Producing Change. In recent years, we have witnessed a rapid increase in the kinds of activities that can be used in management development or OD. Some can be used in both management development and OD; others are primarily suited to either management development or OD.

Typical activities in management development include: (1) in-company workshops and special conferences; (2) specialized training, often outside the organization, including skill training, such as studying public speaking or attending a Managerial Grid seminar, and other more cognitive training, such as attending a seminar at a university; (3) correspondence courses; (4) university programs which typically offer a master's degree; and, of late, (5) the sabbatical (some organizations recently have been granting a sabbatical year during which the person either teaches at some college or university, conducts a research project, writes, or does some combination of all these).

Change strategies in management development, then, involve having the manager participate in one of these educational activities. Efforts are made to free him from job pressures for a specified period of time. He can then concentrate solely on up-grading his knowledge and skills. Another common strategy is job rotation: giving the rising manager a chance to get the feel of various aspects of the organizational system.

In OD efforts, interventions for change take a variety of forms. In some instances, the strategy might be a training intervention for individual managers such as a sensitivity training laboratory. More typically, however, the strategy is to deal with problems *on the job*. There is a deliberate attempt to learn while in the process of solving problems and to solve problems while in the process of learning. A case example of this process follows:

"Recently, a vice president in a large U.S. corporation was having trouble with his division managers' occasionally responding inappropriately to his memos. The vice president had the choice of (a) sending his subordinates to a communications course, (b) attending a communications course himself, (c) both (a) and (b), (d) trying to live with the problem, or (e) working on the problem directly. He chose the last alternative. An external OD consultant and an internal consultant from the Employee Relations Division worked on the problem with the vice president in a team development session. They designed a work session to be held from 9:00 a.m. to lunch on a regular work day in the staff meeting room. Before the meeting, several memos from the vice president to the division managers were selected and prepared on a glass slide which could then be shown on a screen via a projector. With the vice president and consultants present, all division managers considered several of the memos according to a certain procedure. After reading the memo on the screen, they were asked three questions: (1) What do you think the message says? (2) What priority would you give to the message: (a) High, take care of the matter immediately, (b) Medium, take care of the matter relatively soon, or (c) Low, take care of it when I can get to it. (3) What action would you take?

After everyone responded to the three questions by writing their answers, each manager was asked to read his response to the total group. Considerable differences occurred among the managers. Later, the vice president explained what he meant the memo to say, what priority he desired, and what action he wanted. As might be expected, a number of misunderstandings were corrected and learning resulted, learning on both the vice president's part as well as the division managers'.

An interesting side effect resulted later in time; the vice president's memos decreased in number by 40 percent. Also, after a year of collecting relevant data, a considerable monetary savings amounting to approximately $20,000 was realized as a result of changes in communications procedure."[3]

In organization development, the underlying strategy is to plan and develop a process which will bring about change in the organization's culture. A fundamental change effort in OD, then, is to change group norms. For example, if a group norm is such that competitive behavior on the part of individuals is expected and implicitly rewarded, but the organization's effort is hurt as a result, then an OD strategy is to develop an intervention which will help the group to change this competitive norm to one that is more collaborative — provided individuals will be rewarded appropriately for this change in behavior.

Referring again to the case study above, a norm concerning interpersonal communication was changed as a result of this particular team development session. Prior to the session, there was an implicit norm between the subordinates and the vice president that few of the subordinates after receiving a memo from the VP communicated with him directly to question or seek clarification of the memo even when the message might have been ambiguous. During the months following the team development session, the VP's memos decreased in number. Further exploration (by interviews) as to why showed that more communication between the VP and his subordinates was now being conducted via the telephone and in face-to-face dialogue. Thus, the norm of one-way-communication was modified such that a norm of two-way communication began to develop.

This case not only represents the kinds of results that are possible from team development sessions like this one, it illustrates one type of OD intervention as well. Representative of the range of interventions in the OD arena are the following: (1) team building (or team development), which may include off-site meetings of a training or problem-solving nature as well as long-range planning, (2) techno-structural intervention, such as a confrontation meeting[4] or a change in the organization chart, (3) action research,[5] (4) specific training programs, such as laboratory training,[6] or specific skill training, like the programs in decision making and problem solving by Kepner-Tregoe, (5) survey feedback,[7] and (6) intergroup or interdepartmental interfaces for training and/or problem solving.[8]

To summarize, the strategy for change in management devleopment is to improve the individual manager's knowledge and skill and, in some cases, to modify his attitudes. Typical interventions are those of an educational nature represented by courses, conferences, seminars, and the like. The strategy for change in OD is to develop a process which will help the organization to diagnose its problems, plan ways to solve them, and implement these plans. Stated somewhat differently, the strategy is to change the organization's culture from one of dealing with problems "as we have always done" to a culture that (1) takes full advantage of the human resources the organization has available, and (2) allows for a process to develop which will insure that the organization can plan and implement needed change at all levels rather than having to adjust to change that is already in process.

Time Frame. Due to the nature of management development, the time frame, with respect to the manager's degree of involvement, is relatively brief. The longest time span would probably be a university master's or doctoral program which covers anywhere from 12 to 36 months. The shortest might be a one- or two-hour session where managers hear a speaker from some graduate school of business or from some other industrial organization.

Like any other kind of activity, OD has a beginning, but, ideally, there is no end, since the process of OD is continuing one. There is a time frame, however, regarding the use of outside consultants, and, to some extent, the same holds for internal consultants. At the outset, an organization's use of consultants is usually quite heavy, with a tapering off as progress is made. After a time, external OD consultants work themselves out of a job by helping to develop personnel within the organization who can perform many of the services that they do early in the relationship. Subsequently, an organization may want to retain the external consultant's services periodically to check matters and to receive help on special concerns or projects.

OD, then, is continuous in the sense that the organization strives to renew itself as times, requirements, and people change. This renewing process means that the organization is able to change social and technical relationships as it becomes necessary without waiting for a crisis. Ultimately, the organization functions in such a way that these internal changes are systematic rather than haphazard.

Staff Requirements. The critical factors affecting the success of any program in management development are the design and implementation of the learning experience. It is essential that the training staff have both considerable skill in planning and conducting a training session and also a working understanding of the dynamics of human learning. Managers of programs in management development may have these abilities and knowledge themselves, they may hire skilled staff, they may engage outside instructors, or they may combine all of these possibilities in their training efforts.

Thus, an important — perhaps the critical — capability which a management development staff must possess is that of skill and knowledge in the educational process.[9] This is not the only capability required, however. Today, persons in management development are being called on for such things as career development (helping managers to plan their careers more systematically) and managerial counseling (helping managers to deal with some of the problems they face in supervising subordinates). In fact, the management development function in many organizations is expanding to such an extent that the staff is beginning to work in the broader area of organization development. Let us now consider the staff requirements for this organizational function.

Persons who are called "OD practitioners," or "internal consultants," or "change agents," and who perform the staff functions of OD do not have a university degree in organization development. Their formal education has most likely been in a variety of fields, but the behavioral sciences are probably predominant. They have organizational backgrounds in such areas as management development, personnel, industrial relations, personnel research, operations research, and manpower development. The common denominator with respect to background is commonly in the "people" area, whether it be training people, studying them, or planning for their utilization in the organization.

At least five general areas of competence should be represented on an OD staff:

1. *The ability to diagnose accurately problems of an organization nature,* such as the appropriateness of various organizational structures for different tasks. To be an effective diagnostician in this area requires a thorough understanding of the consequences of different structures like a pyramidal structure, the matrix principle of organization, decentralization, team management, temporary systems, and so on. The OD practitioner should also be competent in diagnosing human problems within the organization, especially in the areas of small group behavior, interpersonal relationships, and intergroup competitiveness.

2. *The ability to function as facilitator and/or catalyst within the organization.* This ability reflects itself in interventions which are appropriate, timely, and facilitating. Interventions may take the form of suggesting to a manager how he might design his next staff meeting or helping to plan the strategy for a major change in the reward system. An OD practitioner can also facilitate team building by helping the team: (a) to diagnose its blocks for more effective work, (b) to improve interpersonal relationships, (c) to make long-range plans, set goals, and perform related activities. There are, of course, other catalytic and facilitating functions which the OD practitioner can and should implement. These examples are not exhaustive; they are intended to provide only a general idea of the various activities.

3. *Understanding and skill in the consultative process.* A substantial portion of an OD practitioner's activity is to give help to other prople. Being able to render help effectively to others is not easy. The successful OD consultant should (a) be able to work in such a way that he is as nonthreatening and nonjudgmental toward the client as possible, (b) focus on a joint exploration of the problem area with his client, and (c) be able to assess his client's readiness and capacity for change.

4. *An understanding of the dynamics and realities of planned change.* Bennis[10] has pointed out that "...adaptability to change becomes increasingly the

most important single determinant of survival," Although at this point
Bennis was talking about American life in general, he later stresses that this
ability to adapt to change is just as critical and relevant for organizations in
particular. If Bennis is correct in this proclamation, and we believe that he is,
it behooves modern organizations to develop resources which will enable
them to respond to change not only by adapting but also by learning to *plan*
needed change before the onset of crises. The most effective way to adapt to
change is to plan for it. It is a matter of learning to control change and not
being controlled by it. The organization can facilitate this adaptability-to-
change process by having access to people who are knowledgeable in the
literature of planned change[11] and who also know how to apply this knowledge. The OD practitioner, or organizational change agent, plays a key roll in
this planning and adapting process. He is the educator and the facilitator in
the planning of change.

The OD practitioner is not an advocate of change for the sake of change.
He helps the manager in the organization to diagnose the problems he faces to
see if change is needed. If change is needed, he helps the manager and
relevant others plan for the changes in such a way that the least amount of
resistance will develop. He continues to help the manager during the changing period, to identify and diagnose the causes of resistance and to plan ways
of working with the resistance, whether it be to try to overcome the resistance
or to accept it and not push for change if it makes sense not to do so. It could
be that what a manager may learn in the process is that change in a certain area
is really not called for after all.

In effect, the OD practitioner should be (a) knowledgeable about planned
change and the effects thereof, (b) skillful in applying this knowledge, and
(c) capable of adapting to resistance to change.

5. *Skill and knowledge in applied behavioral science in general, and reasonable competence in experienced-based learning or laboratory training in
particular.* Since OD is a process of applying behavioral science knowledge,
it is important that the OD practitioner have some theoretical background and
research knowledge about behavioral science. Being competent in the particular area of experienced-based learning is highly relevant because many of
the interventions a practitioner makes in OD are based on principles derived
from laboratory training. Interventions in OD commonly serve a dual purpose: (a) They help a person or group solve a problem, and (b) they illustrate a
procedure by which a person or group can learn to solve problems more
efficiently in the future.

The OD practitioner will find that improving his skill and knowledge in
experienced-based learning will help him to have a better understanding of
his own strengths and limitations, so that he can more effectively use himself
as an instrument of change.

In summarizing this section on the five general areas of competence for an OD practitioner, it can be seen from the space devoted to each that effective work in OD requires a wider range of skills and knowledge than is required for the practitioner in management development. This is not to say necessarily that one activity is more important than the other. What we mean to imply is that the field of OD is complex and diversified, and is difficult for any one person to be highly competent in all of its aspects.

Common Problems and Criticisms. As with most training programs, the major problem in management development is transferring learning to the job situation. In training programs, it is always difficult to create conditions similar to those faced on the job. In more technical areas this is often easier than in areas of human behavior. Most training programs teach general principles rather than specifics — making transfer difficult for many participating managers.

Even if the program does include elements of learning that are easily transferable, there is also the problem of follow-up and reinforcement. All too often a manager will attend a program, learn something new about management, return to his job, and never try to apply it. Or, if he tries to put into practice what he has learned, he is frequently faced with questioning and lack of support from his boss and/or subordinates.

Other problems in managment development include (1) a heavy dependence on a small number of outside "experts" with no expertise being developed within the organization; (2) the paying of lip service to management development with little, if any, actual support from top management (often revealed in the rapid abandonment of training when financial conditions worsen); and (3) the restricting of participation in management development programs, the majority of attendees being from middle management. Little attention is paid to the development of first line supervisors or top management. Some organizations still assume that when a person has reached a certain position, he no longer requires any development as a manager. (Fortunately, the number of such organizations is shrinking.)

One other criticism of management development programs is that in the design, planners rarely incorporate plans for continuity of the program elements. Many programs represent a smorgasbord of content sessions. On one day of a program, Professor X from Ivy U. speaks on Subject A. The remainder of the day is spent on Case B, which has nothing to do with Professor X's Subject A, and so it goes throughout the week or the two weeks. Seldom do these programs have a central theme.

There are just as many, if not more, problems in OD as in management development. Currently, OD faces the problem of being seen as "just another program," or "it is only a passing fad." In fact, in some organizations with which we are familiar, OD is really nothing more than a new name for sensitivity training or management development. As with any new area of professional activity, OD (less than ten years old as an approach to organizational change) suffers the growing pains of being seen as something which is only temporary.

Since it is important that top management give support to any OD effort, a pitfall is that top management may give lip service "support" only, without fully understanding the consequences. Support for change efforts from managers at all levels in the organization is critical to the success of OD. Better yet is for all relevant levels of management to be involved in any change process.

Related to this issue of support is the matter of risk-taking. OD typically involves change of one kind or the other, and managers must take some risks if they are to be involved in the process. For example, when two departments in an organization are having difficulty with one another, the conflict is often handled by bucking the problem "upstairs" for some superior to resolve, or the two department heads get together to negotiate and reach some compromise. In OD, an interdepartmental conflict, which concerns many persons in both departments and not the department heads only, is frequently managed by arranging what is sometimes called an interface problem-solving session. This is a session which involves as many of the persons who are relevant to the conflict as possible. Briefly, the two departmental groups gather to (the events may not occur in exactly the order described here) (1) explain to one another their view of the conflict, (2) describe to the other group what they *think* their (the other group's) view of the problem is, and (3) work together in small groups (with the groups being composed of individuals from both departments) to develop ways in which the conflict can be managed and, if possible, resolved. More managerial risk is involved when conflict is handled in this manner. Responsibility and authority for managing the conflict is not exclusively in the hands of the two department heads nor is the conflict exclusively up to them to resolve. The advantage of sharing the responsibility and authority for managing the conflict is that with the greater involvement of departmental personnel participating together in confronting the problems, the commitment to implementing plans for resolving the conflict will be considerably greater than if only the superiors dealt with the problems.

Sharing responsibility is not too risky for most managers, but when this is coupled with sharing of authority as well, managers tend to view the process as one of considerable risk. The payoff in such risk-taking is often unclear to managers. A basic problem facing the OD practitioner, then, is to help the manager understand the potential advantages if he takes an "OD approach" to problem solving. Futhermore, the OD practitioner must be willing to counsel, challenge, and support his client throughout the entire effort.

To summarize, we can say that the problems and criticism of management development programs are familiar. Typical problem areas are (1) difficulty in transferring the program learning to the job, (2) lack of systematic follow-up, and (3) need for organizational support, particularly from top management. A basic problem confronting OD is that it is not well known. Naturally, managers are reluctant to become involved in something that requires change and implies a continuing process if it seems strange and unfamiliar.

Summary and Conclusions

We began this article by asking some questions. We would like to conclude by posing questions again and by responding to each.

For the organization which desires maximum effectiveness in its functioning and output, which will help most, management development or OD? If our bias regarding this question has not been apparent in the paper thus far, let us now make it clear. We do not believe that this question can be answered with an either/or response. The effective organization must have both management development and OD. In an attempt to clarify differences and issues, we have chosen the method of comparing management development and OD. While we have found this method useful, the method should not dictate the message. We contend that management development and OD are not incompatible processes in an organization. The two are not only highly compatible, but, more importantly, they are complementary. Our view is that management development is an arm of OD; it is in practice a slice of the OD pie. But each slice of the pie is different. While one slice is management development, another is techno-structural interventions, and another is survey feedback, and so on. Management development is the educative slice.

To be more specific about our belief in the complementary nature of management development and OD: The first step in any OD process is data gathering and diagnosis, the second step is intervention. (Technically speaking, the distinction may not be so clear. When a person enters a system to gather data, an intervention is being made in the process.) Suppose that in the diagnostic phase we find the following problem: "We have to make a significant number of decisions in groups, and our managers and staff people seem to know very little about group decision-making." An appropriate intervention in this case might be that of calling on our management development staff to develop a training program in group decision making.

Now to return to our bias again. Stated somewhat differently, but still holding to our complementary notion, we maintain that management development programs should *respond* to diagnosed needs in the organization and not establish programs for the sake of maintaining a management development program. This is not to say that needed OD interventions cannot derive from some management development program. What we are saying is that most often the appropriate OD intervention, whether it be training or something else, is one that originates from a diagnosis of current and relevant data.

Although the Grid approach to OD[12] combines management development and OD in a complementary manner, Blake and Mouton's bias with respect to this combination is somewhat different. Their approach to OD is a highly educative and sequential one. The beginning phase is that of management development, especially in the area of developing, and, possibly, changing one's managerial style. Their diagnosis assumes that managerial styles in the organization should be considered initially. Other phases in Grid OD, such as teamwork development and intergroup development, follow, but management development is first on the list.

How does one decide whether his organization needs OD? A manager may be able to answer this question by reflecting on his responses to some more specific questions. Do people in his organization feel that they are doing meaningful work and their abilities are being fully utilized? Are meetings of committees, task forces, staffs, and other groups productive, interesting, and considered a good use of one's time? Do young persons who have recently graduated from college or obtained an MBA tend to stay with the organization? Does the competition that may exist between organizational departments lead to higher efficiency for the overall organization? There are other questions which could be raised. Asking questions is the easy part. If our hypothetical manager's answers to these questions tend to be "no," then we can conclude that OD would be valuable for his organization. This is not to say that OD is a cure for all organizational ills. When an organization is deeply immersed in OD, problems continue to arise and crises may develop overnight. What OD does provide is a process for handling these problems that leads to (1) the maximum use of human resources, (2) the learning of procedures for diagnosing causes of problems and innovative ways of dealing with them, and (3) a greater integration of individual needs with organizational goals.

Our attempt in this concluding section has been to respond to the two questions raised. In so doing, we have also been responding to the original question posed in the title of this paper, "What should be the target for change?" In our opinion, the two processes, management development and OD, are inextricable related or, at least, they should be. In the OD process, problems will undoubtedly arise which a management development program can handle. During a management development program, on the other hand, a member of the organization may see the need for individual as well as organizational change. The OD process should be such that these changes, provided they are needed, will be supported and implemented. And so it goes.

References

1. J.P. Campbell and M.D. Dunnette, "Effectiveness of T-Group Experiences in Managerial Training and Development, " *Psychological Bulletin*, Vol. 70 (1968), pp. 73–104.
2. Taken from "What is OD?," NTL Institute *News and Reports*, Vol. 2, No. 3 (June 1968).
3. From a paper by J.B. Harvey and C.R. Boettger to be published in a future issue of the *Journal of Applied Behavioral Science*. Reprinted by permission of the authors.
4. This type of intervention is explained in an article by Richard Beckhard, "The Confrontation Meeting," *Harvard Business Review*, Vol. 45, No. 2 (March-April 1967), pp. 149–155.

5. A fairly formal discussion of this technique may be found in the following article: I. Chein, S. Cook, and J. Harding, "The Field of Action Research," *American Psychologist*, Vol. 3 (1948), pp. 43–50. Succinctly, action research is "research" undertaken to solve a problem for a client. At the simplest level, it involves the gathering of data from the client, feeding it back for understanding and ownership, and then helping the client to take action in order to solve the problems identified in the initial data collection phase.

6. A discussion of the relationship between laboratory training and organization change may be found in Chapter 10, "Principles and Strategies in the Use of Laboratory Training for Improving Social Systems," in E.H. Schein and W.G. Bennis, *Personal and Organizational Change through Group Methods: The Laboratory Approach*, New York: Wiley, 1965.

7. An explanation of this type of intervention may be found in M.B. Miles, H.A. Hornstein, P.H. Calder, D.M. Callahan, and R.S. Schiavo, "Data Feedback and Organization Change," in W.G. Bennis and R. Chin (Eds.), *The Planning of Change*, rev. ed., New York: Holt, Rinehart and Winston, 1968. See also F.C. Mann, "Studying and Creating Change: A Means to Understanding Social Organization," in C.M. Arensberg et al. (Eds.), *Research in Industrial Human Relations*, New York: Harper & Row, 1957.

8. Pertinent references for this type of activity are as follows: R.R. Blake, H.A. Shepard, and J.S. Mouton, *Managing Intergroup Conflict in Industry*, Houston, TX: Gulf Publishing Co., 1964; R.R. Blake, J.S. Mouton, and R.L. Sloma, "The Union-Management Intergroup Laboratory," *Journal of Applied Behavioral Science*, Vol. 1, No. 1 (1965), pp. 25-47; H.S. Shepard, "Changing Interpersonal and Intergroup Relationships in Organizations," in J. March (Ed.), *Handbook of Organizations*, Chicago: Rand McNally, 1967.

9. A description of trainer characteristics may be found in G.L. Lippitt and L.E. This, "Is Training a Profession?" *Journal of the American Society of Training Directors*, Vol. 14, No. 2 (1960).

10. W.G. Bennis, *Changing Organizations*, New York: McGraw-Hill, 1966, p. 19.

11. Two of the most important books in this area are R. Lippitt, J. Watson, and B. Westley, *The Dynamics of Planned Change*, New York: Harcourt, Brace & World, 1958; and W.G. Bennis, K. Benne, and R. Chin, *The Planning of Change*, rev. ed., New York: Holt, Rinehart and Winston, 1964.

12. R.R. Blake and J.S. Mouton, *Corporate Excellence through Grid Organization Development*, Houston, TX: Gulf Publishing Co., 1968.

W. Warner Burke is professor and chairperson of the Department of Management, Clark University.

Warren H. Schmidt is assistant dean and director of Continuing Education, Graduate School of Business Administration, University of California at Los Angeles.

Disengagement and Closure

In our original thinking, and in the model we propose, there are two different phases. One is disengagement, and the other is closure. Little has been written which is specifically labeled disengagement. The phase does exist, but is generally combined with closure in most writing. We feel disengagement should be discussed as a separate phase and it is hoped that writers and practitioners will give more consideration to making it a distinct phase.

Disengagement

During disengagement, the relationships between the client and the consultant begin to change. The purpose of disengagement, as the name implies, is to start the process in which the consultant leaves the situation. At this point in the relationship, the problem or purpose of the consultation will have been resolved or well on its way to solution. It is often a tentative phase where the consultant might have to recycle back to response, and even to diagnosis. Disengagement is characterized by a period of testing whether or not the client and the client system are able to function in the new situation caused by the response, and whether they can cope with the new relationships which have emerged.

An analogy, although a harsh one, is to compare disengagement to the practice of certain colonial powers in the past half century as they granted freedom to colonies. In some cases, the granting of freedom (i.e., the allowance for new behavior) was done with too little preparation and only the briefest time for the novice nationals to become acquainted with their new system. Often, the result of this abrupt transition was civil war and chaos during ruthless struggles for power, as factions competed to fill the gap left by the departing colonial power.

The departure of the consultant may not produce such dramatic and world shattering results, but it certainly can create a power vacuum, the need for new, untried behaviors and development of fresh emerging relationships.

An abrupt departure by the consultant can be quite threatening to the client — an unnecessary distraction sure to impact the project's effectiveness. Fortunately, it is possible to alleviate this problem. The departure of the consultant can be carefully planned and recognized by both the client and the consultant. The reduced involvement by the consultant in the life of the client system — at least for this particular assignment — can be envolved.

Unfortunately, the consultant who wishes just to emphasize the need for his or her services can easily demonstrate this need by departing in an unplanned and precipitous manner. The consultant might even tell the client that it is "for his or her own good," or "that it's time for the client to stand on his or her own feet." The result can be an insecure client, unsure, and highly dependent on the consultant. An anticipated result is that the client asks for more, even though the need for the consultant is no longer essential. If so, the consultant will have put the client in a position where he or she thinks help is still needed, rather than concluding this particular assignment and leaving a client who is able to function independently of the consultant.

The tendency to overlook a carefully planned disengagement can also occur when the consultant is on some kind of retainer. There is the implication that funds are still available and the temptation to continue until those funds are exhausted. In that case, disengagement will reflect the money available, rather than the completion of the assignment.

An internal consultant may have more difficulty in disengaging than an external consultant. The internal consultant is still evident within the total organization and may even have some geographic proximity to the client. This requires even more attention to the disengagement phase to ensure the relation does not limp along until actually forced to terminate by some external force demanding closure.

During disengagement the process of evaluation should be very evident. There may be some evaluation during response but that will be more of the formative kind of evaluation designed to influence the situation while in progress. By the disengagement phase, however, the evaluation should become the focused, summary type to determine specifically if the response has met the needs of the organization as identified during diagnosis.

As the consultation unfolds, changes may have occurred which render the earlier diagnosis either partially or completely invalid. To push ahead is to court failure. If the situation has changed, it may be necessary to go back to diagnosis or to alter the response. Hopefully, this has occurred. If not, it should be addressed during disengagement.

Consultation frequently produces new behaviors, relationships, or processes within the organization. At disengagement, the client and the consultant should verify whether the organization has the resources to continue in the preferred direction. If there are new relationships, determination must be made regarding whether these are to be supported so they will continue after the consultant leaves. During disengagement, the consultant may be available on an "as needed" basis while the client system tries to work with the changes which have been introduced.

Closure

Assuming disengagement has proceeded successfully, it is then time for closure. This should be distinctive and both the client and the consultant should acknowledge that they are now moving into this final phase. They can continue their relationship, but it should be based on other problems or concerns. It is important that each task or problem be brought to some kind of finality. Where the consultant is working with more than one client within the same client system, this process can easily become obscured. Closure should not be seen as a rejection of the consultant, but rather as a signal of the successful completion of a particular assignment and relationship.

Evaluation was mentioned earlier. It should have been planned in some fashion during the early stages of the response. During closure, the results of the evaluation should be shared. However, there are many times when the final effect of a consultation may require several months or even years before a meaningful evaluation can be conducted. Both sides should recognize this and understand that closure can take place, and that the final evaluation can come later. Meanwhile, it should be possible to agree on what would constitute an acceptable evaluation before the consultant departs.

If the evaluation discloses that the objectives of the consultation have not been met, further work might be needed. This should have surfaced during disengagement, but it is possible for it to become evident only in this final stage. Frequently, there is little that can be done about working further at this point, which is why it is crucial to do the evaluation during the disengagement phase. If the summary evaluation is done during closure, then both sides must agree that all they can do is to live with the data and the situation as presented. It may raise the need for further consultation, or the need for a different consultant.

Reducing the involvement of the consultant during disengagement should also bring about reduced dependency by the client. It is always desirable to keep dependency at the lowest possible level. Still, dependency does occur. If it has not been adequately dealt with by disengagement, it can become a horror during closure. The client may present excuses and see reasons why the consultant should continue. We have known clients who have suddenly discovered new financial resources just so the relationship could be sustained. Or, the problem suddenly changes, creating a desperately renewed need for the consultant. Such actions on the part of the client can build the bank statement and ego of the consultant. But if they are reflections of contrived client–dependency, then the behavior of the consultant becomes suspect. They should both be working toward closure as the normal, expected stage of their relationship. That does not prevent either from exploring the possibility of working together on other problems or in other relationships.

The physical aspects of closure take several forms. Frequently, a written report is required. This ranges from a brief memo to a comprehensive analysis or log. In consulting with the federal government, a written report is almost always required. However, this direction may not be stipulated in the initial discussions or subsequently in the contract, purchase order, or other legal obligating documents. Some of our colleagues have negotiated a contract, blocked their time, and made the necessary preparations for the consultation. When the written contract arrived, they found it mentioned a written report which was not previously mentioned or implied. The report, of course, entailed additional costs not anticipated. The consultant should query early in the contracting phase, if a written report is required by the terms of the contract.

Working with the private sector does not present this kind of problem. There are other problems, however, which differ from organization to organization. For example, some organizations require a written report when an external consultant is used, while there may not be the same requirement for an internal consultant. Generally, we have found that most organizations do not require a formal written document on closure of the consultation.

There should be a clearly identified closure meeting. Both parties should have agreed that this particular meeting is for the purpose of closure of this assignment. If all has gone well, and both parties are satisfied, the closure meeting is frequently in the form of a social experience. It may take place in a restaurant or some other environment conducive to social as well as business activities. This signifies that both parties are satisfied and there is nothing substantive which needs to be discussed at this time. Others might be invited to this meeting, as appropriate. It is a form of farewell to the consultant — at least for this assignment — and can become a warm occasion in the relationship.

At the same time, this would be when the consultant presents the final bill for services and related expenses. The client should have the assurance that no other financial requirements are outstanding. The consultant can expect that payment will follow and that no additional bills can be charged to this activity.

Some people consider it unprofessional or beneath their dignity to discuss the financial arrangements. This can be very unrealistic. It is not necessary to belabor the financial aspect, but to ignore it is to court financial disaster, particularly by the consultant. If the consultant has used a group, they must be paid. In some cases, they may require payment early, even before the lead consultant has been paid by the client. For those who consult with the federal government, the expected time lag in payment can cause severe cash flow problems. Such a situation has encouraged many good consultants to avoid contracting with the federal government.

Private companies usually present no problem here, but there are times when the client may have forgotten to push the right buttons or to put the appropriate paper into the system. By having a closure date, the consultant can follow-up the payment from a specific given date.

And so, closure is final. The particular assignment is completed. Neither the client nor the consultant is foreclosed from continuing with other tasks or from creating new relationships. Some clients keep going back to the same consultants time after time. This may be due to the successful work of the consultant, or the client's comfort with the relationship which has developed. There is nothing unethical about a consultant following up, at a later date, to determine whether the client has any additional needs which the consultant can help resolve.

If all has gone well, closure should bring a feeling of satisfaction to both the client and the consultant. They should feel they have been mutually helpful and have a high personal regard for each other. With great satisfaction, we have experienced, as have others, that old clients can become new friends.

Chapter 19
"Evaluating the Consulting Process"
Donald Swartz and Gordon Lippitt

The authors offer some sound, specific questions which should be asked as part of evaluation. They present a model, and areas to be evaluated. We do have a minor difference with one aspect of their material. They write of the "consulting/training" event. Within this book, we separate consulting from training as two different kinds of activities. Despite this distinction, the material they present can be very useful for evaluating consulting activities.

It is important to note that Donald Swartz and Gordon Lippitt encourage evaluating the client–consultant relationship. Too often, this is an overlooked area, though the results of this evaluation can be extremely helpful to both parties. Note, too, their use of a "contractual agreement for consultative services." Such a document proves extremely helpful during disengagement, as it provides the basis for identifying whether the mutual expectations have been met. Of course, it is always possible that the expectations have changed since the initiation of that document. Reference to the expectation of written reports could improve the utility of the document for the closure phase.

Chapter 20
"Evaluation of Results and Disengagement"
Edgar H. Schein

This is one of the few sources we have found which specifically discusses disengagement. Schein emphasized the need for both parties to agree that disengagement is actually taking place. When the point is made that "involvement not zero" it does raise the question of whether this is rightly disengagement or another part of the response phase. For process consultation, which the author clearly espouses and is noted for, it is probably acceptable to describe disengagement as he does.

Note particularly his last section about reinvolvement with the client. This comes closer to what we are describing as part of the closure activity. This article is taken from Schein's book *Process Consultation*.

Evaluating the Consulting Process

Donald Swartz
Gordon Lippitt

There are some key questions to ask about evaluation — These questions should be asked as part of the contract-setting discussion with the client:

1. What should be evaluated?
2. Why is this important to you? What will you gain from measuring it?
3. How will you measure it? Can you use existing data sources and processes?
4. Who will do the measurement data collection and analysis?
5. Who will do the evaluation based on the data?
6. When will the measurement be done? How often?
7. Who will/should see the results of the evaluation?
8. What will it cost in time and dollars to do this evaluation?
9. Are the benefits of the evaluation worth the cost?

It's easy to ask questions. It's quite another thing to get good answers that will result in a realistic and relevant evaluation system for the client. The model in Figure 19-1 has helped our clients to focus on possible areas of evaluation and appropriate levels of measurement sophistication for their projects.

Explanation of the Evaluation Model

The model points out four interdependent elements to consider when designing an evaluation system:

— Evaluation areas
— Evaluation criteria
— Sources of data
— Methods of data collection

Some brief explanations and definitions of these elements will lead us into a more detailed look into each evaluation area later in this article.

Reprinted from *The Journal of European Training*, Vol. 4, No. 5, copyright 1975, M.C.B. Publications, Ltd., Bradford, England.

Figure 19-1. Evaluating the consulting process.

Evaluation Areas

Client – Consultant Relationship. This area relates to the evaluation of the personal and professional relationships between client, client system, and consultant. These behavior relationships often have a major impact on the final outcome of the consulting process.

Consulting/Training Events. This area relates to the evaluation of significant consulting interventions such as survey-feedback meetings; skill training; conflict resolution meetings and other important "milestone" activities. Assessing the impact and contribution of each of these types of event on the overall project can provide important information for designing future projects with the client — and for improvement of similar events that will take place in the current project.

Progress Toward Specific Goals. This area relates to the client system's progress toward achievement of pre-stated goals and the possible contribution that the consultation help made to this progress. Overall results evaluation helps to answer the client's question, "Was the money I invested in consulting help at least returned by the results achieved?"

Evaluation Criteria

Cost/Profit-Related. These "hard measure" criteria are developed to determine as directly as possible the effect of consultation on the achievement of specified results. Some examples of cost/profit-related specified results are:

— Consulting time and expense estimate vs. actual
— Consulting event outcomes resulting in increased sales, decreased costs, etc.
— Trend changes in safety record, grievances, turnover, absenteeism, theft

Within the cost-related evaluation criteria there are three approaches to measurement that can be considered:

— Specific goal attainment by a specified time
— Trend tracking vs. plan or estimated performance
— Spot checks of performance vs. hoped for change, e.g. down-turn trend has been reversed

Behavior Observation. These criteria call for documentation of significant factual observed changes in individual and in organizational behavior that resulted directly from the consulting process or from an event influenced by the consulting process. Some examples of observed behavior change are:

— Client much more relaxed and functioning in a more assertive manner
— Change in organization structure, simplifying lines of communications
— Event participants' demonstration that they can plan for and conduct problem-solving meetings

Reaction. These criteria relate to the reactions of client and client system to the consulting process. They report feelings, attitudes, points of view, as these change over time. Some examples of reaction criteria measurements are:

— Client's expressed feelings about the consulting relationship
— Participants' evaluation of a training event
— Client system's reactions as expressed through a series of attitude surveys during the course of the consulting process

Sources of Data

There are four sources of data for an evaluation system. We define each of them as follows:

The Sponsor. A person or persons who can significantly influence the consulting process; who has (have) strong interest in the initiation, progress and final outcome of the consulting process. In some instances the sponsor is the client's "boss." Many times (particularly when working at the top of the organization) the sponsor is the client, e.g. the President. The sponsor could also be a group of people such as City Council, advisory board, executive committee, board of directors, etc.

The Client. The person who makes the "go or no-go" decision about events and directions within the project scope.

The Client System. Any person or group directly involved in or affected by the consulting project.

The Consultant. The helper(s) whose expertise has been contracted for by the client. Helpers may be internal to the client system or external to it. They may be a combination of internal and external helpers.

Methods of Data Collection

Data can be collected in a wide variety of ways. The following five methods are most frequently used to collect data for evaluation of the consulting process:

— *Observation*. The observation and recording of individual and group behavior as it relates to the job to be done. Also, the observation and recording of the way systems are functioning; e.g. flow-charting, decision trees, PERT charting, etc.
— *Questionnaires*. Specially designed or standardized formats that ask for individual written responses concerning attitude, viewpoints, opinions, perceptions.
— *Interviews*. Face-to-face or telephonic live interviews with individuals or groups to gain in-depth perceptions, specific examples, ideas and feelings.
— *Documentation*. The use of archival records, current records, and specially recorded data to show trends and changes resulting from the consulting process.
— *Instruments*. Specially designed data collection devices whose purpose is to stimulate individual feedback about a situation and to provide a framework for evaluation discussions between client, client system and, consultant.

We'll next illustrate how the four evaluation elements interact by looking at evaluation examples in each of the three "evaluation areas".

Evaluating the Client–Consultant Relationship

The success of the consulting relationship is not just a matter of consultant competency and/or creativity. The trust and acceptance of client–consultant are key factors along with appropriate definition of roles. Some guidelines in assessing the consulting relationship are as follows:

1. *Does the consultant form sound interpersonal relations with the client?* A consulting relationship is based on trust developed by effective interpersonal relations. Does the consultant allow time for exploring this relationship in sufficient depth so both parties feel that changes are likely for developing confidence and trust?
2. *Does the consultant build dependence on his resources with the client?* A responsible and ethical consultant does not make the client dependent on him, or his methods. Instead, he recognizes the need for people to develop their own competence and capabilities, while he assists only when needed. He can do this without creating dependency.

3. *Does the consultant focus on the problem?* Beware of the consultant who so much wants to please everyone with his work that he glosses over problems and conflict. The realities of organizational life and interpersonal dynamics mean that there will be people who feel threatened, upset and unhappy about the results of any organizational change. The problem or need, however, must be confronted or we are dealing with "flight", not coping behavior.

4. *Does the consultant respect the confidences of his clients?* Another sign of a professional consultant is his ability to keep confidential his dealings with clients.

5. *Does the consultant achieve influence appropriately in the organization?* The professional consultant makes every effort to build the resources or the department or person who brought him into the consultation. His influence is by expertise and he does not put on a political show to impress others.

6. *Does the consultant indicate the skills he possesses relative to the client's problem?* Many consultants who are good in one field may not be expert in the resources required to help an organization to investigate the total aspects of its structure, finances, technology, and human processes. Be wary of the consultant who may be venturing far beyond the limits of his actual skills and abilities.

7. *Does the consultant clearly inform the client as to his role and contribution?* A consultant should clarify his role with the potentials and limitations inherent in such a clarification.

8. *Does the consultant express willingness to have his services evaluated?* One sign of the non-professional consultant is an unwillingness to have his work reviewed or evaluated by persons in the organization. He will muster up comments such as: "My kind of services cannot be evaluated," or "The nature of my work is so scientific and technical that there is no way it can be accurately measured." Exercise caution with the consultant who is reluctant to get "feedback" on his own performance.

These suggested assessment guidelines are based on our experiences from both the sending and receiving sides of consulting services. Of course, this is not meant to be an exhaustive list, but is indicative of some of the concerns which should be brought to the attention of managers and organizations that use consultants and wish to evaluate the process.

In Table 19-1 we have attempted to illustrate a number of possible ways to organize the evaluation of the relationship between consultant and client and between consultant and client system. Most of the criteria are dependent upon behavior observation and reaction data.

Evaluating the Consulting/Training Event

Most consulting interventions include key training and group process events. It is often helpful to client, client system, and consultant to evaluate these events so

Table 19-1

Evaluating the Client–Consultant Relationship

What to Evaluate	Why Evaluate	How Evaluate	Who Will Evaluate	Who Will Get Evaluation	When Evaluate
Client-Consultant Contract Agreements: Role Clarity Commitments Schedule Cost vs. Estimate	Project success depends on it. May need to re-negotiate due to changes	Open discussion	Client or consultant	Consultant or client	As desired by either party or between phases
Interdependency or Dependency	To determine if client is becoming too dependent on consultant	Open discussion	Sponsor, client or consultant	Client and/or consultant	As desired by either party
Consultant's Influence	To determine if the consultant is exerting too little or too much influence	Instrument observation	Other consultant, sponsor or client	Consultant	As desired by the client
Consultant's Ethics	To determine if consultant's behavior is helpful to the project	Observation Client system reaction	Client system, client, sponsor, other consultant	Consultant	As desired by client
Consultant's Arena	To determine if the consultant is staying within the bounds of his expertise and competence	Observation Client system reaction	Client system, client, sponsor, other consultant	Consultant	As desired by client
Consultant's Ability	To determine if the consultant's work is performed adequately	Reaction interviews with client system Observation Questionnaire	Other consulting professional	Client, consultant	As desired by client

that learning reinforcement and needed corrective action take place. Much has been written about event measurement. We have included here the methods we have used most frequently.

Post-event Measure (only)
Use this method when:

— There is no opportunity or little need for comparative pre- and post-measurement.
— The trainer/consultant is interested in the immediate reaction to the content and methodology of the event.
— Consultant and client are satisfied with reaction data as the main basis for evaluation.
— The event is not designed to result in a specific measurable behavior change. Rather, its purpose is to create awareness, internal motivation, inform, educate.

Evaluation Criteria

— Behavior observation: consultant/trainer's observation of behavior changes in participants during the event
— Reaction data: post-event questionnaire is frequently used for these data
— Post-event interviews of individuals or group by consultant or client

Pre-event and Post-event Measure
Use this method when:

— The event is designed to help to cause a specific observable behavior change in the participants.
— The event is designed to increase the participants' knowledge or understanding of a subject area and it is worth measuring the degree of improvement.

Evaluation Criteria

— Cost/profit related: summaries of decisions made and problems solved as a result of the event, including cost/benefit estimate of each. This summary should be made by the participants and *they* should report it to the client or sponsor.
— Behavior observation: documented observation of participant behavior by consultant and/or client before and after the consulting event. For example, participant ability to plan and conduct effective staff meetings.
— Reaction data: participant response to a pretest and to a posttest, demonstrating an increase in knowledge and understanding; or expressing a change in attitude about an issue with which the event was concerned (e.g., attitudes about minority employment).

Table 19-2
Performance Data Summary

Condition	Premeasure Bags/Man-Hr	Postmeasure Bags/Man-Hr	Change	Cost Difference
Control Group	0.1027	0.1020	− 0.7%	-0-
Continuous ($2)	0.0813	0.1081	+33.0%	−$4.14/Bag
VR-2 ($4)	0.1010	0.0929	− 8.0%	+$3.61/Bag
VR-4 ($8)	0.1151	0.1359	+18.1%	+$0.15/Bag

Pre-event and Post-event Measure with Control Group

Group A (Trained)	Measure Performance	Training	Measure Performance
Group B (Not Trained)	Measure Performance	————	Measure Performance

This is a more sophisticated method of evaluating the payout from consulting events in terms of performance on the job. All three Evaluation criteria could be used as under "Pre-event and Post-event Measure" above.

Table 19-2 illustrates the use of this method for evaluating the performance change of tree planters in a large wood products company in a consulting event versus the performance of those who had not participated.

The Control Group method can also be used for comparing Post-event measurement between training group and control group.

The Control Group method should be used when:

— It is possible to identify a control group who are experiencing similar variables as the training or consulted group (e.g., working conditions, supplies, tools, climatic conditions, terrain, etc.).
— The Control Group and the training group each contain 15 or more persons, so that the results are statistically reliable.
— The consultant and/or client need good comparative performance data.
— Identifying a "control" group will not create a "have" and "have not" feeling in the client system.

Time Series Pre-event and Time Series Post-event Measure with Control Group

In this design, a series of performance measures are taken prior to and again following the consulting event.

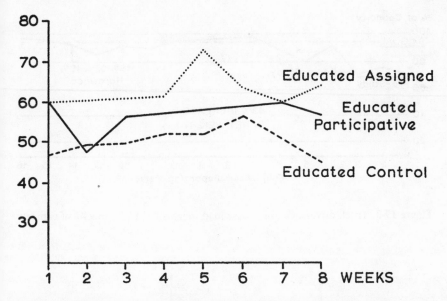

Figure 19-2. Cutting units per manhour across weeks for educated workers.

					Design		
Group A	O_1	O_2	O_3	Event	O_4	O_5	O_6
(Trained)							
Group B	O_1	O_2	O_3		O_4	O_5	O_6
(Not Trained)							

where O = Observation, reaction or cost/profit measure data.

Figure 19-2 demonstrates the use of this type measure design used to determine the effectiveness of goal setting practices as related to production rates of educated wood workers.

The charts in Figure 19-2 show the comparative effects of a consulting event with occurred in weeks 4 and 5 of the time series.

The time series can also be used without control group. Figure 19-3 illustrates the use of time series without control group in measuring the effect of a goal setting consulting event on the productivity of truck drivers in a logging operation.

The time series method should be used when:

— Sample sizes of training or control groups are less then 15.
— When there are a great many variable factors that could cause an actual decrease in performance during the measurement period (for example, bad weather may cause a decrease in productivity for all outside operations).

Figure 19-4 illustrates the value of using time-series, control group measure.

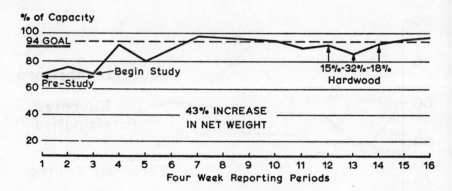

Figure 19-3. Truck drivers. Goal-increase load weights from 73% to 94% of capacity.

Figure 19-4. In this hypothetical situation, the control group's performance dropped significantly, while the training group maintained production despite the rain. Since the employees were randomly assigned to the two groups and their performance was approximately the same prior to training, and since both groups were exposed to the same factors prior to and again during training (with the exception that the control group did not receive training), the only logical conclusion that can be drawn is that training maintained production.

Evaluating Progress Toward Specific Goals

In evaluation of the overall system's progress toward specific goals it is usually difficult to isolate the effect of the consulting process. The cost in time and money to isolate the consulting process to show its contribution to the end result may be higher than the value returned to the client.

One way to evaluate progress is for the client and consultant actually to develop a written "contract" between the client and consultant so expectations on goals, terms, and roles are spelled out for all parties concerned. An example of such a form used by internal consultants in a large voluntary agency is indicated in Table 19-3.

Our experience indicates that it is good practice to review the overall measurement possibilities with the client and then to determine the level of sophistication in measurement he can live with. Regardless of the level of sophistication or methods chosen, they must be part of the initial understanding between client and consultant — even if the cleint says, "I'll know if this consulting has helped because I'll feel better."

Here are some examples of Evaluation Criteria methods as applied to evaluating client system progress toward goals:

Cost/Profit-Related Criteria

Specific Goal Attainment by a Specified Time. Example: To have a career development system in operation by 1st January 1976 at a cost not to exceed $15,000 for printing, training, and outside consultation. To attain an annualized production rate of 15 tons per hour by reducing downtime required for maintenance through a concentrated continuous training and problem-solving process for maintenance employees between 1st January 1976 and 1st July 1976.

Trend Tracking vs. Plan or Estimated Performance. Figure 19-5 shows how historical performance and projected estimates might be used as a base-line performance against which to track client system performance over time.

Trend Tracking and Comparative Analysis with Similar Systems

Table 19-4 shows a sophisticated comparative analysis of the safety performance of a large pulp mill as compared with the performance of other similar mills in the area. Note that the statistical analysis is accompanied by a documented account of significant planned and unplanned events which the consultant considers to have had an impact on the safety performance change.

(Text continued on page 229)

Table 19-3
Contractual Agreement for Consultative Services

Client _____ Consultant_____
Duration: from _____ 19____ to _____ 19____
Reason for Requested Service:
Client Expectations/Time Frame:
Description of Service: (estimated number of days _____)
Goals and Evaluation Method:
Personnel Involved:
Signatures:
client_____ date_____
consultant _____ date_____
project manager_____ date_____

Instructions for Completing Contractual Agreement

Client: Name of group or individual requesting service.
Consultant: Name of person designated to render service.
Project Manager: Name of Staff Member co-ordinating project services.
Duration: Total length of agreement for services, to include preparation, on-site
                           and follow-up service.
Reason for Requested Service: (completed by client) Give statement of situation or
                           problem for which consultant services are requested.
Client Expectations/Time Frame: (completed by client) Define expectations and give
                           time frame for results of service to be provided by consultant.
Description of Service: (completed by consultant) Describe design of service as related to
                           fulfillment of client expectations.
Goals and Evaluation Method: (completed by consultant) Describe anticipated results of
                           service, method of measuring results, follow-up required by client or
                           consultant.
Personnel Involved: (completed by client and project manager) Designate groups or
                           individuals within client complement with whom consultant will work.
                           Identify person(s) to receive written report if required.
Distribution: Client   2 copies
                           Client   1 copy
                           Consultant
                           Project Manager
                           File

Figure 19-5. Tracking client system performance over time.

Table 19-4
Cost-Related Criteria

Measurement Area No. 1: Safety Results

The purpose of this analysis was to *test* the hypotheses that (a) the number of accidents in Mill A was significantly higher than that of the BC pulp and paper industry average *prior* to the OE intervention; and, that (b) the number of accidents decreased significantly after the OE intervention.

The null hypothesis* was that the difference between the number of accidents in Mill A and those that occurred in the industry in general would remain relatively constant. A Mann-Whitney U test was used to test this hypothesis. This test combined the scores from Mill A and those reflecting the industry average and ranked them in order of increasing size.

Data were collected from January, 1973 until August, 1974. The OE intervention process was completed in November, 1973. The data were analyzed by comparing the preintervention data for Mill A with the preintervention data for the industry. Similarly, the postintervention data for Mill A were compared with the postintervention data for the industry.

---

*The null hypothesis assumes that no significant differences or changes occur as the result of an intervention.

(Table continued on pages 228 and 229)

Table 19-4 (continued)
Premeasure — Safety

Month	Mill A Accident Frequency	Rank	BC Average Frequency	Rank
January	70.87	22	18.82	11
February	64.18	21	15.15	10
March	50.66	20	14.61	4
April	44.20	19	14.30	3
May	41.77	18	14.28	1
June	40.92	17	14.95	7
July	38.04	15	15.03	9
August	38.15	16	14.90	5
September	36.56	14	14.87	5
October	35.79	13	14.29	2
November	34.02	12	15.02	8
$p<.001$	$R_1 =$	187	$r_1 =$	66

Postmeasure — Safety

Month	Mill A Accident Frequency	Rank	BC Average Frequency	Rank
December	30.30	17	15.45	10
January	10.07	8	12.65	9
February	9.39	7	15.55	11
March	8.94	6	16.08	13
April	7.28	3	15.96	12
May	7.76	4	17.04	14
June	8.03	5	17.54	15
July	6.82	1	18.13	16
August	7.19	2		
$p<.001$	$R_1 =$	53	$R_2 -$	100

Conclusions: The odds are 1 in 1000 that these results are due to chance†. The Mill A accident frequency is significantly lower than that of the BC industry average.

†Odds of 5 in 100 (or 1 in 20) are considered sufficient in science for assuming that the results are not due to chance. The present results exceed even this stringent criterion.

Table 19-4 (continued)
Significant Interventions/Events — Safety

November 1973
1. Top management commitment to establish a comprehensive safety program.
2. Safety co-ordinator job position filled by a respected "line" management employee.
3. Supervisors meetings held with mill manager to fix accountability for safety at first line supervisor's level.
4. Arranged schedules, etc., so that every employee attends at least one departmental safety meeting/month.
5. Safety work order system revised and published to all employees. (See Appendix 1 for effect on work orders received and processed in December 1973 and January 1974).

December 1973
6. Revised safety induction procedure.
7. Ceased hiring "casual" labor.
8. Revitalized and reconstituted Labor-Management Safety Committee.
9. Established environmental protection joint committee.

January 1974
10. Revised and posted mill safety rules.

March 1974
11. Revised Tag Out procedure and trained crews in its applications.
12. Instituted new accident investigation procedure.
13. Instituted new "near miss" investigation procedure.
14. Instituted monthly safety themes and methods for departmental meetings.

July 1974
15. Reviewed and standardized safety equipment in mill.

Behavior Observation Criteria

There are two ways to use behavior criteria measurements:
— To test an assumption about what changes will be observed in individuals and groups as a result of the consulting intervention
— To demonstrate the effect of the consulting process based on observations made after completion of the process

Some examples of preprocess assumptions about expected behavior change are:
— The average time for coffee breaks will decrease from 25 minutes to within 15 minutes.
— Employees will make greater use of industrial relations counseling services.
— Engineering and production will work more collaboratively in new product development activities.

An actual example of an observation measurement made after the process was completed is shown in Table 19-5. These observations data and conclusions were jointly developed by the internal consultant and the client.

Table 19-5
Behavioral Observations

Observable change in individual and organizational behavior was the second set of criteria used to measure the effectiveness of the OE intervention. The seven observations reported here can be related directly to various OE intervention events such as Survey-Feedback decision/action meetings, team development sessions, personal consultation, productivity and effectiveness study, etc. In many instances, the "interventions/events" contributing directly to the observed change are themselves direct results of a specific OE intervention activity.

Observation No. 1 — Mill Supervisors' Unionization Attempt

Observed Behavior Change	Interventions/Events Contributing to Change	Transferable Learnings
Before: March 5, 1973 Mill supervisors filed for certification to unionize. **After:** Nov. 1, 1974 No threat of supervisors unionizing.	Corrected inequities in salaries and compensation for overtime worked during construction and start-up phases. (July-August 73).	Develop controllable S.O.P's and conduct performance/reward reviews against these standards vs. giving across-the-board "merit" increases.
	Conducted objective salary reviews (August 73). Disclosed salary ranges. Instituted performance bonus plan (July 74).	Do not reward extra work with trips of dollars is the expectation. At least give a choice.
		Do not allow unrewarded overtime to "pile up."
	Team-building meetings to socialize front-line supervisors into management (November 73 — April 74).	Over-staff with supervisors during start-up to reduce fatigue and provide adequate training time.
	Heavy involvement of supervisors in labor relations strategy and procedures (November 73 forward).	Be absolutely open related to salary administration plan and details. Any other behavior creates suspicion and distrust.

Reaction Criteria

As in the other evaluation criteria methods there are multiple levels of sophistication. Some examples of these levels are shown here:

Sponsor/Client Reaction. The sponsor and/or client are invited to make spot-check observations of the project, and record their reactions in writing. (We are noting an increasing tendency for sponsors and clients to be satisfied with this level of sophistication as a measure of the value of the consulting process to their project).

Client System Reaction. This can be obtained through spot-check interviews by client or an evaluation consultant. Client system reaction can also be determined through the multiple application of attitude questionnaires. These questionnaires can range from homemade one-pagers to highly sophisticated and validated computerized attitude surveys (e.g., Survey Research Centers at University of Michigan and University of Chicago). Figure 19-6 illustrates the use of an employee survey to indicate attitude changes related to 11 work climate dimensions and issues. The base document from which these data were summarized on the chart was designed for use as a diagnostic instrument during the consulting process. By collecting data from the client system at the beginning of the consulting process, again at 6 months after the start, and again at 18 months after the start, the consultant and client were able to see attitude trend changes that were consistent with behavior observation and cost/profit-related changes.

Summary

Evaluation of the consulting process must always be considered as part of the initial contract between client and consultant. Ideally, evaluation will serve several important purposes:

1. Give the consultant feedback that will support professional growth.
2. Give the consultant feedback so that corrective actions can be made during the consulting process.
3. Give the consultant accomplishment feedback necessary for his psychological needs.
4. Provide progress and final accomplishment data as positive reinforcement for client behavior, or as a basis for needed change in the behavior.
5. Justify the time and expense of the consulting process (and this should be the least important reason of all).

Evaluation should be helpful to the projects goals, not hindering. The time and money expenditure for evaluation must be weighed carefully by the client against expected payout.

Figure 19-6. Organization climate profile.

The following questions give some of the criteria for determining whether a particular consultation lends itself to evaluation:

1. *How complex is the consulting problem?* If the problem is really a number of problems, or is very complex, it may not be possible to evaluate the process.
2. *How much time will be required to get the information?* If a consultation covers a scope of years, it may not be possible to do evaluation.
3. *Is the question one of values or operations?* If a question is a matter of policy rather than measurable operations, it may raise a question of whether evaluation is possible.
4. *What will be cost demands in securing the facts?* If the financial demand of such an evaluation is too great, it might make data collection impractical.
5. *What will be the nonfinancial demands on the consultant and client?* Any consulting relationship should assess such matters as need for support, time, possible public relations, stress tolerance, etc., in determining the possibility of doing evaluation.
6. *How feasible is it that consultation success can be answered through the obtaining of evidence?* If the data are difficult or impossible to obtain, it might make it questionable that evaluation will be possible.

This may sound as if we are making evaluation difficult. No, our point is that in *some* cases evaluation may be difficult but that a subjective evaluation of consultation will *always* take place, and we suggest that *some* attention be given to make it an objective part of the process as frequently as possible.

There is no "one right way" to evaluate. Consultants and clients need to "invent" evaluation systems appropriate to their needs and based on proven principles of evaluation.

It is our hope that this article provides internal as well as external consultants with some bases upon which to develop some useful evaluation processes with their clients, so that consultation becomes a professional part of the improved effectiveness of individuals, groups and organizations.

Donald H. Swartz is president of Effectiveness Resource Group in Tacoma, Washington.

Gordon Lippitt is professor of behavioral science in the School of Business Administration, George Washington University.

Disengagement: Reducing Involvement with the Client System

Edgar H. Schein

The process of disengagement has, in most of my experiences, been characterized by the following features:

1. Reduced involvement is a mutually agreed-upon decision rather than a unilateral decision by consultant or client;
2. Involvement does not generally drop to zero but may continue at a very low level;
3. The door is always open from my point of view for further work with the client if the client desires it.

Let me comment upon each of these points and give some examples.

Joint Decisions

In most of my consulting relationships there has come a time when either I felt that nothing more could be accomplished and/or some members of the client system felt the need to continue on their own. To facilitate a reduction of involvement, I usually check at intervals of several months to see whether the client feels that the pattern should remain as is or should be altered. In some cases where I have felt that a sufficient amount had been accomplished, I have found that the client did not feel the same way and wanted the relationship to continue on a day-a-week basis. In other cases, I have been confronted by the client, as in Company A, with the statement that my continued attendance in the operational group meetings was no longer desirable from his point of view. As the president put it, I was beginning to sound to much like a regular member to be of much use. I concurred in the decision and reduced my involvement to periodic all-day meetings of the group, though the initiative for inviting me remained entirely with the group. Had I not concurred, we would have negotiated until a mutually satisfactory arrangement

---

Edgar H. Schein, *Process Consultation,* ©1969, Addison-Wesley, Reading, Massachusetts. Reprinted with permission.

had been agreed upon. I have sometimes been in the situation of arguing that I remain fully involved even when the client wanted to reduce involvement, and in many cases I was able to obtain the client's concurrence.

The negotiation which surrounds a reduction of involvement is in fact a good opportunity for the consultant to diagnose the state of the client system. The kinds of arguments which are brought up in support of continuing (or terminating) provide a solid basis for determining how much value and skill change has occurred. The reader may feel that since the client is paying for services, he certainly has the right to make unilateral decisions about whether or not to continue these services. My point would be that if the consultation process has even partially achieved its goals, there should arise sufficient trust between consultant and client to enable both to make the decision on rational grounds. Here again, it is important that the consultant not be economically dependent upon any one client, or his own diagnostic ability may become biased by his need to continue to earn fees.

Involvement Not Zero

If the client and consultant agree on a reduced involvement, it is important that both should recognize that this does not necessarily mean a complete termination. In fact, a complete termination is not desirable because the diagnosis on which reduced involvement is based may not be accurate enough to warrant termination. A more desirable arrangement is to drop the level to perhaps a half-day every three or four weeks, or attendance only at certain kinds of special meetings, or an interview with key members of the client system once every two or three months. Through this mechanism it is possible for the client and the consultant to reassess periodically how things are going.

In Company B, there was a period where I felt that a plateau had been reached. At this point I suggested that I reduce my involvement to a half-day every other week, and even then only if specific individuals wanted to have some time to talk over problems with me. After a few months at this reduced level, a number of events made it more important than ever for the top management group to increase their level of effectiveness. The group decided to have more meetings and asked me to become reinvolved at an increased level. This decision was much easier to negotiate from a reduced involvement than it would have been from a situation where I had terminated the relationship completely.

In my relationship with Company F, there are long periods where I do not pay any visits, but it is understood that as problems or issues come up the client is free to call on me with the expectation that I will respond positively. The only problem with this kind of arrangement is that it makes it difficult for the consultant to plan his time. Obviously if several clients decide to increase their involvement all at the same time, it may be impossible for the consultant to respond. If this occurs, the consultant has to be open about his dilemma and determine from the various clients whether or not they can wait for a month or so. I have found from experience that I can carry about four clients at any given time, with two of them being more active (one half-day every week), while two others are "dormant" (an occasional visit every three weeks to a month).

Reinvolvement Is Always Possible

This point is closely related to the previous one, but I want to separate it to bring out a special aspect of the obligation of the process consultant. In any P-C consulting relationship with a client, I think the consultant should make it clear that the door is always open to further work once the relationship has begun. The reason for this obligation is that a good relationship with a consultant is difficult for a client to develop. Once both the consultant and the client have invested effort in building such a relationship, it does not terminate psychologically even if there are prolonged periods of lack of contact. I have had the experience with a number of clients of not seeing them for many months and yet being able to tune in on the group very quickly once contact has been reestablished.

As a general rule it should be the client who reestablishes contact, but I would not advocate sticking to this rigidly. I have, after some period of no contact, called a client and asked if I could talk with him to find out what was going on. In several cases such a call was welcomed and served as the basis for some additional counseling or process observation. The consultant must be careful not to violate his role by selling himself back to the client. It must be an honest inquiry which can comfortably be turned down by the client should he desire to do so. I have been turned down often enough to know that there is nothing inherent in the situation to force an artificial contact. Rather, it sometimes helps a client who wanted help anyway to ask for it in a face-saving way.

Edgar H. Schein is professor of organizational psychology and management in the Sloan School of Management at Massachusetts Institute of Technology.

Part VII

Issues

One way of defining the word "issue" is "a point of view subject to dispute." The propensity for dispute is generally a function of the relative value placed on the point of view. We get some sense of valuing occurring when we hear phrases like, "That's an issue for me" or "I take issue with you on that."

Conventionally, issues come in continuums; the larger the crowds at either end, the more likely a point of view will come to be labeled an issue. While our Eastern neighbors encourage us to transcend duality and experience a reality in which all views are part of a larger framework, our Western heritage entices us to define values as a collection of continuums and dichotomies — for every up, there must be a down; for every left, a right.

Issues are borne out of values; values give our lives meaning, purpose, and parameters. They provide a type of control aimed at fostering freedom without anarchy; fairness without apathy. The comparative judging of people, things, and ideas insures diversity, creativity, and progress.

Conventional issues in the client–consultant relationship generally have to do with rightness, goodness, and openness. Few words have more quickly recognizable opposites. Since the definition of right–wrong, good–bad, and open–closed is solely in the eye (value) of the beholder, the three continuums make a useful framework for exploring conventional issues.

Rightness

If issues spring out of valued points of view, the greatest recoil is from those viewpoints dealing with rightness. At their greatest breadth, right–wrong continuums are legal or ethical boundaries; at their narrowest, they revolve around our sense of fair play. Gross and flagrant misrepresentation of professional skills by a consultant, for instance, is clearly unethical and in some circumstances illegal. Subtle misrepresentation of some minor skill (the ability to use a particular training exercise) is, at a minimum, unfair to the client.

Consultation in the behavioral sciences has yet to achieve the kind of professional stature which is accompanied by enforceable codes of conduct. Nevertheless, even the most casual client is concerned with malpractice. Just as the use of inappropriate drugs can be physiologically damaging, using an inappropriate technique on a naive client can be as psychologically damaging.

237

Sex and money are frequently regarded within a right–wrong context. The consultant who allows the client–consultant relationship to evolve to a point incorporating sexual behavior is clearly courting charges of unethical, if not illegal, behavior. Likewise, inflated consultant fees which are negotiated via the inexperience of the bargaining client are unfair and potentially unlawful.

The list of issues which can fall on a right–wrong continuum are numerous. They can be short-circuited best by consultants employing codes of conduct which favor the client and by facilitating a client–consultant relationship which is built on honesty, effectiveness, and a keen sense of fair play.

Goodness

The road to goodness in the consultation is paved with standards, competencies, and qualities. The continuum relates most to the worth or value of the effort to parties involved. A consultative relationship falling on the good side of the continuum connotes congruence of expectation and outcome, mutuality of purpose, and interpersonal satisfaction. The bad side is laden with labels of conflict, confusion, and ambiguity.

The worth of the consultant in the client–consultant relationship is largely shaped by the qualities and competencies he or she possesses. Many writings have offered a taxonomy of consultant competencies. Central to most are (1) the ability to see things with minimal bias, (2) awareness of personal needs and motives and their potential impact on the effort, (3) an understanding of a body of knowledge related to the consultation, and (4) skill in solving problems and helping others solve problems. Other qualities include such things as trust, imagination, intuition, honesty, and flexibility.

Little has been written about client qualities and competencies which effect the goodness of the client–consultant relationship. Essentially, they are the same qualities required of a consultant, viewed differently. An honest consultant and a dishonest client, for instance, are likely to make rather uncomfortable bedfellows.

A client may not be expected to have diagnostic ability, but nevertheless may be expected to exercise resourcefulness and responsiveness in helping the consultant obtain the required data for an accurate organizational diagnosis. Client self-awareness increases the chances the consultative intervention will be implemented smoothly during the response phase. Disengagement and closure will be made smoother if the client has warded off consultant dependence by maintaining sufficient humility to learn from the relationship.

Whether client or consultant, the goodness of the relationship is typically a function of the commitment of both to consistently stay sensitive to relationship tensions. Likewise required of both is the willingness to test the authenticity of each other by confronting disruptions and uncertainties with caring candor and ruthless integrity.

Openness

Chris Argyris, *Intervention Theory and Method,* stated that if consultation is to be helpful in an ongoing sense, it is critical the client have "free, informed choice." For such choice to be possible, it is important the client have a cognitive map of what he or she wishes to do. Provision of a cognitive map requires a relationship characterized by openness.

Few people relish being coerced or having things done to them in mysterious ways. The relational climate needed is one in which members of the client system find increasing options open to them and a perpetual high return from their personal employment of behavorial science knowledge.

The openness of the relationship is increased as the consultant discovers ways to be helpful to the client rather than cementing the client's dependence on the consultant. The client has the responsibility of being honest in a manner which confronts any real or perceived deception in the relationship.

Consultants are often drawn to the behavioral science field out of personal needs for relationships, affiliation and social acceptances. This magnetic force, left unchecked, can lead to consultant action incompatible with consultant belief. The consultant's failure to function with congruence and genuineness dooms the client-consultant relationship to something less than authentic. Not only does it fail to provide the client a solid example to model, the lack of authenticity seduces the client into perpetual dependence on the consultant.

The client–consultant relationship marked by the spirit of collaboration and cooperation is likely to be right, good, and open to those touched by that relationship. The challenge to client and consultant is to construct their agreements with appropriate feedback loops which allow effective monitoring by each, or timely renegotiation by both.

Chapter 21
"Toward a Philosophy of HRD Consulting"
Chip R. Bell

An issue which cuts across all three types of client–consultant relationship issues (rightness, goodness, and openness) is the role of belief in impacting consultant behavior. A psychoanalyst friend once stated, "Every action a person takes is to them the best action they could take at the moment. No one ever does anything they personally label stupid or wrong. Given a person's self-perception, their world view, and their desire to meet personal needs, the behavior taken was the best choice of action at the time."

This perspective is useful in replacing blame with insight. It is likewise helpful in better managing the client–consultant relationship. Each party has responsibility for continually assessing the impact personal belief has on behavior in the consulta-

240   The Client—Consultant Handbook

tion. The Bell article describes a number of issues in which belief can bias what behaviors occur. Several suggestions are provided as means for tempering the weight of prejudice on practice.

Chapter 22
"Ethical Considerations in Consulting"
J. William Pfeiffer and John E. Jones

The Pfeiffer and Jones article makes the point that, while some consultant behavior is clearly ethical, other behavior may be ethical but may be irresponsible, imprudent, unprofessional, or incompetent. Many issues dealing with a variety of consultant misbehaviors are organized into four areas of consideration: (1) self and colleagues; (2) individual clients; (3) training groups; and (4) organizations.

The article is particularly useful for better understanding the rightness dimensions of the client–consultant relationship. As earlier discussed, the nature of consultation is such that the level of trust between client and consultant directly impacts the probability of success. That trust is enhanced if the client senses that the consultant operates from a code of conduct which has the welfare of the client as its primary fabric.

Chapter 23
"Organizations as Phrog Farms"
Jerry B. Harvey

Consultant competence lies at the heart of the goodness issue. The Harvey article slices caustically to the core of the issue by allegorically outlining ways consultants prostitute their competence by being seduced into responding to the client's desires rather than the client's needs.

Few articles have dealt more provocatively with the client–consultant relationship and the competency issue than the Harvey article. Already a classic in behavioral science literature, it stimulates reassessment of how honestly consultants utilize their skills to facilitate improvement in the client system. Likewise, the article enables clients to determine how the consultant may be enticed to affirm the client's beliefs rather than, more appropriately, supplying valid information which provides the client with choice of action.

Towards a Philosophy of HRD Consulting

Chip R. Bell

A popular line we frequently hear in our society today goes something like, "When you understand where he's coming from, then what he does makes sense." The implied message is that a relationship exists between belief and behavior; that is, the assumptions we have about life color our perception of our environment and shape our actions in our environment. The importance of the linkages among assumptions, perceptions, and action cannot be overstated.

Assumptions, beliefs, or personal philosophy are derived out of our previous experience of making sense out of the world around us. We build up certain constants we learn to depend on to bring order to chaos and to help us to predict occurrences. These learned constants become our personal philosophy and determine what we perceive in our world. For example, one of the functions of the brain is to protect us from being overwhelmed and confused by the mass of data we daily encounter. As a reducing valve, the brain selects in and selects out information based on the constants we have learned. In the words of Goethe, "Every man takes the limits of his own vision as the limits of the world." Adam Smith in his book *Powers of Mind* implies that if one learns (believes) purple cows do not exist, one is not likely to report seeing one even if the purple cow is truly a part of one's immediate environment.[1]

Elements in perception include: some external stimulus, some process by which the external stimulus is transmitted into psychological experience, and some meaning of that psychological experience given by the person. Because they play an active role in giving meaning to stimuli, different people will see the same thing in different ways, depending on their personal set of constants, beliefs, or philosophy. It is how a person "sees" that determines his/her behavior. In brief, we learn assumptions which shape perception which determine action or behavior.

For the human resource development (HRD) practitioner functioning in a consultant role, the recognition of the connection between personal philosophy and possible consultative response is critical to objectivity. The purpose of this

Reprinted with permission from the *Journal of European Industrial Training*, Vol. 1, No. 3, Copyright 1977, M.C.B. Publication, Ltd., Bradford, England.

article is to discuss varied HRD philosophies and how a particular philosophy can bias what the HRD consultant "sees" during the problem diagnosis and can adversely influence what the HRD consultant recommends as the appropriate response for dealing with the problem. It is hoped this article will create a greater awareness of the potentiality of consultant bias enabling the consultant to take precautionary steps to minimize bias which can inadvertently reduce the accuracy of HRD consultation.

There are many studies on the effect belief has on behavior. A team of Stanford psychologists raised groups of kittens, some in only vertically striped environments, some in only horizontally striped environments. Even after they were adult cats and placed in normal environments, the vertical stripers though the world was vertical, the horizontal stripers thought the world was horizontal. The horizontal stripers literally could not see the vertical world and vice versa. The neural connections had been totally modified by external stimulation[2].

"That's very interesting," you say, "but what does it have to do with people?" Research done by Toch and Schulte found that the training policemen received increased the probability that they would see themes of violence in ambiguous pictures[3]. Hadley Cantril reports research conducted in South Africa by Gordon Allport. A stereogram is an instrument in which the right lens has one picture (e.g., a photograph), and the left lens has a different picture (e.g., a different photo). Using a stereogram with photographs of an equal number of black and white faces, South Africans tended to see more black faces. Indians saw more Indian faces when viewing paired Indian and white photos. In both research efforts, people perceived what was personally significant to them.[4].

The HRD Consultant

There is a myriad of ways one can divide the major roles performed by HRD practitioners. They include such roles as learning specialist, administrator, program manager, and others. Most writers who have dealt with the HRD roles issue indicate that a key HRD role which has emerged in the last decade is that of HRD consultant. The complexity of organizational problems increasingly requires solutions broader than that furnished by the usual learning programs, methods, and technology.

The present era of tight economics has caused HRD practitioners to become more results-oriented in their responses to organizational needs. Learning programs are increasingly more relevant; program delivery, more practical. In this era of pragmatism, HRD practitioners are realizing they have diagnostic competencies and behavioral science-based orientations not only unique in their organization, but needed by their organization in order to cope with complex human system problems.

Practitioners are becoming increasingly reluctant to employ skill deficiency medicine as a cure for will deficiency maladies. Many are realizing their charter is not only to facilitate learning, but to stimulate improvement in the quality of work life. Some practitioners have donned an organization development hat as an important extra garment needed for the achievement of their HRD goals. No longer just the teacher of workshops and overseer of the tuition refund program, the HRD practitioner spends a growing amount of time as a consultant to managers on how best to manage and optimize the human resources for whom they are responsible.

An HRD consultant is a person who, because of competence, experience, status, reputation, or a combination of these, is contacted by a client to provide help in solving a current or potential problem which involves or is concerned with human resources. The HRD consultant is usually external to the client's area of responsibility but may be internal to the organization in which the client is an employee.

Leonard Nadler, in his book *Developing Human Resources*[5], divides the HRD consultant role into four subroles.

1. Advocate: takes a position and attempts to have management adopt his/her views.
2. Expert: responds to management questions regarding the use of HRD, supporting his/her response with research and other evidence.
3. Stimulator: raises questions for management consideration as it explores directions and actions concerned with HRD.
4. Change Agent: assists management in diagnosing and planning for change focusing primarily on the process of change rather than the goals.

Gordon and Ronald Lippitt[6] divide the HRD consultant roles along a directive to nondirective continuum and include the role choices of advocate, technical specialist, trainer/educator, collaborator in problem solving, alternative identifier, fact finder, process specialist, and reflector. The appropriate choice of role is determined through dilemma analysis, an effort aimed at discovering the nature of an organizational dilemma and the determining of the real causes of that dilemma.

The HRD Consulting Process

There are numerous ways of perceiving the HRD consulting process. Like the HRD roles, writers differ on their labels of process steps and on the models or conceptual frameworks they utilize. They do agree that there is entry, some type of diagnosis, some action or response taken based on the diagnosis and at some point, disengagement, closure or termination of the consultation. Most writers agree there is some type of contract agreed upon by client and consultant. Figure 21-1 reflects yet another way of outlining the process and is included to provide visually a simple overview.

Because of some psychological pain or disequilibrium experienced or expected to be experienced by the client and/or client system (e.g., the advent of a new product, employees not sufficiently skilled, supervisors not working as a team,

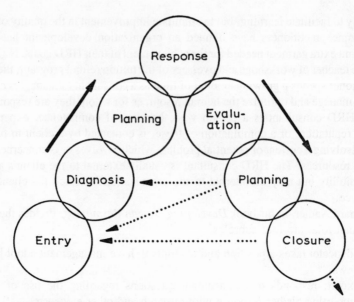

Figure 21-1. The HRD consulting process.

morale or productivity lower than it should be, etc.), a consultant is called onto the scene. During the *entry* phase, problems are jointly explored; roles defined; relationship clarified; goals, objectives, time and budget parameters identified; and a contract (written or psychological) is negotiated. The consultant conducts a *diagnosis* of the situation using one or more data collection methods such as survey, interview, observation, etc.

The results of the diagnosis are fed back to the client (and/or client system); alternative responses are explored discussing the pros and cons of each alternative; priorities are established; and a course of action is *planned,* spelling out goals, roles, and strategies.

The *response* or action phase includes the engagement of structured activities or interventions employed to bring about the needed system improvement. Response could include such activities as workshops, serving as catalytic advisor to the client, survey feedback to the client system, MBO, career planning, team building, job redesign, technostructural changes, intergroup activities, confrontation sessions, process consultation, and many others. Response could also be the action plan itself to be later carried out by the client alone or with a different consultant.

Utilizing procedures to elicit feedback about change progress, the effort is *evaluated* to determine if the consequences of response are consonant with the goals and objectives established at entry and if there is need for response revision or additional resources. Based on that evaluation, *planning* for continuous process maintenance is conducted to insure permanent integration and lasting change.

A part of the postresponse-planning component may include agreement that other aspects of the client system need some type of change process which came to light as a result of the current response. Under this condition the process recycles to diagnosis. For example, in a team building effort, the client and consultant may discover that supervisors in the client system need formal training in decision making and problem solving. A career planning intervention may uncover need for performance appraisal process revision.

The postresponse planning may likewise indicate the need for entry into a different subunit under the jurisdiction of the current client but a subunit not impacted directly by the current response. Other units, not a part of the client system but interfacing with the client system, may require the consultant to work simultaneously with two or more interlocking client systems. Finally, there may be *closure* and termination of the client–consultant relationship with or without a rider or agreement for entry again at a prescribed point in the future.

Admittedly, the HRD consulting process is much more intricate and complex than may be apparent in the overview discussed here. The reader, unfamiliar with the process, might do well to review books which treat the process in more depth. Works by such writers as Fritz Steele (*Consulting for Organizational Change*), Robert Blake and Jane Mouton (*Consultation*), Gordon and Ronald Lippitt (*The Consulting Process in Action*), Ed Schein (*Process Consultation*), Chris Argyris (*Intervention Theory and Method*), and Richard Walton (*Third Party Consultation*) may be particularly helpful.

HRD Consulting and HRD Philosophy

Regardless of the consultant subrole or process used by the HRD consultant, there is difficulty in escaping the impact personal HRD philosophy has on consultation effectiveness. Each of us will tend to hold a primary philosophy regarding how best to understand the dynamics of relationships and organizations. Like the Stanford cats, we have learned cause-and-effect relationships and paradigms which may or may not reflect reality. These learned beliefs predispose us in our diagnosis and recommended responses. While congruence of paradigm and practice is vital, a more critical issue is the relative ease with which consultant philosophy clouds consulting objectivity, resulting in a prejudice inappropriate in meeting the true needs of the client.

What follows is a discussion of the more frequent HRD philosophies and their potential influence on diagnosis and response. Conflicting philosophies are presented as polar opposites, recognizing there is likely greater allegiance to points along the continuum than to those at the extreme ends. Also, the resultant influences discussed are not givens, although they may appear to be in this article.

The influences are rather propensities or inclinations of which one should be aware in order to counterbalance their impact.

Helping Others vs. Helping Others to Help Themselves

There is a measure of ego gratification in the expert subrole. Most of us derive some degree of satisfaction in being needed and in being perceived as a person with good solutions to tough problems. While appropriate in some cases, the expert helper risks seeing only problems which he/she can solve framing diagnosis feedback in a way in which the consultant is the only key to response. Another risk is that the response will be conducted in a manner which reinforces the consultant's expertness reputation. The fallout of client dependence is obvious — the consultant potentially stacks the deck to keep the client forever knocking on the consultant's door for assistance.

The flip side of the coin is the philosophy of "Give me a fish and I eat for a day; teach me to fish and I eat for a lifetime." Diagnosis tends to be collaborative; response, participative. It is the philosophy that true consulting is helping the client and the client system to become better able to learn from their experience. As altruistic as the philosophy is, the real need may be for timely expert advice or research-based advocacy. It is like the HRD consultant whose client exasperatingly said, "I want to learn and you are a great teacher, but right now I just need your recommendation; that's all!"

Process vs. Content

Process-oriented HRD consultants tend to view all organizational dysfunctions as due to maladaptive relationships. They typically focus on the lack of interpersonal communication, lack of shared power, ineffective use of delegation, and interunit conflict. Response takes the form of highly experiential workshops, sensitivity training, process consultation, team building, weekend retreats, etc. Workshops may be designed around simulation exercises and off-the-shelf games rather than developed around the terminal job behaviors needed. They often overlook the fact that problems are sometimes due to inadequate skill training, obsolescent methods, or lack of task knowledge.

Content-oriented consultants see the source of most problems as being lack of clarity regarding organizational goals, absence of or inadequate use of feedback, incomplete information, and skill deficiencies. They believe most problems happen because people do not know what they are required to do or how best to do it. Response is likely to include elaborate orientation programs, technostructural changes, extensive job training, job redesign, work simplification, MBO, and management information systems. Workshops designed by content-oriented HRD consultants are often high on structure and information dissemination, making heavy use of movies, slides, and lectures. Missing from their diagnosis and response are the process factors described above.

Individual vs. Group

There are HRD consultants who view their role as facilitating the meeting of the needs of individuals. They often speak of the enhancement of individual power and freedom, and they fear technocratic control and loss of individuality. Viewing organizations as a collection of individuals, they zero in on such areas as counseling, career and life planning, performance appraisal, boss–subordinate relationships, role clarification, behavior modification, and transactional analysis. They sometimes overlook the synergistic effect of work groups or the role of group norms and pressures. Consultation often centers on the relationship with the client and never directly interfaces with the client's unit.

Group-oriented HRD consultants get lost in the group process and forget the importance of individual needs. They see their primary task as group catalyst and process observer. Responses are likely to be very group-oriented activities such as confrontation meetings, survey feedback, organizational mirroring, family T groups, and third-party peacemaking at group levels.

Behaviorist vs. Humanist

No doubt one of the most hotly debated issues among social scientists is the conflict between behaviorism and humanism. Behaviorists draw their arguments from the works of such people as Watson, Thorndike, Hull, Dollard, and Skinner; humanists from the works of Maslow, Rogers, Allport, May, and Goldstein. Behaviorists tend to believe man is flexible, malleable, and a passive victim of the environment, which determines his/her behavior. While not denying the existence of emotions, feelings, and attitudes, they discard them as unobservable and unmeasurable, and therefore immaterial. Ethics, morals, and values are only the result of associative learning. Diagnosis by behavioristically oriented HRD consultants focuses on reinforcement systems and the quality of feedback; response is built on system feedback, leadership behaviors of supervisory personnel, and the establishing of positive consequences or rewards for appropriate behavior.

Humanists, while not totally rejecting behavioristic theory, assume the human species to be more than just a higher form of animal, but with unique characteristics. It is a belief that we can learn a great deal more about human nature through consideration of the subjective as well as the objective. Humanism stresses the dignity and freedom of the individual. A gestalt approach, the humanistically oriented HRD consultant's diagnosis focuses on barriers to openness, lack of empathy, inclusion, trust, and growth. Response is usually non-manipulative and takes the form of group experiences designed to enhance leveling, honesty, affiliation, and freedom.

Philosopher King vs. Participative Manager

Perceiving leadership parameters in organizational disharmony is likewise subject to consultant bias. The recommended leadership response can easily reflect the style of leadership personally preferred by the HRD consultant. While participative management and adaptive leadership are the "in" prescriptions, a growing number of HRD consultants are leaning more toward leadership with an air of enlightened self-interest; Machiavelli has been resurrected. The era of assertiveness and power is causing some to reconsider the importance of charisma and influence. While not with the rawness of bygone days, the age of uncertainty has created a new homage to the strong, decisive, courageous leader. HRD consultants with philosopher–king orientations tend to work primarily with individual managers and focus on a leadership skills recipe with a twist of politician added. The danger lies in potentially subverting follower opinions, talents, and ultimately their followership.

The shift from hierarchical to horizontal organizational structures carries its own special bias. Caught up in the popularity of matrix organizations and participative management, the HRD consultant may inappropriately see the client's unit as a fertile entree for a novel structure. Diagnosis tends to reveal the need for adaptive and organic structures with the manager serving as the co-ordinator or "linking pin" among various temporary task forces. Response likely includes the alteration of organizational charts reflecting project groups rather than stratified functional groups. Employees and supervisors most probably would be trained in project management with liaisons identified to provide interteam continuity. The danger in such an orientation is that the matrix form may be inappropriate for the people or nature of work and/or introduced too rapidly for effective integration and adaption.

Conclusion

There are other dichotomies which could be included. Proactive creator versus reactive buyer, centralization-oriented versus decentralization-oriented, thinkers versus feelers, grass-roots rebel leaders versus executive suite diplomats are all categories with potential for belief-based bias illustrations. Those discussed in this article are only a few of the major sets.

Most HRD consultants would indicate they are more eclectic, subscribing to a variety of beliefs and philosophies. Granted, some are commonly linked together. Humanists, for instance, are often process, individual, facilitative, participative manager oriented. Some readers will disagree with the manner in which their favorite philosophy has been here described.

My own beliefs no doubt peek through. The crucial point is, however, that we all are tied to certain beliefs or assumptions which shape what we see and how we respond. Think of the interventions you have recommended in the last year. You will no doubt recognize a pattern. If I am a process-oriented consultant, I will very likely see process problems and recommend process solutions.

Guarding against the encroachment of bias is no easy task. Being aware of its likelihood, however, is a useful step in reducing its exaggerated influence. The use of a shadow consultant, a professional peer who can serve as consultant to the consultant, is often helpful in countering the influence of a particular paradigm. A related method is collaborative consulting, that is, working with colleagues who have a slightly different philosophical bias. Choice of perspectives is the first step toward reality-based diagnosis and need-fulfilling response.

It is probably no accident that the word "vision" has connotations regarding both the eye and soul of mankind, for it is through vision we derive meaning and decide direction in life. Yet, our vision and its seductive effect on behavior can deliver a heavy blow to the objectivity foundation of HRD consulting. Widening the brain's reducing valve entails constantly punctuating our declarations of reality with question marks instead of exclamation points. It requires a deliberate search for truth and a never-ending state of personal growth. At stake is not only our personal effectiveness and credibility, but the mental health and productivity of the client system we serve.

References

1. Smith, A., *Powers of Mind,* New York: Random House, 1975, p. 24.
2. Spinelli, D.N., H.V.B. Hirsh, R.W. Phelps, and J. Metzler, "Visual Experience as a Determinant of the Response Characteristics of Cortical Receptive Fields in Cats," *Experimental Brain Research,* Vol. 15 (1972), pp. 289–304.
3. Toch, H., and R. Schulte, "Readiness to Perceive Violence as a Result of Police Training," *British Journal of Psychology,* Vol. 52 (1961), pp. 389–393.
4. Cantril, H., "Perception and Interpersonal Relations," *American Journal of Psychiatry,* Vol. 114 (1957), pp. 119–126.
5. Nadler, L., *Developing Human Resources,* Houston, TX: Gulf Publishing, 1970, p. 235.
6. Lippitt, G., and R. Lippitt, "Consulting Process in Action," *Training and Development Journal,* Vol. 29, No. 5 (May 1975), pp. 48–54; and Vol. 29, No. 6 (June 1975), pp. 38–41.

Chip R. Bell is vice president and director of management development and training for NCNB Corporation in Charlotte, North Carolina.

Ethical Considerations in Consulting

J. William Pfeiffer
John E. Jones

As the field of human relations training grows and the number of human relations consultants and group facilitators increases, it becomes more important than ever to face the question of ethical behavior. It is necessary to consider with care what is ethical, what is not ethical, and what may be ethical but irresponsible, imprudent, unprofessional, or incompetent.

In this article we discuss 19 issues that pertain to human relations consulting. Some of these issues are clearly questions of ethics; other topics do not fit into the ethical–unethical category but rather concern themselves with the responsibilities of prudent, competent professional consultants. We have divided these 19 issues into four areas of consideration, relating to (1) self and colleagues; (2) individual clients; (3) training groups; and (4) organizations.

Self and Colleagues

Presentation of Professional Qualifications

A major ethical issue relating to the individual consultant is the presentation of the consultant's professional qualifications. If a consultant is inaccurately represented by someone else as having extensive experience in a particular area, it is categorically incumbent on that consultant to correct the misrepresentation. The consultant has an ethical responsibility to clear up all actual or implied inaccuracies of qualifications, experience, and/or education.

For example, if someone introduces you as a person who knows a great deal about organization development in government (*nobody* knows a lot about OD in government), you might say, "That sounded good, and I wish I could say that about myself, but it isn't literally true. I have done some work with government trainers, and I have done some work with government departments, but most of my work has been in educational settings."

Reproduced from John E. Jones and J. William Pfeiffer (Eds.), *The 1977 Annual Handbook for Group Facilitators*, La Jolla, California: University Associates, 1977. Used with permission.

It is, of course, possible for facilitators to dwell too much on their limitations. If you give excessive emphasis to your inadequacies, you may severely erode your clients' confidence. It is important to balance the representation of your professional competence in a way that gives equal weight to both your strengths and your limitations.

It is essential to recognize that if you allow *implicit* misrepresentations to stand, you are promoting and encouraging an inaccurate perception of your competencies. A prudent test is to imagine that your most severe critic is present when you are presenting your qualifications to a client or prospective client. Ask yourself if your imaginary critic would take issue with the manner in which you have represented yourself. If you can pass this "test," it is highly likely that you have made an ethical representation of your credentials.

Fees

There are several potential issues concerning consulting fees. It seems to be a fairly common practice for consultants to vary the amount they charge according to their clients' ability to pay. It is clear that, in general, business and industrial clients are used to paying substantially higher consulting fees than either education or government agencies. A free market exists in consulting, and fees seem to reflect a balance between the value that clients place on services and the value that consultants place on their time and contribution. If consultants set their fees too high, they will price themselves out of the market.

Fee setting is a matter of prudence — demand what you are worth and deliver what the client pays for. It is unethical to pad your expenses or to charge the client for either time or materials not delivered. It is your responsibility to see that your agreement with the client is *explicit* in terms of professional fees and agreed-upon expenses.

It is unprofessional to undercut your competition's fees in order to secure a consultation. However, while it is generally a poor professional practice to allow a client to negotiate a reduction in your fee, there may be times when you should weigh the longterm payoffs of a consultation against the immediate budgetary limitations of the prospective client.

The Consultant's Health

Particularly important as it relates to the individual consultant is the issue of health. Consultants are responsible for monitoring their own physical and mental health. If, for any reason, you are emotionally "stretched," your consulting work is going to be affected. There may be times when you have to decline, postpone, or cancel a consultation. You need to recognize that if you are physically ill or emotionally chaotic, you cannot adequately attend to your responsibilities to your clients. If you cannot pay attention to people, you cannot be empathic, and you cannot teach. You may need to take a vacation for a while and "get your own act together."

Because consultants work with other people, it is a major imperative that they keep themselves healthy. Working with people is taxing if you do not maintain yourself; dealing with emotions all day long, every day, can take its toll. Human relations consulting makes special demands on its practitioners. To help others effectively, you must be in good emotional and physical shape. If you are below par, you cannot give the client your best. We believe that you are responsible for delivering the best consultative services of which you are capable.

Meeting Your Own Needs

Not only must consultants be concerned about their own health; they must also be aware of their own needs and whether those needs will be imposed on their clients. Consultants usually get their needs met; it is simply a matter of who is going to "pay." If, for example, you have a big need for power, you are apt to meet that need through your clients, possibly at their expense. If you are first concerned with your own needs, your groups are going to suffer.

Most consultants can recall examples of other consultants forcing their needs on people. If you are very unhappy in your job and/or your marriage, it is very likely that in your groups you will manipulate the members into giving you emotional support. They will be forced to soothe and console you. If you find yourself in such a situation, perhaps you should stop leading groups until you get yourself together. If you do not, you will be jeopardizing the development of your groups. One person should not be allowed to manipulate an entire group to that person's sole benefit — and of course this applies to you, the consultant, as well as to any other individual.

Promises

Consultants are faced with a dilemma: selling their skills but doing it blatantly. Selling professional services takes a special approach. Business-oriented people who work for consultants may not see that selling skills is different from selling shoes and that it operates according to a different set of rules. Brochures, flyers, advertising copy — all have to fit the professional image the consultant wants to project.

Regardless of the kind of consultation to be performed, consultants cannot ethically promise that they will be able to bring about certain types of outcomes. Nothing can be guaranteed in working with people. You cannot promise people what will happen as a result of your efforts. You cannot imply that people are going to be different when you leave or that you will "set them free." People may be unable or unwilling, and you cannot force them to achieve any specific outcomes or learning. You can simply state that they may learn some things they will be able to use.

What consultants can promise to do, in effect, is to be interventionists, to work hard, and to be sensitive and resourceful in any given situation. That is the basis on which a defensible contract can be built.

Public Criticism of Other Consultants

Consultants must be concerned with ethical issues regarding themselves and the way they present themselves, charge for their services, perform their work, meet their own needs, and offer promises. But ethical issues relate also to consultant's behavior toward their colleagues.

If you talk with anyone about other consultants, you should either comment in a positive vein or not comment at all. You should not, either subtly or directly, put down any other professional or consulting organization. It is unethical for a professional to criticize another professional either to another colleague or to the general public.

You may not like what you hear about another consultant or what the consultant does, but you are not obligated to pass judgment; you can simply decline the opportunity to comment. Be sure, however, that you do not, at the same time, give contradictory nonverbal signals. The best test you can apply in this situation is to imagine that the individual concerned is present. If what you say could be said in front of that person, your comments probably pass the test of being ethical.

Confronting

If you do have serious reservations about the competence or behavior of another consultant, you are ethically responsible for confronting that individual. You should let that person know exactly what behavior you believe is unethical. You might say, "in my judgment you're behaving unethically, and I will not lend implicit support to what you are doing." If the person's behavior is not modified, you must register your concern with an appropriate professional organization. That may be an uncomfortable decision. But consultants cannot afford to have their effectiveness undermined by someone else's incompetence or unethical behavior. It is a difficult problem. The strong tendency is to *collude*, not to confront —just to "let it go." But failing to confront when a confrontation is called for can be irresponsible. "Not to decide is to decide."

One slogan a consultant can use is, "When in doubt, confront." As professionals, we must attempt to regulate ourselves, just as bar and medical associations do.

Individual Clients

Ethical issues also exist in relationship to individual clients. Consultants have an obligation to behave in a responsible and professional manner with those who are relying on their expertise.

Evaluating Participants

Doing training for the purpose of evaluating people — the "assessment center" method — can be ethical if everyone understands the rules. But if, on the other hand, a consultant conducts communications training and later is asked how a particular person performed, the only position that is ethically defensible is for the consultant to tell the inquirer to talk directly to the individual concerned. If evaluation is not the purpose of the training, it should not be the result. The consultant may have a great deal of information about individuals and may even have counseled them privately. It would be unethical to reveal such information without a clear previous understanding between the consultant and the participants.

It goes without saying that ethically you must not give specific data about any participant or client to that person's supervisor; be sure that the participants understand that you will not do this. As for giving information to people outside the group, you may generalize or report anonymous data, but you may not be specific or give particular, identifiable details.

Confidentiality

Violating confidentiality is an obvious ethical breach. If someone asks you to keep information private, and you agree to do so but do not, you are being unethical. Very often you, as a consultant, can find yourself caught in a trap. Someone has confided in you, but you cannot use that information, although its disclosure would clearly affect the situation. You have to be very careful about letting yourself be the recipient of a great deal of confidential data. It can tie your hands and stifle your effectiveness. If someone wants to give you confidential data, you can say that you do not accept confidential information — and explain why. You can tell the person that, instead, you are willing to keep the data anonymous. Our experience is that people will still give you the same data — although obtaining it should not be your hidden intent. Refusing to accept information if it is labeled "confidential" makes it much easier for you to deal authentically with a situation.

Sexuality

Consultants and group facilitators, like teachers, therapists, and counselors, have potent roles. That is, participants in human relations training respond to the facilitator differently from the way they would respond to the same individual in a peer relationship. If you, as a consultant/facilitator, use your role to establish a sexual relationship with a participant, you have clearly violated the standards of ethical behavior.

This issue is somewhat complicated; if you are involved with a participant, you are not in a good position to differentiate objectively between your personal attractiveness and your role potency. One test to apply is this: if, as a facilitator, you start a training event with identifiable sexual needs, you will *probably* meet your needs at the expense of someone else.

Logically, a consultant's colleagues should be good sources of balanced judgment on this question, but collusion is common — especially among colleagues who are open to (or seeking) sexual relationships with participants.

The reality is this: if you are heavily involved personally with a participant (either sexually or emotionally), you are (1) less able to attend to your professional commitments and (2) less available to be responsive to other participants. Most participants sense it if a special relationship between the facilitator and a participant exists. Such a situation often generates counterproductive energy that is experienced as jealousy and resentment.

A practical solution is to establish a clear ground rule: observe a cooling-off period of three to six months to allow the relationship to evolve and your role potency to fade before you become involved in a sexual relationship with a participant.

Perhaps it is worth mentioning briefly that engaging in sexual relations with *colleagues* while co-consulting is, at a minimum, likely to be distracting to the work at hand. Your major commitment has to be to your contract with the client, and anything that jeopardizes your effectiveness should be avoided.

Training Groups

In addition to their personal behavior and their behavior toward colleagues and other individuals, consultants must also be concerned with their professional responsibility toward their training groups.

Deception

Sometimes structured experiences and other training techniques involve deception — withholding information from trainees for strategic teaching purposes. If consultants do purposely deceive their training participants, they must be careful to undo the effects. Some structured experiences, for example, require that the facilitator not discuss the goals before the activity. They must, however, be made explicit later. A general training rule that we have found useful is "no surprises."

Cooptation

If a consultant coerces people into doing something they really do not want to do, that consultant is involved in unethical cooptation. For example, in a workshop, part of whose purpose is to involve people in giving each other feedback, someone may not want to participate. You, the facilitator, might put pressure on that person by suggesting the the activity will be harmless. That is coopting the person. Groups, too, can become tyrannical; they can pressure someone to participate when that person does not really want to participate. You should protect the right of individuals not to take part in an activity if they do not want to — particularly if the activity involves their talking about themselves or receiving feedback and even more so if it requires their talking about their emotions, feelings, values, beliefs, and wants.

Inappropriate Techniques

A consultant should be aware that in some settings particular techniques, such as activities that involve physical touching, may be very inappropriate. For example, asking a group of first-line supervisors to explore each other's faces would probably be altogether inappropriate and would undoubtedly create unnecessary anxiety. We believe that you have to be sensitive to the norms of the context in which the training takes place and not use methods that deviate markedly from participants' behavior expectations.

Inattention to Application

It is irresponsible for a consultant to conduct training without paying attention to the application of that training. The integration of learning cannot be left to chance. In using experiential learning, the facilitator must be careful not to cut short its full cycle. Participants should be directed to answer the questions "So what?", "What am I going to do with this learning?", "What implication does this have for new behavior?" Part of your responsibility as a trainer is to help people come to grips with the ways in which they want to change toward more effectiveness.

Rehashing

If consultants do the same training over and over again, by rote, not learning anything new or improving their professional skills, that behavior may be "ripping off" their clients. When you conduct a particular workshop many times, you have a professional obligation to keep it vital. You have to keep yourself generating new ideas, content, and methods. You should strive to experiment, to improve your style, to rethink your procedures — you should not "lecture from old notes." Otherwise, you become stilted, and what you do becomes unimaginative and mechanical. You will not be bringing your best to the people who need what you have to offer.

Organizations

In dealing with organizations, the consultant has similar problems of ethical and responsible behavior, although the applications of the issues are different.

Accepting Organizational Goals

Consultants need to determine what the values of a client organization are, and if they cannot accept those values, either they have to get out or they have to try to change the organization's values. If you are working for a unit whose leader has a philosophy that you cannot accept, then you must either confront that person's values or not work with that unit. In helping a leader to achieve better, you, the consultant, are, in effect, accepting the client's goals by helping to further them. A consultant's techniques are very powerful; they can be used to manipulate people, or they can be used to free people. Techniques themselves are "value free" — it is the purposes for which they are used that determine whether they are ethical. It is you who must decide in which direction you will lend your expertise.

Guerrilla Warfare

If you decide that you cannot accept a particular organization's goals, it is clear that you should not work for that organization; it is even clearer that you must not agree to work for it and then surreptitiously undermine it. If you engage in covert activities that are not correlated with the goals of the organization or that are antithetical to them, you are engaging in unethical behavior. For example, a high school counselor may not like the school system she works in, and she meets with the officers of the student government to reinforce their fight against the system. That counselor is working against the system in a clandestine way, and that is unethical. Besides the fact that consultants who behave that way sooner or later will be "caught," they are not meeting their obligation to be direct in promoting change, and they are not modeling appropriate confrontive behavior.

Assessing Outcomes

After conducting their interventions, facilitators must follow through to identify the effects of what they did and to determine further needed work. That is a difficult task, especially in working with people. In dealing with an organization, consultants are aware of the complex political, environmental, and leadership pressures, inside and outside; they know that the effects of their work may not be immediate or obvious. But even though much of what they do in organization development cannot be specified with any scientific accuracy because of the subjectiveness of the data, they still have to try to determine, in whatever terms they choose, whether they made a difference. Although you will have to live with ambiguity in terms of outcomes, you must ask yourself such questions as these: Did a team-building session improve the work group's meetings? Does the group seem to be cooperating better? Are the training participants improving their supervisory skills on the job?

Hatchet Jobs

Doing someone else's dirty work is neither ethical nor prudent. If consultants do, they will soon gain unsavory reputations. Your image or reputation as a consultant is critical; if you carry out the unpalatable tasks of management, your image will be sullied and your effectiveness will be jeopardized. If, for example, you suspect that a manager's "real" motivation for requesting a team-building session is to provide a basis for firing someone, that suspicion needs to be confronted before you agree to do the work.

Conclusion

Although the consideration of ethics in human relations training is imprecise at present, we believe that the key to understanding the issues lies in a few pertinent words: *power, sensitivity, responsibility, motivation,* and *caring*.

You, as a trainer or a consultant, are in a position of power, simply by virtue of your role. You need to be sensitive to the fact that prople will have different expectations of you than of anyone else in the consulting situation.

Because of these heightened expectations, you must be clearly aware of your responsibilities. Facilitators are responsible for monitoring the climate of the groups with which they work; for facilitating openness, so that people will feel free to explore and experiment; for providing sufficient structure so that learning can take place; and for helping the groups to maintain themselves. You are responsible for *yourself* and the effectiveness of your own helping behavior; you are not directly responsible for the behavior or the learning of others.

Motivation and caring are critical final determinants of ethical behavior: you are less likely to be unethical if you are concerned with benefiting the client than if you are thinking of taking care of yourself at someone else's expense. Too great a desire for contracts, for example, puts your motivation in doubt; a good rule might be that if you cannot say "no" to a proposal, you should not say "yes." In the end, a decision based on your sincere concern for people is likely to be an ethical decision.

J. William Pfeiffer is president and John E. Jones is vice president of University Associates in La Jolla, California.

Organizations as "Phrog" Farms

Jerry B. Harvey

A short time ago I received a telephone call from a friend of mine who was employed as an OD specialist in a large corporation.

"Jerry, I've just been fired," he said.

"Fired? You mean you are out of a job completely?"

"Well, not completely," he replied. "I'm just no longer an OD specialist. In fact, the whole function has been wiped out. They have given me a make-work job in salary administration. It's a nothing job, though. I hate it, I was really interested in doing OD. All I'm doing now is scutt work and drawing a paycheck."

"Why were you fired, Hank?"

"I'm not really sure. I've never heard the reason directly. My boss's boss was the one who really did the firing. He told my boss to do it."

"Why did he tell your boss he wanted you fired?"

"My boss was vague about it. He just said his boss had said I wasn't powerful enough to do the job."

"What did your boss's boss say to you when you asked him about it?"

"I haven't talked with him."

"Why not?"

"That would be violating the chain of command. You don't do that around here."

"Why not?"

"You can get fired for that."

"But Hank," I said, "You *have* been fired."

"Oh!"

And then, perhaps because I had recently read my children the fable of *The Princess and the Frog,* I said, "Hank, your boss's boss is correct. You aren't powerful enough to do the job. In fact, for all intents and purposes, he has turned you into a phrog. I can almost see you in a big phrog pond with your boss's boss sitting on a willow stump saying to himself, 'I think I'll turn ol' Hank into a phrog.' And then he waves a magic wand, mutters some mystical-sounding incantation and concludes with, 'Hank, you are a phrog,' and suddenly you have web feet. Hank, you are now a phrog."

The silence at the other end of the line was seemingly interminable.

Finally, out came the poignant, one-word reply that echoed down the line, "Ribbit."

Organizations as Phrog Farms

After talking with Hank at some length about his life in the phrog pond, I got to thinking that most formal organizations are, metaphorically speaking, phrog farms. By phrog farms I mean that they turn a lot of good people into phrogs. In addition, if we accept the metaphor of organizations as phrog farms, we might conceptualize organization development as the process of draining the swamp. Therefore, building upon that metaphor, I would like to suggest a number of hypotheses, to make some generalizations, and to conceptualize some issues of organization, management, and organization development within the framework of life in the swamp. These various statements are provided, in no particular order of importance and in no conscious linear sequence, as follows:

1. All organizations have two essential purposes. One is to produce widgets, glops, and fillips. The other is to turn people into phrogs. In many organizations, the latter purpose takes precedence over the former. For example, in many organizations, it is more important to follow the chain of command than to behave sensibly.

2. *Phrog* is spelled with a *ph* because phrogs don't like to be known as frogs, and they try to hide their phroginess from themselves and others by transparent means. In short, once one has been transformed into a phrog, one likes to attempt to hide that fact. For one who has been a person, it's a great come-down to be a phrog.

3. Phrogs tend to live a solitary life in the swamp, or as one phrog said, "It's a lonely life on the lily pad." Phrogs compete with one another for insects, vie for the right to head the flicking order of the swamp, and are ultimately evaluated for what they do in their own mud flats. Furthermore, phrogs don't really get rewarded for how well they sing in the chorus. Given that, is it any wonder that a common phrog maxim is, "You can't get involved with other phrogs in the swamp; someday you may have to appropriate their lily pads"?

4. Phrogs speak the Language of Ribbit. The language is simple because it contains only one word, but it doesn't communicate very well. When all the phrogs in the swamp croak "Ribbit," the swamp is noisy as hell, but not a lot of real information is ever exchanged. You see, accuracy of information is not very important in the swamp. In fact, any time a person enters the swamp, he or she is generally told why the Language of Ribbit is the only possible language of the swamp, despite the fact that phrogs don't learn much from one another when they

use it. For that reason, people have a difficult time talking with phrogs. In fact, they seldom talk with phrogs at all.

5. Most phrogs spend more time flicking flies in the fog than in draining the swamp. As best I can tell, their behavior is circular. If they were to spend time draining the swamp, there would be no flies to flick and no phrogs. For that reason, it's very important to phrogs to maintain the swamp as it is rather than to drain it.

6. In phrog farms, bullphrogs generally get to be fresident. Stated differently, the better a phrog can tolerate the loneliness of his lily pad, the more competent he becomes at speaking the Language of Ribbit, the more facile he becomes in flicking flies, the more skillful he becomes at appropriating other lily pads, and the more adroit he becomes at maintaining the swamp, the more likely he is to become fresident.

7. Bullphrogs are greatly revered in the swamp. In fact, other phrogs assume bullphrogs have magical powers because of their unusual abilities to turn people into phrogs. In one sense, such reverence may not be misplaced. They are apparently instrumental in the process of phrog production. It is strange to me, though, that we have devoted so little effort to understanding the role that humans play in permitting phrogs to attack them in the swamp.

8. The magic exercised by bullphrogs comes from humans' belief in it. The tyranny of bullphrogs stems not from the reality of the bullphrogs' power, but from the belief of humans in the Myth of Bullphrog Power.

9. Belief in the Myth of Bullphrog Power prevents one from having to take responsibility for the fog and mud and moss that make up the atmosphere of the swamp.

10. Bullphrogs — particularly fresidents — frequently feel very trapped in the swamp. Many of them are destroyed by it.

They feel trapped because they are trapped. Mr. Nixon was not an aberration.

11. One of the peculiarities of the swamp is that the masses of swamp phrogs both worship and destroy bullphrogs for the very qualities of phroginess that resulted in their becoming fresident.

12. Darwinians say only the strongest go to the top of the phylogenetic scale. Phrogologists say only the weakest go to the top of the same scale. Both say only the fittest survive. One is incorrect.

13. Another perculiarity of the swamp is that cowphrogs seldom become fresident. Cowphrogs apparently don't have the capacity for loneliness, the Language of Ribbit, fly flicking, and swamp maintenance that bullphrogs have. If, by chance, they do develop that revered capacity, they become cowphrogs in bullphrog's clothing, and their croaks deepen.

14. The process of producing phrogs is not sexual — it's magical.

15. OD generally consists of phrog kissing, which is magical, harmless, and platonic.

16. Any activity designed to facilitate phrog kissing is an example of ODD behavior — cosmetic organization development or organization development by deception — or OD as practiced by phrogs. Activities such as phrog chorus-building, interlily-pad conflict resolution, phrog sensing, phrog-style assessment, marsh groups, tadpole development, and phrog coaching in the absence of swamp drainage and area reclamation are examples of phrog kissing by ODDITIES.

17. Phrog kissing is a seductive activity. Frederick Herzberg claims that being seduced is ultimately less satisfying than being raped, because when we are seduced, we are, in fact, part of our own downfall. Stated differently, and in our context, ODD specialists are frequently seduced into phrog kissing, an activity that seldom leads to love-making but frequently adds to the warts on the kisser's face.

18. Many organization members belong to Phrognarian Networks, and Swamp Maintenance Associations. The purpose of such networks and associations is to meet and exchange information regarding the nature of the fog in each member's respective swamp. Since the Language of Ribbit is employed, such exchanges seldom allow one to differentiate one swamp from another. Phrogs seem to get reassurance from noting the similarity among their swamps. Or, as one bullphrog put it, "Misery loves company and miserable phrogs love miserable companies."

19. Occasionally, during meetings of Phrognarians, a phrog pharts in the fog. When that happens, that phrog loses some of his or her phroginess and therefore represents a great threat to the balance of the swamp. Phrog pharts are seldom sanctioned by Phrognarians. They are too real. They put holes in the fog and ultimately threaten the atmosphere of magic required to maintain the swamp.

20. There is a myth on the part of phrogs that kissing another phrog turns that phrog into a prince. I think it should be noted that, in general, kissing a phrog only produces skin irritations. For those who decide to kiss anyway, I think they should also realize that, in all that fog, it is very difficult to determine which way a phrog is facing.

21. Phrogs frequently try to set traps for one another. Phrog traps have a peculiar quality because they catch only the phrogs who set them. Stated differently, if you have to set a phrog trap, there is no need to do so. You are already in it.

22. So that the technology of setting phrog traps is not lost to future generations, phrogfessors of marsh management are hired by Schools of Swamp Maintenance to research and teach. (Phrogfessors of marsh management are not limited to Swamp Maintenance Schools. In fact, they are on the faculties of all kinds of teaching organizations, defined not by what they teach but by the attitude and approach with which they teach it.) The work of such phrogfessors is governed by the underlying credo that is frequently displayed on their respective lily pads. It goes something like this: "If the tadpole hasn't learned, the phrogfessor hasn't taught."

The underlying rationale of that credo is rather peculiar if subjected to close scrutiny. To explain, it clearly implies that the basic responsibility for the tadpole's learning belongs to the phrogfessor. Consequently, if the tadpole does a lousy job, the phrogfessor is at fault. Likewise, following the same logic rigorously, if the tadpole does competent work, the phrogfessor must also get the credit. For all intents and purposes, then, the tadpole doesn't exist, except as some sort of inanimate, passive receptacle for the phrogfessor's competence or incompetence.

23. Given that such a teaching attitude implies that students have no animate existence, is it any wonder that students seem to fit so well into the lonely parallelism of the swamp? Is it also any wonder that when someone accepts responsibility for another's learning, that person ceases to be an educator and becomes a phrogfessor, whose primary job is to prepare tadpoles for life in the swamp?

24. People frequently become phrogs in other kinds of organizations by the same process. After all, a common swamp saying is, "You can delegate authority but you can't delegate responsibility." Translation: "You are responsible for your subordinates' performances. If your subordinates perform competently, it is because of you. If they perform incompetently, it is because of you, too. Like students, they don't even exist, except as extensions of you. They are objects you must manipulate in the best interests of the swamp."

If phrogs don't feel they are responsible for the performance of their subordinates, then why do so many of them go to training programs designed to help them alter their styles of phrogging? As I see it, they do it because they believe they are responsible for their subordinates' performances and that their style (as opposed to their essence) has something to do with how effectively their subordinates perform.

25. All of us are phrogs at one time or another. All have the potential to develop webbing between their toes. All have experienced the terror of the trap, and accepting responsibility for others actions is the bait with which phrog traps are set.

26. Many bullphrogs can't laugh at the absurdity of their lives in the swamp. Such phrogs tend to become steerphrogs and are very poignant creatures. Bullphrogs frequently die laughing, but I have never seen a steerphrog laugh. They just croak.

27. The seat of our government is located in Washington, D.C., in a swampy area of the city known affectionately to some as "Foggy Bottom." For many, it is also the locus of the "bureaucratic mess." Perhaps it should be renamed, "Phroggy Bottom."

28. *Making Waves in Foggy Bottom*, by Alfred Marrow, is a book about an OD effort to clean up the bureaucratic mess in the U.S. Department of State. In its essence, the book is about the failure of that effort. Should you decide to read it, you might come to realize that making waves — in any organization — is a very different process from draining the swamp.

29. The size of the swamp is growing; the world may ultimately be inhabited by phrogs. Air pollution is not really a great a threat to future generations as phrog pollution.

30. The swamp is ultimately evil. Hannah Arendt described how phrog farms, despite their benign appearance, tend to develop bullphrogs with an enormous capacity for evil. Adolph Eichmann was not an aberration either.

31. The job of most swamp mannagers is to maintain and enhance the swamp, not to drain it. For example, Winston Phroghill said, "I was not made marsh minister to preside over the draining of the swamp."

32. The purpose of swamp consultants — in the eyes of swamp managers — is to help the swamp operate effectively, not to drain it.

33. Most OD literature is designed to facilitate swamp management, not area reclamation. Most managers are phrog farmers. Most OD specialists and phrogfessors of marsh management are phrog farmers' helpers. The relationship is symbiotic.

34. Most phrog farmers and their helpers are aware of their lots in the swamp. Most have about all the consciousness they can bear. May God have mercy on their souls.

35. God does have mercy on their souls. Otherwise, God would be the greatest phrog farmer of them all.

Alternatives to Life on the Phrog Farm

With all those objects around, it is indeed a lonely life on the lily pad.

"What is the alternative to life in the swamp?" you ask. After all, isn't that my job as a responsible phrogfessor, to provide some answers to the problems of the dismal swamp?

The temptation is great.

Suddenly, though, I see that sign on my lily pad and realize that another feature of phrogs is that they are frequently afraid to think. It's not that the thoughts are not there. In fact, in the swamp, there are plenty of thoughts to be thought. But who is to think them? Certainly not phrogs, because thinking is as dangerous to the ecology of the swamp as passing gas in the fog.

Not thinking, or getting someone else to be responsible for thinking one's thoughts, is not without its advantages — as long as a phrog can get someone else to take responsibility for changing the climate of the swamp.

I do know, though, that noncosmetic organization development involves swamp drainage and area reclamation and is done by humans, not phrogs. Ultimately, that process of drainage and reclamation destroys the swamp and includes such modifications in the swamp's environment as building habitats that allow people to cooperate — rather than compete. Such habitats allow people to:

• Get paid as pairs, teams, organizations rather than as individuals. If two individuals get paid for working as a pair, it is amazing how much interest they take in helping one another succeed.

- Work in nonzero-sum climates when it comes to promotion, layoffs, salary, performance appraisal, and grades. For example, during bad times, phrogs lay others off in terms of seniority. People don't lay one another off at all. They all take proportionate pay cuts and therefore learn that they can rely on one another during both good and bad times.

People with zero-sum attitudes believe that the outcome of any interpersonal encounter is zero, that is, "If you get a pay off of plus one, I must get a payoff of minus one, and the outcome is zero." Stated in day-to-day language, people with that attitude say, "If you win, I must lose." People with nonzero-sum attitudes believe that the outcome of any human encounter can be other than zero, that is, we can both win and, if we do, under certain conditions, it is not one plus one equals two but rather, with synergism, three.

- Leave the environment when they lose interest in it. For example, when it comes to vesting (of rights), people don't wear vests, phrogs do.

- Accept personal responsibility for their own activities in the habitat. Phrogs, for instance, demand that bullphrogs take responsibility for the swamp. People will not permit others to take over their responsibilities for the habitat and its operation.

- Trust one another in a wide variety of situations. Phrogs distrust 'most everybody. Given their distrust, they put in time clocks which say, "We don't trust you to do an honest day's work, so prove that you did." They demand doctors' certificates when someone calls in ill. They have private offices so that others access to them is limited and so that their conversations and work with other phrogs can't be observed and overheard. They demand close verification of expense accounts because "Everyone knows those slick swamp salesmen would rob the marsh blind if a bullphrog doesn't keep tabs on them." They keep just-in-case (JIC) files to protect themselves from other phrogs' poisons.

People have, by contrast, very few rules and procedures that question the honesty of others. In fact, they assume other people can be trusted and live with the reality that in a few cases such trust will be violated.

- Be treated as subjects — not objects. R.D. Laing has pointed out that one way to make others mentally ill is to treat them as depersonalized objects or things, (that is, objectively) rather than as "personalized" subjects (that is, subjectively). Bullphrogs try to treat others objectively. They try to gauge the performance of others objectively, and they try to "keep their feelings out of the situation." However, when you treat another objectively (that is, as an object), you should know that the price of being objective — eliminating one's feelings from the situation — is that you become an object yourself, since you have denied the very essence of your own humanness. Thus are bullphrogs born.

Humans don't treat one another as objects. They try instead to build a work environment in which human subjectivity is accepted as an integral part of the habitat's problem-solving process.

"You still haven't answered the question of "What do we do to save ourselves from the swamp? You are too vague, too idealistic and too impractical. You certainly have not fulfilled your responsibilities as an article writer."

I hope you don't feel that way, but if you do about all I say is: "You're right. I haven't tried."

"Ribbit."

Jerry B. Harvey is professor of behavioral science in the School of Business Administration, George Washington University.

Bibliography

Alderfer, C.P.,"Organizational Diagnosis from Initial Client Reactions to a Researcher," *Human Organization,* Vol. 27 (1968), pp. 260–265.

Anderson, Florence, and B. Shangold, "The Role of the Consultant in Adult Education," *Adult Education Bulletin,* Vol. 14 (1950), pp. 14–20.

Arendt's, Hannah, *Eichmann on Jerusalem,* New York: Viking, 1965.

Argyris, Chris, "Explorations in Consulting–Client Relationships," *Human Organization,* Vol. 20, No. 3 (1961), pp. 121–133.

Argyris, Chris, *Intervention Theory and Method,* Reading, MA: Addison–Wesley, 1970.

Baker, John K., and Robert H. Schaffer, "Making Staff Consulting More Effective," *Harvard Business Review* (January–February 1969), pp. 62–70.

Barber, William H., and Walter Nord, "Transactions Between Consultants and Clients: A Taxonomy," *Group and Organization Studies,* Vol. 2, No. 2, (June 1977), pp. 198–214.

Becker, Stephen, "How to Work With — and Manage — Outside Training Consultants," *Training: The Magazine of Human Resources Development,* Vol. 13, No. 7 (July 1976), pp. 14–16.

Beckhard, Richard, "A Leader Looks at the Consultative Process," Leadership Resources, Inc., Washington, D.C., 1965.

Bell, Chip R. "The HRD Managers 'Rules for Living,' " *Training and Development Journal,* Vol. 30, No. 12 (December 1976), pp. 38–39.

Beene, Kenneth D., "Some Ethical Problems in Group and Organizational Consultation," *Journal of Social Issues,* Vol. 15, No. 2 (1959), pp. 60–67.

Bion, Wilfred, *Experiences in Groups,* New York: Basic Books, 1961.

Blaha, M.J., "When and How the Consultant Can Be Used Most Effectively," *Educational Leadership,* Vol. 10, No.4 (1952), pp. 96–100.

Blake, Robert R., and Jane S. Mouton, *Consultation,* Reading, MA: Addison-Wesley, 1976.

Block, Kenneth L., "The Professional Consultant," *The Office* (January 1972).

Blumberg, Arthur, "The Consulting Function of Leadership," *Adult Leadership,* Vol. 8 (1960), 265–266.

Boehm, W., "The Professional Relationship Between Consultant and Consultee," *American Journal of Orthopsychiatry,* Vol. 26, No. 3 (1956), pp. 241–248.

Bordin, E.S., "Effective Consultation," *Adult Leadership,* Vol. 3, No. 1 (1955), pp. 13–26.

Bowman, P.H., "The Role of the Consultant as a Motivator of Action," *Mental Hygiene*, Vol. 43, No. 3 (1959), pp. 105–110.

Bradford, Leland P., "How to Diagnose Group Problems," *Adult Leadership*, Vol. 2, No. 7 (December 1953), pp. 18–26.

Brandon, David, *Zen in the Art of Helping*, New York: Dell, 1976.

Brown, T.H., "The Business Consultant," *Harvard Business Review*, Vol. 21 (1944), pp. 183–189.

Browning, Larry D., "Diagnosing Teams in Organizational Setting," *Group and Organization Studies*, Vol. 2, No. 2 (June 1977), pp. 187–197.

Burke, Warner W., ed., *Contemporary Organization Development: Conceptual Orientations and Interventions*. Washington, D.C.: NTL Institute for Applied Behavioral Science, 1972.

Carkhuff, Robert R., *Helping and Human Relations: A Primer for Lay and Professional Helpers*, New York: Holt, Rinehart and Winston, 1969.

Carr, Rey A., "Principal-Centered Preventive Consultation," *Group and Organization Studies*, Vol. 1, No. 4 (1976), pp. 455–473.

Chalofsky, Neal E., and Joseph A. Cerio, "Professional Development Program for Federal Government Trainers," *Training and Development Journal*, Vol. 29, No. 12 (December 1975), pp. 18–20.

Charters, W.W., "Stresses in Consultation," *Adult Leadership*, Vol. 3 (1955), pp. 21–22.

Cocking, W.D., "The Role of the Educational Consultant," *School Executive*, Vol. 75, No. 8 (1956), p. 7.

"Consultation as a Training Function," *Exploration in Human Relations Training*, Washington, D.C.: NTL Institute for Applied Behavioral Science, 1953.

Cooper, Lloyd, "How to Make More Effective Use of Your Training Consultants," *Training and Development Journal*, Vol. 31, No. 3 (March 1977), pp. 16–18.

Crissy, William J., "Are You Hiring a Consultant — or a Parasite? *The Management Review*, Vol. 42, No. 10 (October 1953), pp. 8–11.

Custer, G.E., "A Look at the Personnel Consulting Business," *Personnel Administrator*, Vol. 22 (1956), pp. 24–31.

Dekom, Anton K., "The Internal Consultant," *AMA Research Study #101*, New York: American Management Association, 1969.

Dyer, William G., *Team Building: Issues and Alternatives*, Reading, MA: Addison–Wesley, 1977.

Egerton, Henry C., and Jeremy, Bacon, "Consultants: Selection, Use and Appraisal," *Managing the Moderate-Sized Company, Report No. 13*, New York: National Industrial Conference Board, 1970.

Fordyce, Jack K., and Raymond Weil, *Managing With People: A Manager's Handbook of Organization Development Methods*, Reading, MA: Addison–Wesley, 1971.

Fox, Robert S., Richard Schmuck, Elmer Van Edmond, Miriam Ritvo, and Charles Jung, *Diagnosing Profesional Climates in Schools,* Fairfax, VA: NTL Learning Resources Corp., 1975.

French, Wendell L., and Cecil H. Bell, Jr., *Organization Development: Behavioral Science Interventions for Organization Improvement,* Englewood Cliffs, NJ: Prentice-Hall, 1973.

Friendlander, Frank, "A Comparative Study of Consulting Processes and Group Development," *Journal of Applied Behavioral Science,* Vo.l. 4, No. 4 (1968), pp. 377–399.

Gluckstern, Norma B., and Ralph W. Packard, "The Internal–External Change Agent Team: Bringing Change to a 'Closed Institution,' " *Journal of Applied Behavioral Science,* Vol. 13, No. 1 (1977), pp. 41–52.

Goodstein, Leonard D., *Consulting with Human Service Systems,* Reading, MA: Addison–Wesley, 1978.

Green, Howard L., "Management Consultants: How to Know What You're Getting and Get What You Pay For," *Management Review,* Vol. 52, No. 12 (December 1963), pp. 14–17.

Goldman, Samuel, and William Moynihan, "Strategies for Consultant–Client Interface," *Educational Technology,* Vol. 12, No. 10 (October 1972), pp. 27–30.

Guder, R.F., "How to Choose, Abuse and Misuse Consultants," *Management Review* (December 1963).

Guss, L.M., "Consultants Need Client's Cooperation," *Chemical and Engineering News* (April 1965).

Harrison, Roger, "Role Negotiation: A Tough-Minded Approach to Team Development," in *Interpersonal Dynamics* (Warren G. Bennis et. al., eds.), Homewood, IL: Dorsey Press, 1973.

Harvey, Jerry, "It's Not My Dog: Eight Myths OD Consultants Live and Die by," *OD Practitioner,* Vol. 7, No. 1 (February 1975), pp. 1–5.

Harvey, Jerry, and Richard Albertson, "Neurotic Organizations: Symptoms, Causes, and Treatment," *Personnel Journal,* Vol. 50, No. 9 (September 1971), pp. 694–699; Vol. 50, No. 10.

Harvey, Jerry, "The Abilene Paradox," *Organizational Dynamics* (summer, 1974), pp. 63–80.

Haslett, J.W., "Decision Table for Engaging a Consultant," *Journal of Systems Management* (July 1971).

Havelock, Ronald G., and Mary C. Havelock, *Training for Change Agents* Ann Arbor, MI: Institute for Social Research, 1973.

Herzberg, Frederick, "One More Time: How Do You Motivate Employees?", *Harvard Business Review,* Vol. 46 (January-February 1968), pp. 53–62.

Hunt, Alfred, *The Management Consultant,* New York: Ronald Press, 1977.

Huse, Edgar, *Organization Development and Change,* New York: West Publishing, 1975.

Jorz, J.J., and L.M. Richards, "A Curriculum Plan to Develop Training Professionals," *Training and Development Journal,* Vol. 31, No. 10 (October 1977), pp. 22–24.

Kaplan, Robert E., "Stages in Developing A Consulting Relation: A Case Study of a Long Beginning," *Journal of Applied Behavioral Science,* Vol. 14, No. 1 (January–March 1978), pp. 43–60.

Kelman, Herbert C., "Manipulation of Human Behavior: An Ethical Dilemma for the Social Scientist," *Journal of Social Issues,* Vol. 21, No. 2 (1965), pp. 31–46.

Kintzer, Fredrick C., and Stanley M. Chase, "The Consultant as a Change Agent," *Junior College Journal* (April 1969).

Kolb, D., and A. Frohman, "An Organization Development Approach to Consulting," *Sloan Management Review,* Vol. 12, No. 1 (fall 1970), pp. 51–65.

Laing, R.D., *The Divided Self,* Pelican Books, 1965.

Lawler, Marcella R., "The Role of the Consultant in Curriculum Improvement," *Educational Leadership,* Vol. 8 (1951), pp. 219–225.

Leach, Wesley B., and Vyrle W. Owens, "Training and the Change Agent Role Model," *Training and Development,* Vol. 27, No. 10 (October 1973), pp. 40–47.

Levinson, Harry, *Organizational Diagnosis,* Cambridge, MA: Harvard University Press, 1974.

Lorsch, Jay W., and Paul Lawrence, "The Diagnosis of Organizational Problems," *The Planning of Change* (Warren G. Bennis, Kenneth D. Benne, and Robert Chin, eds.), New York: Holt, Rinehart and Winston, 1969.

Luke, Robert A., Peter Block, Jack M. Davey, and Vernon R. Averch, "A Structure Approach to Organizational Change," *Journal of Applied Behavioral Science,* Vol. 9, No. 5 (1973), pp. 611–635.

Lundberg, C.C., and A.P. Raia, "Issues in the Practice of Organizational Development Consultancy," in *Proceedings of the Academy of Management,* Thirty-Sixth Annual Meeting, Kanasas City, MO, 1976.

Lippitt, Gordon, and Ronald Lippitt, *The Consulting Process in Action,* La Jolla, CA: University Associates Press, 1978.

Lippitt, Gordon, "Operational Climate and Individual Growth: The Consultative Process at Work," *Personnel Administrator,* Vol. 23 (1960).

Lippitt, Gordon, "The Criteria for Selecting, Evaluating and Developing Consultants," *Training and Development Journal,* Vol. 26, No. 8 (August 1972), pp. 12–17.

Lippitt, Ronald, "The Dimensions of the Consultant's Job," *Journal of Social Issues,* Vol. 15, No. 2 (1959), pp. 5–12.

Lippitt, Ronald, J. Watson, and B. Westley, *Dynamics of Planned Change,* New York: Harcourt, Brace and World, 1958.

Lippitt, Ronald, "On Finding, Using and Being a Consultant," *Social Science Education Consortium Newsletter* (November 1971).

Mager, Robert F., and Peter Pipe , *Analyzing Performance Problems*, Belmont, CA: Fearon Publishers, 1970.

Marguiles, Newton, "Implementing Organization Change Through an Internal Consulting Team," *Training and Development Journal*, Vol. 25, No. 7 (July 1971), pp. 26–33.

Maynard, H.B., "How to Select a Management Consultant," *Management Methods* (February 1957).

Merry, Uri, and Melvin E. Allerhand, *Developing Teams and Organizations: A Practical Handbook for Managers and Consultants*, Reading, MA: Addison–Wesley, 1977.

Mitchell, M.D., "Consultant Burnout," in *The 1977 Annual Handbook for Group Facilitators*, (J.E. Jones and J.W. Pfeiffer, eds.), La Jolla, CA: University Associates Press, 1977.

Morris, Jud, "Why Management Consultants Are Not Needed," *Manage*, Vol. 20, No. 8 (June 1968), pp. 50–55.

Nadler, David A., *Feedback and Organization Development: Using Data-Based Methods*, Reading, MA: Addison–Wesley, 1977.

Nadler, Leonard, *Developing Human Resources*, Houston, TX: Gulf Publishing Company, 1970.

Nadler, Leonard, "How is Your Organizational Health?" *Management of Personnel Quarterly*, Vol. 9, No. 1 (spring 1970), pp. 18–28.

Paster, Irving, "So You Want to be a Consultant," *Personnel Journal*, Vol. 50, No. 11 (November 1971), pp. 827–833, 871.

Rapoport, Anatol, and Albert Chammah, *Prisoner's Dilemma*, Ann Arbor, MI: Ann Arbor Paperbacks, 1970.

Redding, William J., "Confessions of an Organizational Change Agent," *Group and Organization Studies*, Vol. 2, No. 1 (March 1977), pp. 33–41.

Reiff, Robert, "The Control of Knowledge: The Power of the Helping Professions," *Journal of Applied Behavioral Science*, Vol. 10, No. 3 (1974), pp. 451–461.

Ricks, Don M., "Sure, Pal. Plunge Into the Fun and Profitable World of Consulting," *Training: The Magazine of Human Resources Development*, Vol. 13, No. 5 (May 1976), pp. 46–48.

Rogers, Rolf E., "The Human Element in Systems and Consulting Work," *Personnel Journal*, Vol. 46, No. 8 (September 1967), pp. 516–519.

Roos, H.W., "How to Make the Best Use of Consultants," *Management Review* Vol. 41 (1952), pp. 421–422.

Schmuck, Richard A., and Matthew B. Miles, *Organizational Development in Schools*, La Jolla, CA: University Associates Press, 1971.

Schroder, Marjan, "The Shadow Consultant," *Journal of Applied Behavioral Science*, Vol. 10, No. 4 (October–December 1974), pp. 579–594.

Steele, Fritz, "Interpersonal Aspect of the Architect–Client Relationship," *Progressive Architecture*, Vol. 50, No. 4 (1968), pp. 32–133.

Steele, Fritz, "Potter Unearthed for the Consultant," *Journal of Applied Science*, Vol. 8, No. 5 (1972), pp. 513–526.

Steele, Fritz, and Stephen Jenks, *The Feel of the Work Place*, Reading, MA: Addison–Wesley, 1977.

Swartz, Donald, "How Not to Sabotage Your OD Consultant," *Successful Meetings Magazine* (October 1973).

Swartz, Donald, "How to Use an OD Consultant," *Organization Renewal Newsletter*, Vol. 4, No. 5 (July–August 1974), pp. 1.

Swartz, Donald H., "Similarities and Differences of Internal and External Consultants," *Journal of European Training*, Vol. 4, No. 5 (1975), pp. 258–262.

Terreberry, Shirley, "The Evolution of Organizational Environments," *Administrative Science Quarterly*, Vol. 12, No. 4 (March 1968), pp. 590–613.

Tichey, Noel, "An Interview with Roger Harrison," *Journal of Applied Behavioral Science*, Vol. 9, No. 6 (1973), pp. 701–726.

Tichey, Noel M., Harvey Hornstein, and Jay N. Nisberg, "Participative Organization Diagnosis and Intervention Strategies," *Academy of Management Review*, Vol. 1, No. 2 ((1976).

Tichey, Noel, and Jay Nisberg, "Change Agent Bias: What They View Determines What They Do," *Group and Organization Studies*, Vol. 1, No. 3 (September 1976), pp. 286–301.

Tilles, Seymore, "Understanding the Consultant's Role," *Harvard Business Review*, Vol. 39, No. 6 (November–December 1961), pp. 87-99.

Titles, S., "Ideas for a Better Consultant–Client Relationship," *Business Horizons* (summer 1963).

Trentin, H.C., "Are You a Full-Time Consultant?" *Management Services*, Vol. 6, No. 2, (March–April 1969), pp. 19–26.

U.S. Civil Service Commission, *Improving the Effectiveness of Employee Development Specialists*, Bulletin 410–85, Washington, D.C.: U.S. Civil Service Commission, July 31, 1975.

U.S. Civil Service Commission, Bureau of Training, *The Employee Development Specialist Curriculum Plan: An Outline of Learning Experience for the Employee Development Specialist*, Washington, D.C.: The Civil Service Commission, November, 1976.

Van De Van, Andrew H., "A Framework for Organization Assessment," *Academy of Management Review*, Vol. 1, No. 1 (January 1976), pp. 64–78.

Varney, Glenn H., *An Organization Development Approach to Management Development*, Reading, MA: Addison–Wesley, 1976.

Walton, Richard E., *Interpersonal Peacemaking: Confrontations and Third Party Consultation*, Reading, MA: Addison–Wesley, 1969.

Weisbord, Marvin R., "Organizational Diagnosis: Six Places to Look for Trouble With or Without a Theory," *Group and Organization Studies*, Vol. 1, No. 4 (1976), pp. 430–447.

"What to Do Before the Consultant Comes," *Management Review,* Vol. 58, No. 6 (June 1969), pp. 14–19.

Woody, R.H., and J.D. Woody, "Behavioral Science Consultation," *Personnel Journal,* Vol. 50, No. 5 (May 1971), pp. 382–391.

Subject Index

Author Index

NOTES

NOTES

NOTES

NOTES

NOTES

NOTES

NOTES

NOTES

NOTES